MACROECONOMIC PROSPECTS FOR A SMALL OIL EXPORTING COUNTRY

INTERNATIONAL STUDIES IN ECONOMICS AND ECONOMETRICS

Volume 11

1. Harder T: Introduction to Mathematical Models in Market and Opinion Research With Practical Applications, Computing Procedures, and Estimates of Computing Requirements. Translated from the German by P.H. Friedlander and E.H. Friedlander. 1969.

2. Heesterman ARG: Forecasting Models for National Economic Planning. 1972.

3. Heesterman ARG: Allocation Models and their Use in Economic Planning. 1971.

4. Durdağ M: Some Problems of Development Financing. A Case Study of the Turkish First Five-Year Plan, 1963–1967. 1973.

5. Blin JM: Patterns and Configurations in Economic Science. A Study of Social Decision Processes. 1973.

6. Merkies AHQM: Selection of Models by Forecasting Intervals. Translated from the Dutch by M. van Holten-De Wolff. 1973.

7. Bos HC, Sanders M and Secchi C: Private Foreign Investment in Developing Countries. A Quantitative Study on the Evaluation of its Macro-Economic Impact. 1974.

8. Frisch R: Economic Planning Studies Selected and Introduced by Frank Long. Preface by Jan Tinbergen. 1976.

9. Gupta KL: Foreign Capital, Savings and Growth. An International Cross-section Study. 1983.

10 Bochove CA van: Imports and Economic Growth. 1982.

11. Bjerkholt O, Offerdal E: Macroeconomic Prospects for a Small Oil Exporting Country. 1985.

Macroeconomic Prospects for a Small Oil Exporting Country

edited by
Olav Bjerkholt and Erik Offerdal

1985 **MARTINUS NIJHOFF PUBLISHERS**
a member of the KLUWER ACADEMIC PUBLISHERS GROUP
DORDRECHT / BOSTON / LANCASTER

338.27282
M174

Distributors

for the United States and Canada: Kluwer Academic Publishers, 190 Old Derby Street, Hingham, MA 02043, USA
for the UK and Ireland: Kluwer Academic Publishers, MTP Press Limited, Falcon House, Queen Square, Lancaster LA1 1RN, UK
for all other countries: Kluwer Academic Publishers Group, Distribution Center, P.O. Box 322, 3300 AH Dordrecht, The Netherlands

Library of Congress Cataloging in Publication Data

```
Main entry under title:

Macroeconomic prospects for a small oil exporting
   country.

   (International studies in economics and econometrics ;
v. 11)
   Based on papers originally presented at a seminar in
Ullensvang, Norway in May 1984, organized by the Central
Bureau of Statistics, Oslo.
   1. Petroleum industry and trade--Norway--Congresses.
2. Petroleum industry and trade--Congresses.  3. Norway--
Economic policy--Congresses.  4. Economic policy--
Congresses.  I. Bjerkholt, Olav, 1942-  II. Offerdal,
Erik.  III. Norway.  Statistiske sentralbyrå.  IV. Series.
HD9565.N82M33  1985    338.2'7282'09481      85-8994
```

ISBN 90-247-3183-6 (this volume)
ISBN 90-247-2730-8 (series)

Copyright

PRINTED IN THE NETHERLANDS

CONTENTS

PART THREE: PRODUCTION. PROFITABILITY AND TAXES

PART FOUR: OIL REVENUES AND LONG-TERM MACROECONOMIC PLANNING

THE AUTHORS

IULIE ASLAKSEN   Central Bureau of Statistics, P.O. Box 8131, Dep 0033 Oslo 1, Norway

ROAR BERGAN   Central Bureau of Statistics, P.O. Box 8131, Dep 0033 Oslo 1, Norway

OLAV BJERKHOLT   Central Bureau of Statistics, P.O. Box 8131, Dep 0033 Oslo 1, Norway

JAQUELINE BOUCHER   CORE, 34 Voie Roman du Pays, 1348 Louvain-la-Neuve, Belgium

ADNE CAPPELEN   Central Bureau of Statistics, P.O. Box 8131, Dep 0033 Oslo 1, Norway

LORENTS LORENTSEN   Central Bureau of Statistics, P.O. Box 8131, Dep 0033 Oslo 1, Norway

ROBERT McRAE   Department of Economics, University of Calgary, 2500 University Drive N.W., Calgary, Alberta, Canada T2N 1N4

HOMA MOTAMEN   Departement of Social and Economic Studies, Imperial College, 53 Prince's Gate, Exhibition Road, London SW7 2PG, Great Britain

ERIK OFFERDAL   Central Bureau of Statistics, P.O. Box 8131, Dep 0033 Oslo 1, Norway

KJELL ROLAND   Central Bureau of Statistics, P.O. Box 8131, Dep 0033 Oslo 1, Norway

ALETTE SCHREINER   Central Bureau of Statistics, P.O. Box 8131, Dep 0033 Oslo 1, Norway

BIRGIR BJØRN
SIGURJONSSON   Lagmula 7, 105 Reykjavik, Island

TOR SKOGLUND   Central Bureau of Statistics, P.O. Box 8131, Dep 0033 Oslo 1, Norway

YVES SMEERS · CORE, 34 Voie Roman du Pays, 1348 Louvain-la-Neuve, Belgium

STEINAR STRØM · Departement of Economics, University of Oslo, P.O. Box 1095, Oslo 3, Norway

SWEDER VAN WIJNBERGEN · Development Research Department, The World Bank, 1818 High Street N.W., Washington D.C. 20433, USA

ASBJØRN AAHEIM · Central Bureau of Statistics, P.O. Box 8131, Dep 0033 Oslo 1, Norway

NA

The theme of this book is the macroeconomic planning and policy issues confronting a small open economy with considerable reserves of oil and natural gas. Most of the articles included deal more specifically with the situation of Norway which made her first oil discoveries as recently as in 1969, and in the following fifteen years has grown to become a major oil exporter. Experiences of other countries are also dealt with and compared to those of Norway. Most of the papers have a strong emphasis on methods, and the editors hope that these may be found to be of interest in a wider context.

The contents of the book are edited from papers originally presented at a seminar in Ullensvang, Norway in May 1984. The seminar was organised by the Central Bureau of Statistics, Oslo, to present results from a project on petroleum economics within the institution together with five invited contributors from other countries.

The papers included in the book is divided thematically into four parts. The first part is concerned with the adjustment problems that arise in the transition towards an oil-rich economy that has been experienced by Norway as well as e.g. the United Kingdom, the Netherlands and Canada. In the Norwegian case this adjustment process almost coincided in time with the international recession that followed the oil price increases in 1974 and 1979. The emphasis here is on the need for public policy to ease this transition in a small open economy, and on the importance of oil revenues in adjusting macroeconomic policies. Part two deals with the functioning of international oil and gas markets, and includes modeling approaches to long-term projections of crude oil prices, and the European gas market. Part three comprises papers on the cost and profitability structure of oil and gas fields on the Norwegian continental shelf, and on the relative merits of different petroleum taxation systems, namely those of Canada and the US. The final part deals with long-run issues such as the regional impacts of oil and gas revenues, the optimal depletion and spending profiles of an oil exporting country and macroeconomic strategies to cope with uncertainty of future oil prices.

A number of persons - apart from the authors - have contributed to make this book appear. The editors would especially like to express their gratitude toward The Norwegian Research Council and the Ministry of Oil and Energy which jointly sponsored the project on petroleum economics in the Central Bureau of Statistics as well as the seminar. Lorents Lorentsen has been in charge of the project, and has acted as advisor to all teams of authors. Similarly, Michael Hoel of the University of Oslo and Dominique Thon of the Christian Michelsens Institute have given valuable comments on some of the papers. The technical staff of the Research Department of the Central Bureau has contributed substantially to many of the papers. Especially we would like to thank Dagfinn Aa for technical computer assistance, Esther Larsen who has drawn the bulk of the figures, and Elin Berntzen, Elisa Holm, Heidi Munkelien, Marit Presthus and Sylvia Staalesen for extraordinary efforts in typing and text processing.

Oslo, March 1985.

Olav Bjerkholt and Erik Offerdal

PART ONE:

BOOMING OIL SECTOR, STRUCTURAL CHANGE

AND MACROECONOMIC POLICY

OIL DISCOVERIES, INTERTEMPORAL ADJUSTMENT AND PUBLIC POLICY

BY

SWEDER VAN WIJNBERGEN

ABSTRACT

There is increasing suspicion that high but temporary oil revenues may be somewhat of a mixed blessing, unless proper public policy eases the adjustment process to an oil-based economy and, where relevant, prepares for "re-entry" once the oil wells have run dry. The paper discusses to what extent public intervention is needed within the framwork of a two-sector, disequilibrium model. The analysis is focused on two issues. Firstly the possibility that spending of oil revenues may result in classical unemployment in a situation with real wage indexation, and which policy measures will be effective in ameliorating this situation. And secondly, the case for subsidies to the non-oil traded goods sector if there are substantial learning-by-doing externalities arising in this sector.

1. INTRODUCTION

"The Economist" (April 9, 1981) compared Norwegian economists to New York psychiatrists, specializing in the diseases of the rich. There is indeed increasing suspicion that high but temporary oil revenues may be somewhat of a mixed blessing, unless proper public policy eases the adjustment process to an oil-based economy and, where relevant, prepares for "re-entry" once the oil wells have run dry. In this paper we will discuss to what extent that is justified; is public intervention needed or not?

Horror stories abound about labour shortages and bottlenecks in the Gulf countries. On the other hand employment benefits of oil bonanza's did not materialise in Latin American oil producers, or for that matter the Netherlands, whose response to gas export revenues gave rise to the phrase "Dutch Disease". In all oil or gas producers, exporters feel pressure from appreciation, either via high domestic inflation, a strong currency or both. Accordingly most of these countries have seen their traded goods sector decline faced with real wage pressure. The explanation of the real appreciation is clear enough: part of the oil revenues are spent on Non-Traded goods which leads to an increase in the relative price of NT goods (a real appreciation). This in turn draws resources out of the traded goods sector.

Two major problems emerge; one has to do with the adjustment from a non-oil economy to an oil based one, and the other with the "re-entry" problem, or the return to a manufacturing based export sector after oil revenues run out. The first issue concerns the surprising increasing unemployment in Latin-American oil exporters and in Holland that accompanied the increase in oil and/or gas revenues, and its failure to respond to Keynesian demand expansion (Holland in the mid seventies).

The second issue is whether a real appreciation and the concomitant negative effects on the T-goods sector call for (increased) public intervention. This could arise when there exist infant industry type learning by doing externalities in traded goods production. Clearly this is more of an issue in the case of a temporary appreciation, so it plays mainly a role in countries that will run out of oil in the foreseeable future.

Before proceeding to the theoretical analysis it is instructive to briefly look at the experience of Norway and Holland where both issues have come up with remarkably different policy response and outcome.

Although Norway's oil revenues started to flow in significant amounts only when the Statfjord field came on stream in 1979, bringing oil and gas revenues to 15% of GNP in 1980, government spending against oil wealth started earlier in the 70 ties, rising above 50% of GNP in the second half of the seventies. Much of that was spent on grants and subsidies to "sunset" industries, under pressure from a steady appreciation of the Krone (about 20% in real, trade weighted terms) and accompanying increases in unit labour cost.

The resulting current account deficit and increase in foreign debt clearly was a perfectly sensible response to the anticipated future oil revenues, the more so since foreign real interest rates were negative throughout most of the seventies.

More contentious is the channeling of all that extra expenditure towards subsidies for sunset industries, with predictable lack of success. Manufacturing output has been declining or stagnant from 1974 onwards although the devaluation cum wage-price controls in February 1978 provided temporary relief at the cost of delayed, but much increased inflationary pressure. Labour productivity performance in manufacturing was dismal as a consequence of the featherbedding by the government, especially when compared with similarly placed Holland (cf. fig. 1).

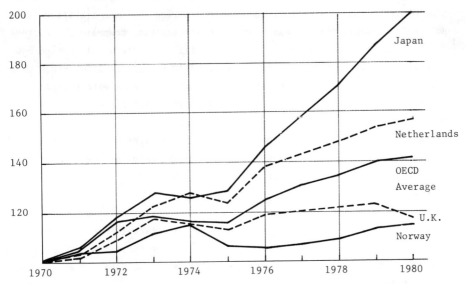

Figure 1. Labour productivity in Manufacturing industry (from Hall and Atkinson (1983)).

Not surprisingly relative unit labour costs (relative to trading partners) were 25% above 1970 levels around 1980.

The micro-economic costs of such King Canut-like fighting-the-tide policies are obvious although not easy to quantify. As the theory developed in the following sections predicts, however, they were highly successful in fighting unemployment, much more so than the more orthodox Keynesian fiscal demand stimulus policies followed in Holland. There is a good reason for that difference in success on the unemployment front as we will see in section 3, where we demonstrate that unemployment, if it arises in response to higher oil revenues, will be classical rather than Keynesian, making demand stimuli an inappropriate policy response.

On Holland we can be brief; we will focus on the two major differences in policies followed. Starting positions are roughly similar, although Holland had a proportionally larger manufacturing base but probably substantially smaller mineral reserves (consisting predominantly of natural gas rather than oil). Holland also witnessed a steady appreciation of the guilder and increases in labour costs.

There are two major differences in policies followed, however. The Dutch relied much more on expansionary demand management and less on targeted subsidies to combat unemployment, and used gas revenues to build up an extensive social security system. This system has clear humanitarian plus points but has now turned into a severe economic liability since Holland's economic fortune has been in an accelerating downward slide since 79/80. Demand expansion was a conspicuous failure in terms of holding down unemployment, which increased from 1.2% in 1970 to 5.3% in 1980; since then the bottom has fallen out under the Dutch economy with unemployment reaching depression era levels (currently around 18%). Fiscal policy, which provided a stimulus when none was called for in the seventies, is now actively used to deepen the recession, with the government arguing that the large deficits inherited from the misguided expansion of the seventies do not leave it any choice but retrenchment in the middle of a collapsing economy.

The combined effect of increasing unemployment and absence of government subsidy policies on manufacturing has however been spectacular (cf. fig. 1). Labour productivity and output have increased substantially over the seventies. The structure of manufacturing has changed substantially, however.

Summing up, Norway subsidized its sunset industries with as a result a sheltered, inefficient manufacturing sector, but a sector that continued to provide employment on a pre-oil scale. Unemployment has therefore not been a problem in Norway.

Table 1: Index numbers of Industrial Production for the Netherlands

	1970	1975	1977	1978	1979	1980
Industry total	100	123	133	134	138	137
Mining & quarrying	100	238	245	226	238	221
Manufacturing	100	109	119	121	125	128
Food, beverages, etc.	100	119	127	132	135	136
Textiles	100	81	81	77	79	74
Leather goods	100	62	61	57	57	56
Printing & publishing	100	104	115	120	123	125
Chemicals	100	125	151	156	170	164
Basic metal industries	100	100	107	114	115	112
Electricity, gas, water	100	153	164	175	178	175

(Source: Hall and Atkinson (1983))

Holland has not followed such subsidy policies, with positive effects for productivity and competitiveness of its manufacturing sector, but relied on Keynesian demand management to combat unemployment, without success on that front. In the theoretical analysis presented in the next three sections we will focus on these two issues:

A.   How and when can unemployment arise in the aftermath of increased oil revenues, and which policy measures will work and which will not?

B.   Under which conditions, if ever, are subsidies to non-oil traded goods producers called for in such circumstances.

In section 2 we set up a "core model" which is then used to analyse (real) exchange rate effects of increased oil revenues; a variant of this model, incorporating wage-price rigidities and therefore the possibility of unemployment, is used in section 3 to look at potential unemployment effects of increased oil revenues and the likely consequences of various policy measures. A different variant of our core model is put to work in section 4 where we derive conditions under which increased subsidies to non-oil traded goods producers will be welfare improving. We do this both for the case of imperfect and perfect external capital markets. Section 5 concludes.

2. REAL APPRECIATION AND OIL: THE CORE MODEL

In the following two sections we will discuss employment problems (section 3) and externalities in Traded goods production (section 4) using slight variants of a "Core Model". It is that model we present now and use to show the effects of oil revenues on the real exchange rate and sectoral allocation of production factors. We will use the "dual approach" (see for example Dixit and Norman (1980)) to analyse the model, because relative prices and welfare effects of various interventions play an important role in what follows.

Since much interest attaches to consequences of oil running out one day we need an intertemporal structure. We take the simplest one, a two period model. Also we assume there are two produced goods in the economy, apart from oil: a Traded good (which we will use as numeraire, so its price is one by choice of normalization) and a Non-Traded good, with price Q in period one and q in period 2.[1)]

Production of oil will be assumed to require no resources in most of the analysis, although we will briefly discuss the case where oil production requires capital at the end of this section.

No attempt is made to fully endogenise oil production since that issue can, under the assumption of perfect capital markets, be completely separated from the effects of oil wealth on the non-oil economy. Capital market imperfections will be introduced at various places in the paper later on, however.

We will describe production structure by using a revenue function, relating the maximum revenue to be obtained from efficient use of factor supplies given relative prices and factor supplies:

(1) $R = R(Q, 1; K, L),$ $r = r(q, 1; k, l)$

Clearly second period capital $k = K + I$, ignoring depreciation; I is first period investment.

Similarly, consumer preferences can be described by the use of an expenditure or cost function, giving the minimum discounted value of expenditure needed to achieve utility level U, given the relative price structure:

(2) $E = E(\Pi (Q, 1), \delta\pi(q, 1), U).$

U depends on current and future consumption of T and NT goods in the usual way. The existence of aggregate price indices Π, π and the particular structure of equation 2 require U to be weakly identically homothetically separable. This allows us to write U as $U(Z(C_N, C_T), z (c_N, c_T))$ where Z and z are within-period utility indices.

The derivatives of R(E) with respect to prices give the corresponding output (Hicksian demand) functions. δ equals $1/(1 + r^*)$ where r^* is the real rate of interest on world capital markets.

We can now write down the economy's intertemporal budget constraint:

(3) $R(Q, 1; K, L) + \delta r(q, 1; K + I, 1) - \phi I + O + \delta o =$

$$E(\Pi(Q, 1), \delta\pi(q, 1), U)$$

where I is aggregate investment, O and o period one and two oil revenues and ϕ the reproduction cost of capital, everything deflated by the price of traded goods (i.e. T-goods are the numeraire). ϕ can be interpreted as a unit cost function with T and NT goods as inputs so that $\phi_Q I$ is use of NT goods for investment purposes.

Period one NT good market clearing is given by

(4a) $R_Q = E_Q + \phi_Q I$

and similarly for period two:

(4b) $r_q = E_q$

Value maximization of the firm leads to an implicit investment function

(5a) $\delta r_k(q, 1; K + I, 1) = \phi$

or

(5b) $I = I(Q, q, \delta)$

with $\dfrac{\partial I}{\partial Q} = \dfrac{\phi_Q}{\delta r_{kk}} < 0,$ $\dfrac{\partial I}{\partial \delta} = \dfrac{-r_k}{\delta r_{kk}} > 0$ and $\dfrac{\partial I}{\partial q} = \dfrac{-r_{kq}}{r_{kk}} < 0$

I_Q is zero or negative depending on whether ϕ_Q is zero or positive ($\phi_Q = 0$ implies first period investment uses T-goods only), I_δ is of course positive (i.e. higher interest rates mean lower investment), while I_q depends on the sign of the Rybczynski term r_{kq}. If the NT-sector is more capital intensive than the T-sector, $r_{kq} > 0$ and vice versa. Capital intensity of NT goods is probably a reasonably assumption given such "NT industries" as power generation, housing etc., so that is the assumption we will usually make. Tracing out the consequense of $r_{kq} < 0$ is simple and left to the interested reader.

After (3) has been used to substitute out the welfare level, (4a) presents an upward sloping schedule in Q -q space labeled QQ in fig. 2:

(6) $\dfrac{dQ}{dq}\bigg|_{QQ} = \dfrac{(E_{Qq} + \phi_Q I_q)}{R_{QQ} - E_{QQ} - \phi_Q I_Q - I\phi_{QQ}} > 0$

Concavity of E and ϕ, convexity of R and the separability assumption on U (quaranteeing $E_{Qq} > 0$ by ruling out complementarity) quarantee that dQ/dq > 0. The intuition is simple. An increase in q (an anticipated future real appreciation) will shift consumer expenditure away toward all other goods (since the separability assumptions and the resulting two-by-two structure of U rule out complementarity), and thus increasing demand for current NT goods. Also a higher future exchange rate will increase current investment spending under our assumption of a relatively capital intensive NT sector, which increases todays demand for NT goods further if $\phi_Q > 0$.

Similarly for the NT goods market schedule in period 2, locus qq:

$$(7) \qquad \frac{dQ}{dq} \bigg|_{qq} = \frac{(r_{qq} - E_{qq} + r_{qk}I_q)}{E_{qQ} - r_{qk}I_Q} > 0$$

A higher first period exchange rate decreases investment via its impact on the cost of capital and therefore reduces the second period supply of NT goods via standard Rybczynski effects, while demand substitution away from current NT goods will increase the demand. Accordingly q will have to go up to restore equilibrium. In stable configurations qq is steeper than QQ.

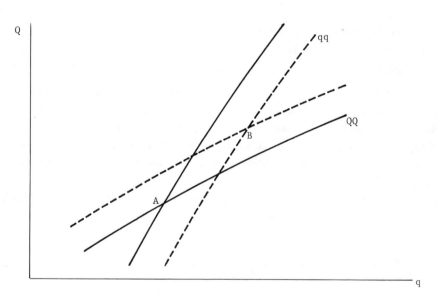

Figure 2. Effects of an oil discovery on current and future exchange rates.

We are now ready to look at the effects of increased oil revenues. Because of our assumption of perfect capital markets (relaxed in later sections) the time pattern of oil revenues is irrelevant, all that matters is their discounted value (the _rental_ value of existing reserves), $T = 0 + \delta o$.

Higher oil wealth will lead to more consumer expenditure in both periods, some of which will fall on NT goods in each period, leading to incipient excess demand in current and future NT markets; therefore the QQ schedule shifts up and the qq schedule shifts to the right:

(8a) $\quad \dfrac{dQ}{dT}\bigg|_{QQ} = \dfrac{C_N}{R_{QQ} - E_{QQ} - \phi_Q I_Q - \phi_{QQ} I} > 0$

and

(8b) $\quad \dfrac{dq}{dT}\bigg|_{qq} = \dfrac{C_N}{r_{qq} - E_{qq} + r_{qk} I_q} > 0$

where $C_N \, C_N$ is the marginal propensity to spend on current future NT goods out of wealth.

The net effect can be seen in figure 2, where A represents the pre-oil and B the post-oil equilibrium. To accommodate the higher oil wealth both the future and the current exchange rate need to rise, in perfect analogy with the standard Salter Swan analysis of the transfer problem.

This discussion, simple as it is, summarizes the content of the vast majority of "Dutch Disease" papers, which are nearly all variations on the transfer problem. An extra mechanism, baptized "Resource Movement" effect by Cordon and Neary (1982) focuses on additional complications, when oil extraction diverts capital from the non-oil economy (this only matters to the extent that the capital goods needed can not be imported in the short run, but exist in and can be diverted from domestic use). This can easily be incorporated in our model and diagram. To do that replace K in both revenue functions by $K - K_0$, with K_0 representing capital used in the oil sector; oil revenues are now a function of the stock of oil θ and the amount of capital K_0 used to extract it:

(9) $T = T(K_0; \theta)$, $T(K_0; 0) = 0$ for all K_0

                          $T(K_0; \theta) > 0$ for all $K_0, \theta > 0$

                          T_{K_0} , T_θ, $T_{K_{0,\theta}}$ > 0   for all $K_0, \theta > 0$

and add an equation determining the allocation of the capital stock over the oil and non-oil economy:

(10) $R_K = T_{K_0}$

An oil shock is represented by an increase in θ .

        Figure 3 shows the results. <u>For given value of K_0</u> the equilibrium will shift to B.

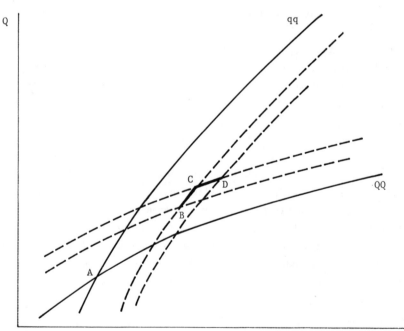

Figure 3.   Corden-Neary Resource Movement effects.

The oil discovery will, however, increase the marginal productivity of capital in the oil sector, raising it above the rate of return prevailing in the non-oil economy. This will, via equation (10), lead to a shift of capital from the non-oil to the oil sector. The result is an upward shift in QQ via standard Rybczynski effects; if investment consists completely of T-goods ($\phi_Q = 0$) the qq-locus will <u>not</u> shift[2] because investment I will adjust to increase the second period non-oil capital stock to its old value. The new equilibrium will therefore be at C (fig. 3).

However if $\phi_Q > 0$, investment will fall short of that because in that case the cost of capital has gone up. But a smaller period 2 capital stock will via Rybzcynski effects shift the qq-locus to the right (since we assumed the NT sector to be capital intensive an excess demand for NT goods develops if the capital stock declines). Accordingly the equilibrium now becomes point D (figure 3). The conclusion is obvious: the resource movement effect will reinforce the upward pressure on the exchange rate exerted by the transfer effect if $R_{QK} > 0$ (i.e. if the NT sector is relatively capital intensive). It is easy to check that the reverse holds if the NT sector is labour intensive ($R_{QK} < 0$).

Two points are worth mentioning before we continue. First, these results are completely independent of the time pattern of the oil revenues because of the perfect capital market assumption. Even if all oil comes today (T = 0) there will be no depreciation in the post oil period two. That result of course depends crucially on the perfect capital market assumption and assumes that any excess of current revenues over the permanent income equivalent is used to accumulate foreign assets.

The second point is as least as obvious but surprisingly widely ignored. <u>Under the assumptions made so far</u> the real appreciation is an efficient, competitive and optimal response to the increase in oil revenues and in itself in no sense of the word a "Disease". Given these assumptions, the appreciation is essential to effect the reallocation of resources out of the T-sector and into the NT-sector that is necessary to accommodate the oil boom. Nearly the entire literature on the "Dutch Disease" (see the survey by Corden (1984)) demonstrates that more oil leads one way or another to an appreciation and concludes that there is indeed a "Disease", ignoring this point. It is quite possible that there is indeed a Dutch Disease, but to demonstrate that one needs to identify a market failure preventing the appropriate adjustment which would take place without such failures, or existing, unmovable distortions made worse by the oil boom or something like that. That is exactly what we will do in the next three sections.

3. OIL REVENUES AND EMPLOYMENT: A SHORT RUN DISEQUILIBRIUM ANALYSIS

In the introduction we noted that increased oil revenues have not uniformly led to employment benefits, pointing especially to the UK and Latin-American oil producers. We will present a modified version of the "core model" to facilitate discussion of this issue. The model we will use is simpler than the core model in that it has been reduced to a static model, more complex in that it explicitly incorporates disequilibrium.

3.1 ONE-PERIOD DISEQUILIBRIUM VERSION OF THE CORE MODEL

The building blocks used are similar to those of the core model with some exceptions. In view of the Short Run Nature of the analysis, we assume a Ricardo-Viner structure with sector-specific capital, and introduce the possibility of disequilibrium in labour and NT-goods markets by assuming the existence of wage-price rigidity.[3] Investment is assumed constant, and, for convenience, set equal to zero.

The budget constraint is

(11) $R(Q, 1; L) + T = E(Q, 1, Z)$

using the notation of the previous section. A labour demand curve can be derived from the requirement that the marginal value product of labour should equal its wage:

(12a) $R_L(Q, 1; L) = W$

or

(12b) $L = L(W, Q), \quad L_W = R_{LL}^{-1} < 0, \quad L_Q = - R_{LQ}R_{LL}^{-1} > 0$

The Rybczynski-term R_{LQ} is always positive in Ricardo-Viner models. In fact we will use later on the fact that $W/Q > R_{LQ} > 0$ (Dixit and Norman (1980)).

To construct the disequilibrium model consider first labour market equilibrium under excess demand for NT goods. In that situation firms can sell whatever they want and will therefore be on their notional (ie.

unconstrained) demand curve for labour along the labour market equilibrium schedule NN. We furthermore assume a fixed labour supply in line with the one-period nature of the model. This leads to a labour market equilibrium schedule under excess demand for NT goods (ie. to the left of the Walrasian equilibrium A in figure 4):

(13) $\bar{L} = L(W, Q)$

(13) corresponds to LL in figure 4. Clearly LL is positively sloped in W-Q space.

(14) $\dfrac{dW}{dQ}\bigg|_{LL} = \bar{R}_{LQ} > 0$

The rationale is simple: an increase in Q given W will not affect labour demand in the T-sector but will increase it in the NT-sector. To get back to equilibrium, an increase in W is called for. This increase will be less than proportional to the increase in Q because for given Q an increase in W affects labour demand in both sectors:

$$\frac{Q}{W}\frac{dW}{dQ}\bigg|_{LL} = \frac{Q}{W} R_{LQ} < 1.$$

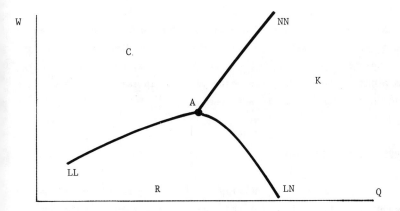

Figure 4. A one-period disequilibrium version of the Core Model.

Consider now NT-goods market equilibrium under excess supply of labour (i.e. above A in figure 4). Firms are once again unconstrained since we have excess supply of labour, and are on a goods market equilibrium locus by construction. Supply of NT goods can therefore be derived from the revenue function by taking the derivative with respect to Q. Consumers are rationed in the labour market, but that is incorporated via the budget constraint so that we can use the expenditure function E to derive demand for NT goods along the NN locus:

(15) R_Q (Q, 1; L(W, Q)) = E_Q(Q, 1, Z)

Z can be obtained from the budget constraint (11).

This locus also slopes upwards and in fact is steeper than LL:

(16) $\left. \dfrac{dW}{dQ} \right|_{NN} = R_{QL} - \dfrac{(R_{QQ} - E_{QQ})}{R_{LQ}} > R_{QL} > 0$

The first inequality holds because revenue functions are convex in prices (so $R_{QQ} > 0$) and concave in factor use (so $R_{LL} < 0$). See figure 4.

The labour market equilibrium locus under excess supply of goods and the NT goods market equilibrium locus under excess demand for labour collapse into one locus, LN, since in any area between them firms would demand more labour than obtainable while being unable to sell the products of the workers already hired. Such double rationing of firms is incompatible with rational firm behaviour, leading to the collapse of these two loci, and the disappearance of a Marxist under-consumptionist regime as incompatible with rational firm behaviour.[4] If T-firms are under rationing in the labour market, LN has a negative slope, but other rationing mechanisms might lead to a different outcome. This is immaterial for what follows, so we will not pursue this further.

3.2 OIL REVENUES AND EMPLOYMENT

We can use the machinery developed into section 3.1 to trace out the consequences of an oil boom for the real exchange rate and employment. From (12) we can see that increased oil revenues will have no direct impact on employment for a given wage-price structure,[5] the LL locus does not shift. This is not true for the NN and LN loci: higher revenue will lead to higher spending, some of which will fall on NT goods; a real appreciation is needed to accommodate that (see also figure 5):

$$\frac{dQ}{dT}\Bigg|_{\substack{NN \\ W=\bar{W}}} = \frac{C_N}{R_{QQ} - R_{QL}^2 \,/\, R_{LL}} > 0$$

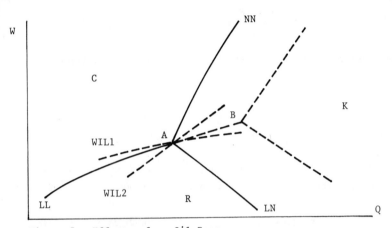

Figure 5. Effects of an Oil Boom.

Since wages and prices are rigid, the economy will stay at point A, on the borderline between the Classical Unemployment region C and Repressed Inflation R, but with excess demand for NT goods (since we are now to the left of the NN and LN schedules).

The new Walrasian equilibrium at B is characterized by a higher real exchange rate; from (11), (12) and (15) one gets:

(17a) $$\frac{dQ}{dT} = \frac{C_N}{R_{QQ} - E_{QQ}}$$

The higher exchange rate induce a higher supply of NT goods and somewhat slows down demand for them. The higher supply implies a transfer of workers out of the T-sector into the NT-sector; to effect this structural adjustment, which is necessary to fully reap the benefits of the oil boom, real traded product wages W will go up:

(17b) $\quad \dfrac{dW}{dT} = \dfrac{R_{LQ} \, C_N}{R_{QQ} - E_{QQ}} > 0$

and real non-traded product wages W/Q will have to fall:

$$\dfrac{dW/Q}{dT} = \dfrac{1}{Q} \left(\dfrac{dW}{dQ} - \dfrac{W}{Q} \right) \dfrac{dQ}{dT}$$

(17c) $\qquad = \dfrac{1}{Q} \left(R_{LQ} - \dfrac{W}{Q} \right) \dfrac{C_N}{R_{QQ} - E_{QQ}}$

Using homogeneity properties of the revenue function it is simple to show that the term between brackets is negative:[6]

(17d) $\quad \dfrac{d(W/Q)}{dT} = \dfrac{-R_{LT} \, C_N}{(R_{QQ} - E_{QQ}) Q^2} < 0$

    The big question is whether the economy will be able to reach the new Walrasian equilibrium B without having to go through a phase of unemployment or not.

    To answer that question we will follow van Wijnbergen (1984b) and make the standard augmented Phillips curve assumption that _real consumption wages_ can only be brought down by having temporary unemployment. The crucial issue then is whether the real consumption wage at B is higher or lower than it is at A.

    Our duality framework allows us to get an exact answer, since we can use the expenditure function structure to get an exact price index measuring the unit cost of aggregate consumption. Remember our assumption in section 2 of homotheticity of the subutility functions Z and z. This allows us to write the expenditure function E(Q, 1; Z) as Π(Q, 1)Z, where Π is the true price index corresponding to the aggregate consumption bundle. It is simple to show that Π is also a unit-expenditure function.[7]

    We can now define the real consumption wage as W/Π. Clearly

$$\dfrac{\Pi}{W} \dfrac{d(W/\Pi)}{dT} = \dfrac{1}{W} \dfrac{dW}{dT} - \dfrac{1}{\Pi} \dfrac{d\Pi}{dT}$$

$$= \dfrac{C_N \, R_{LQ}/W}{R_{QQ} - E_{QQ}} - \dfrac{\Pi_Q}{\Pi} \dfrac{dQ}{dT}$$

$$= \dfrac{C_N \, R_{LQ}/W}{R_{QQ} - E_{QQ}} - \dfrac{Q\Pi_Q}{\Pi} \dfrac{1}{Q} \dfrac{dQ}{dT}$$

(18) $\qquad = \dfrac{C_N}{(R_{QQ} - E_{QQ})Q} \; (\Psi_T - R_{LT}/W)$

where we used $\dfrac{R_{LQ}\,Q}{W} = 1 - R_{LT}$ and $\Psi_T = 1 - \Psi_N$.

There is a straightforward diagrammatic counterpart to this expression, for which we have to rewrite (18) as

(19) $\quad \dfrac{\Pi}{W} \; \dfrac{d(W/\Pi)}{dT} \; \alpha \; (R_{LQ} - \dfrac{W\Psi_N}{Q})$

R_{LQ} is the slope of the LL line in figures 4 and 5, and $\dfrac{W\Psi_N}{Q}$ is the slope of the line in W-Q space along which the real consumption wage W/Π is constant (Wage Indexation Line):

$$\dfrac{dW}{W} - \dfrac{d\Pi}{\Pi} = \dfrac{dW}{W} - \dfrac{Q\Pi_Q}{\Pi}\dfrac{dQ}{Q} = 0 \Rightarrow \dfrac{dW}{dQ} \Big|_{WIL} = \dfrac{W}{Q} \Psi_N \; .$$

Two such lines are draw in fig. 5, labeled WIL1 and WIL2. If the economy is at a point of full employment, like A, our Phillips curve assumption implies that it can move away along a WIL line (in our case to the right pushing up Q since there is excess demand for NT goods at A). The issue then becomes : is that WIL line steeper or flatter than the LL curve?

If it is steeper (WIL2 in fig. 5)), the economy will move into the C region. This corresponds to (18) being _less_ than zero, or a fall in the real consumption wage between A and B. To reach B the real consumption wage has to fall in this case, but indexation will prevent this initially, forcing the economy to move along line WIL2 into the C region with classical unemployment. To see what is going on one should realize that an appreciation will increase the real traded product wage W but lower the real nontraded product wage W/Q. Unemployment will result if indexation requires too large an increase in W to offset the effect of the required fall in W/Q on the real consumption wage. This will happen if the share of NT goods in the consumption basket is "large" in a sense to be made precise below.

Conversely, if the WIL line is flatter than LL, the economy will move into the R region of Repressed Inflation, along WIL1. In that case (18) is positive, T-goods have a "large" share in the consumption bundle and the required fall in W/Q, given the real consumption wage W/Π will lead to much of a decline in W and as a result excess demand for labour.

All this seems to accord well with the stylized facts mentioned in the introduction : the gulf countries, which import virtually all their consumption goods, had excess demand for labour after the oil price shocks lead to skyrocketing revenues; on the other hand Latin American oil producers, which have a long history of prohibitive tariff barriers against imported consumption goods making them effectively NT-goods, saw no employment benefits and in some cases (Venezuela, Mexico) increasing unemployment after higher oil revenues.

(18) can be made more precise in the context of the Ricardo-Viner model used here. It can be shown that (18) boils down too:

$$\frac{\upsilon_T}{\upsilon_T + \upsilon_N} > \Psi_T => \quad \text{economy moves into C region}$$

$$< \Psi_T => \quad \text{economy moves into R region}$$

where $\upsilon_T = \phi_T \sigma_T / (1 - \theta_T)$ and $\upsilon_N = \phi_N \sigma_N / (1 - \theta_N)$. ϕ_i is the share of the labour force employed in sector i , σ_T is the substitution elasticity in sector i and θ_T is the wage income share in sector i.

So a high capital intensity in the N sector $(1 - \theta_N > 1 - \theta_T)$ would increase the likelihood of moving into the C region. Again our Latin American parallel works : prohibitively high tariff barriers have typically favoured capital intensive industries. On the other hand if $\sigma_N = \sigma_T$, $\theta_N = \theta_T$ the expression boils down to

$$\phi_T \lessgtr \Psi_T$$

Under those circumstances ϕ_T is also the share of T-goods in total non-oil input; it is easy to show that $\theta_N = \theta_T$ and $\phi_T < \Psi_T$ implies that countries for which this holds run a non-oil Current Account deficit. Accordingly a large non-oil CA deficit increases the change of a move into the R- region after increased oil revenues, since it implies high (relative to T- production share in output) expenditure. So our model would predict excess demand for labour in countries like the Gulf-oil producers, with small T-goods production sector and most of T-consumption imported.

3.3 EFFECTS OF SOME POLICY MEASURES

In this section we will give a brief diagrammatical analysis of some policy measures which have been taken or discussed in response to the appreciation.

First consider a devaluation of the exchange rate in response to the upward pressure on the real exchange rate (fig. 6). Although a satisfactory treatment of devaluation would require explicit introduction of asset markets, we can use our framework to trace the consequences of a devaluation that is successful in the short run in the sense that it does lead to a real depreciation, at least initially.

If there is no response by nominal NT goods prices and wages at all, a devaluation can be represented by a move back to the origin, say from   A towards C, since under that assumption W and Q will go down proportionally (keep in mind that LL is flatter than L so C is below LL). Clearly the Walrasian equilibrium A will not be affected, there will be no long run real effects, since the cause of the pressure for appreciation is not removed by a devaluation. The result will be increased excess demand for NT-goods, and if nominal wages do not respond, excess demand for labour   (E is below LL, in the R-region).

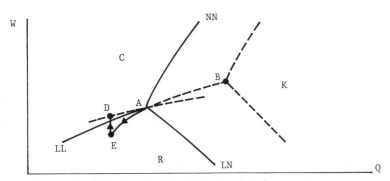

Figure 6. Effects of a nominal devaluation.

Consider, however, if real wages are sticky, rather than nominal wages, eg via CPI indexation. In that case we will move away from A along a Wage Indexation Line, one of which is drawn in figure 6. If the WIL is steeper than LL ($\Psi_T < R_{LT}/W$) we will still be in the R-region, above E but below LL, so no qualitative change here. However, if $\Psi_T > R_{LT}/W$, if the LL is steeper, a move back from A will push us back into the C-region, causing classical unemployment (cf point D in fig. 6)! If the share of T-goods in the indexation formula is large enough, a devaluation will cause such a large increase in nominal wages to offset the increased costs of imported consumption goods that the traded product wage will fall but less than

22

proportionately with the exchange rate times Ψ_T, and the non-traded product wage will go up to such an extent that classical unemployment results.

Consider next import of labour as was done in the Gulf countries; this is clearly only an interesting option if the economy has moved into the R-region with excess demand for labour in the aftermath of the increase in oil revenues like for example E in fig. 7.

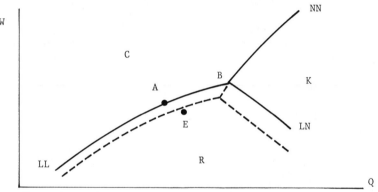

Figure 7. Effects of Import of Foreign Workers.

The increase in L caused by the influx of foreign workers will not affect the location of the NN curve, but will of course shift down the LL locus, alleviating labour market pressure (E is now closer to the LL locus). It will also reduce the equilibrium appreciation of the real exchange rate from Q_A to Q_B since the new workers will produce NT-goods but spend only part of their income on NT-goods, thus increasing the net supply.

A further policy option often discussed is the extension of subsidies to the T-sector to cope with the increased real wage pressure (we will return to this issue in the next section). We will look at wage subsidies set up in such a way that the pre-oil shock traded product wage is maintained [8] at say, W^*. This would rotate the LL-schedule upwards around point A in figure 8: the new LL schedule becomes

$$L_T (W^*) + L_N(W/Q) = \overline{L}$$

which is a line through A and the origin. The Wage Indexation lines are always flatter than one (their slope is $\Psi_T < 1$), so now classical unemployment is impossible. This is not surprising: because of the subsidies no workers will be fired in the T-sector so that the oil revenue increase cannot lead to unemployment, at the cost of allocational distortions and a larger long run real appreciation ($Q_E > Q_B$ in fig. 8). The higher long run appreciation comes about because the wage subsidies fixing of labour costs in the T-sector eliminates any incentive for labour movements out of that sector, leaving demand shifts to do all the adjustment.

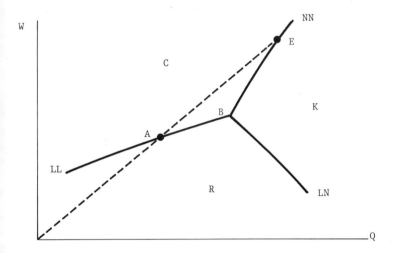

Figure 8. Effects of wage subsidies to the T-sector.

Finally if unemployment results because wage indexation does not allow a sufficiently large fall in the real non-traded product wage for the NT-sector to absorb all the workers fired in the T-sector, an obvious policy response would be to use changes in taxation to drive a wedge between real consumption wages and real product wages. Cuts in indirect taxes, unemployment insurance contributions etc. would all allow lower real product wages without lower real consumption wages, leading to a way out of Classical Unemployment.

What will not work, however, is expansionary fiscal policy. Transitional unemployment during an oil-boom obviously is not due to lack of effective demand but to wage rigidity; consider our diagram again

24

(fig.9). Fiscal expansion would shift the goods market loci NN and LN to the right without _directly_ affecting the labour market locus LL. The new post-oil, post-fiscal-expansion Walrasian equilibrium is now at E with an even higher real exchange rate than would obtain without the fiscal expansion; this will over time put even more pressure on T-firms, causing them to lay off more workers, which in turn will not be absorbed in the NT-sector as long as downward real wage rigidity persists. Fiscal expansion in these circumstances will add to real exchange rate pressure while exacerbating rather than alleviating transitional unemployment!

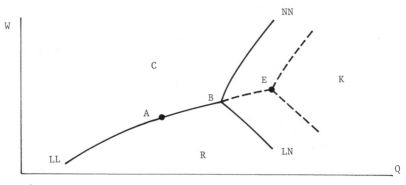

Figure 9. Effects of Expansionary Fiscal Policy.

4. TEMPORARY REAL APPRECIATION, EXTERNALITIES IN TRADED GOODS PRODUCTION AND THE CASE FOR T-SECTOR SUBSIDIES

In this section we go back to the market clearing, two period framework used in our core model of section 2. We extend that model however, by incorporating Learning by Doing (LD) induced technological progress in the T-goods sector.[9] There is empirical evidence indicating that technological progress takes place predominantly in the T-sector (Balassa (1964)); we assume it _only_ takes place in the T-sector for clearer focus. What is more contentious is our assumption that LD effects on technology are external to the firm. Van Wijnbergen (1984b) presents some a priori arguments in favour of the point of view that substantial parts of LD benefits will not be internalized, but solid empirical evidence is entirely missing.

We will first discuss the case where capital market constraints prevent smoothing out of temporary oil revenues, leading to a corresponding time pattern of expenditure; we then look at the other extreme, perfect capital markets allowing complete separation of expenditure from current income subject to the intertemporal budget constraint.

Consider then first the case where expenditure patterns do follow the temporary increase in oil income, as a consequence of the assumption of an exogenous (zero for convenience) current account. That implies that the intertemporal budget constraint (3) is replaced by two within-period budget constraints:

(20a) $R(P + S, Q) + T-SR_p = E(P, Q, Z)$

and

(20b) $r(p,q; R_p) = e(p, q, z)$

T represents first period oil revenues. S is a first period subsidy on T-goods production discussed below. SR_p are the costs of the subsidy financed by non-distortionary taxes. The second period revenue function already embodies our assumption of technological progress in the T-sector via a shift factor-proportional to the output of traded goods X_T in period 1 (which is by properties of the revenue function, R_p):

(21) $r = r(p, q; R_p)$ with $r_R > 0$, $r_{pR} > 0$, $r_{qR} > 0$

where $r_R = \partial r/\partial R_p$ etc. The signs of the cross effects indicate that the outward shift occurs in the T-sector. For analytical convenience we will assume that $r_{RR} = 0$. Oil revenues are temporary, which is incorporated by setting them equal to zero in period 2. P and p are set equal to one by choice of normalization.

NT goods market equilibrium is given by equations (4a and 4b):

(22) $R_Q = E_Q$, $r_q = e_q$

We assume that the LD effect is not internalized, so that a first best intervention rule calls for subsidies to T-goods production in period 1 (not for tariff protection as often claimed in such infant industry type arguments, since that would lead to unnecessary welfare losses for consumers). To determine the optimal subsidy level one needs to maximize social welfare subject to the constraints set up so far. A natural choice for that welfare function is the private welfare function $U(Z, z)$ introduced in section 2. Differentiation of U with respect to S using the budget constraints (20a,20b) to find derivatives $\frac{\partial Z}{\partial S}$ and $\frac{\partial z}{\partial S}$ yields:

$$(23) \quad \frac{\partial U}{\partial Z}\frac{\partial Z}{\partial S} + \frac{\partial U}{\partial z}\frac{\partial z}{\partial S} = -U_z E_z^{-1} S + U_z e_z^{-1} r_R = 0$$

or

$$S^* = \lambda r_R \quad ; \quad \lambda = \frac{\Pi}{\pi}\frac{\partial U/\partial z}{\partial U/\partial Z}$$

λ is the ratio of the marginal utility of expenditure tomorrow (z) to the marginal utility of expenditure today. In a perfect capital market λ would equal the world discount factor $\delta = 1/(1 + r^*))$, but with capital market imperfections that equality need not obtain. The formula has a nice intuitive interpretation: if private producers receive the benefits generated on the margin by the LD externality (δr_R), corrected for any wedge between λ and δ caused by capital market imperfections, they will produce the socially optimal level of T-goods in period 1. If there is no such wedge the formula simplifies to $S^* = \delta r_R$. The presence of λ in (23) indicates there is an intertemporal trade off involved in S^*; an increase in S will lead to a decline in welfare today because of the increased static price distortion it causes today; but to an increase tomorrow because of the dynamic benefits associated with the larger future outward shift of the production function in the T-sector. If on the margin expenditure tomorrow generates less additional welfare than expenditure today because capital market imperfections prevent intertemporal arbitrage ($\lambda < \delta$) a smaller subsidy is called for than would otherwise be the case.

Now what happens when first period oil revenues go up? We will use a diagrammatical representation of the equation system (20) - (23) to help in the analysis (figure 10).

NT1 in figure 10 represents the first period goods market schedule in Q-S space where S equals the _actual_ subsidy level (by assumption $S = S^*$, the _optimal_ level, before the increase in oil revenues). Z has been substituted out using (20a). NT slopes upwards; a higher subsidy S to production in the T-sector draws resources out of the NT sector, reducing

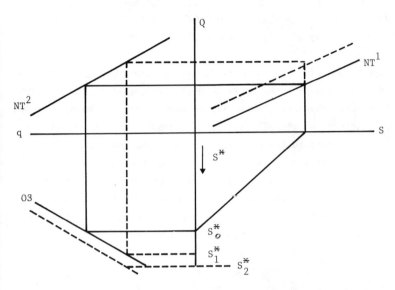

Figure 10. Effects of an increase in Oil Revenues in period 1 on
optimal subsidy level and period 1 and 2 real exchange
rates.

supply of T goods; a return to equilibrium requires a higher real exchange
rate Q, so NT1 slopes up.[10] Moreover, higher oil revenues in period one
will be spent partially on NT goods in period one, shifting the schedule
upwards (to NT1 in figure 10).

NT2 represents NT goods market equilibrium in period 2. Z has been
sustitute out using (20b). Because of our assumption of an exogenous CA,
there is only one rather indirect intertemporal channel left; the one via
LD externalities. A higher real exchange rate today will draw resources out
of the T-sector today, leading to lower productivity in that sector
tomorrow because of lost LD experience. This in turn will lead to a shift
of resources out of the T-sector tomorrow into the NT sector, necessitating
a lower second period real exchange rate. Accordingly NT2 has a negative
slope. An increase in first period oil revenues will not directly affect
NT2 under our exogenous current account assumption.

Finally the OS schedule, representing equation (23) in S*-q space,
with S* the optimal subsidy level. A higher second period real exchange
rate implies a lower value of second period T-goods, therefore, given
everything else, the value of the extra future productivity benefits of an
additional unit of first period T-goods production declines and so does the
optimal subsidy level: OS has a negative slope. First period increases in

oil revenues shift OS out under our exogenous CA assumption: more expenditure today for given expenditure tomorrow increases λ, the ratio of marginal utility of expenditure tomorrow over that of expenditure today because of the concavity of $U(Z, z)$. Since $S^* = \lambda r_R$, the OS schedule shifts out.

We now have all the building blocks in place to work through the effects of more oil today on the optimal subsidy to the T-sector. As argued above, higher oil revenues today will at least partially be spent on NT goods today, shifting out the NT1 curve and leading to a first period real appreciation for standard Dutch Disease reasons. The resulting decline in T-goods production will lead to a decline in second period productivity in that sector as technological progress slows down. The resulting resource shifts into the NT sector will lead to a real depreciation in period 2.

For given location of the OS schedule this in itself would already be enough for an increase in the optimal subsidy level: the negatively sloped OS schedule tells us that a lower second period exchange rate (higher value of period 2 T-goods) calls for higher first period subsidies: the post-oil-increase optimal subsidy S_1^* exceeds the pre-oil-increase one S_0^* (cf. SE quadrant in figure 10).

Moreover we have already seen that higher oil revenues today will increase λ, the social discount factor, shifting out the OS schedule. This leads to a further increase in the optimal subsidy towards S_2^*[11)]

We therefore have a clear-cut result: if the CA cannot or is not used to smooth expenditure , subsidies to the non-oil traded goods sector should be increased if that sector shows the potensial of significant Learning by Doing induced increases in productivity external to the firm. In this sense the Dutch Disease is indeed a disease.

What however if the link between current income and expenditure can be broken via the current account? In that case income from foreign assets (and running down of the principal) accumulated in period one will provide another source of foreign exchange in period 2, reducing the need to switch back into T-goods production. Accordingly the case for increased subsidies to the T-goods sector during the period of high oil revenues will be weakened.

Not much adjustment to the model is needed to introduce perfect capital mobility into the system, in fact several simplifications obtain. First of all, now that capital markets are perfect, $\lambda = \delta$ via inter-temporal arbitrage, leading to a simplified formula for S:

(24) $S^* = \delta r_R$

Moreover several complicating income effects disappear now that current losses and future gains can be offset against each other.

The two within-period budget constraints are now replaced by one intertemporal budget constraint:

(25) $R + \delta r + T - SR_p = \tilde{E} (\Pi(P, Q), \pi(p, q), U)$

where $\tilde{E}$ gives the minimum discounted value of expenditure today and tomorrow needed to achieve welfare level U given the relative price structure. The NT goods market clearing equations remain basically the same except that E_Q and e_q have to be replaced by $\tilde{E}_Q$ and $\tilde{E}_q$.

Once again we will use a diagram to show what is going on (figure 11). The NW quadrant in figure 11 shows the negative relation between S^* and the second period exchange rate q that we already discussed. The NE quadrant shows the two NT goods market schedules NT1 and NT2. The first period slopes up unambiguously; a higher real exchange rate tomorrow leads to substitution towards future and current foreign goods and current NT goods since the structure of the utility function (separable over time) and the fact are only two goods per period rule out complementarity in con-

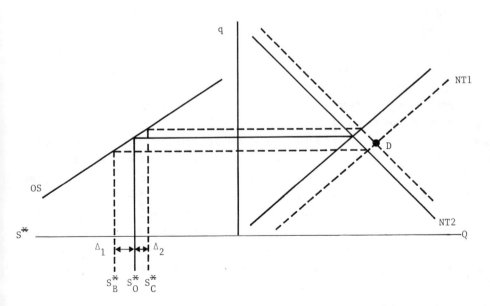

Figure 11. Optimal Subsidy and Real Exchange Rate Effects with an Endogenous Current Account.

sumption. To get the first period NT goods market into equilibrium, the first period real exchange rate has to increase. The curve will shift out after an increase in oil revenues for standard Dutch Disease reasons.

The second period NT goods market schedule NT2 is more complicated. On the one hand the mechanism behind the negative slope in the exogenous CA case (the channel via the LD externality) is still there; on the other hand the same substitution mechanism that causes a positive NT1 slope is also at work here (in the opposite direction of course, dQ > 0 leads to excess demand for period 2 NT goods pushing up q via substitution effects). No strong statements can be made, NT2 can slope either upwards or downwards (although it will always be flatter than NT1 in stable configurations). Here we only represent the case where NT2 has a negative slope but we will briefly discuss the implications of a positive NT2 schedule at the end. Whatever its slope, the NT1 schedule shifts up after an increase in oil revenues as some of the revenues will be spent on second period NT goods.

Consider now the effect of higher oil revenues on the optimal subsidy. The increase in oil revenues leads to some extra expenditure today and some tomorrow. The expenditure effect today leads to excess demand for NT goods today, pushing up the first period exchange rate Q: NT1 shifts out (cf fig 11, NE quadrant). By tracing the effects of a higher Q along the NT2 and OS schedules to the level of optimal subsidy (from B via OS to S_B^*) it can be seen that this shift in itself makes for increased subsidies: $\Delta_1 = S_B^* - S_0^* > 0$. The mechanism is now familiar, a higher first period exchange rate draws resources out of the OT sector leading to less beneficial LD induced productivity increases tomorrow, therefore a second period depreciation ($Q_B < Q_A$) and accordingly an increase in the optimal subsidy from S_0^* to S_B^*.

On the other hand some of the oil revenues will be spent tomorrow leading to upward pressure on the real exchange rate tomorrow (NT2 shifts up and $q_C > q_A$), reducing the value of second period T-goods (=1/q) and therefore reducing the optimal subsidy from S_0^* to S_C^* with Δ_2.

The net effect is ambiguous. The final outcome in Q-q space will be D with a higher real exhange rate today but either a higher or a lower real exchange rate tomorrow, leading to an optimal subsidy $S_D^* = S_0^* + \Delta_1 - \Delta_2$. Since $\Delta_1 - \Delta_2$ can have either sign, the optimal subsidy can go either way (although it will always remain positive).

Diagram 11 shows that the optimal subsidy will <u>increase</u> whenever a <u>future depreciation</u> of the real exchange rate is anticipated, leading to a fairly strong conclusion: if the real appreciation caused by the oil boom is temporary (in the strong sense that the future exchange rate is anticipated to fall back <u>below</u> the current pre-oil shock level), the subsidy to the T-sector needs to be increased.

In that case the Dutch Disease will still be a "Disease" despite the existence of perfect international capital markets, in that more government intervention is called for.

5. CONCLUSIONS

The survey of problems oil producers have run into, presented in the introduction, identified two major issues of concern. The first one has to do with employment problems that may arise during the sectoral reallocation necessary during the transition towards an "oil economy" (or more in general when large increases in oil revenues occur). The second question is whether an oil-induced real appreciation and accompanying pressure on the Traded goods sector, calls for (increased) assistance to that Traded goods sector. This issue is especially important when the real appreciation is likely to be of a temporary nature.

On employment, we identified and spelled out conditions under which downward rigidity of the real consumption wage will cause transitional unemployment during the adjustment towards higher oil revenues. Those higher oil revenues will cause excess demand for Non-Traded goods, and over time a real appreciation, necessitating a transfer of labour (and, in the medium run, capital) from the T-sector to the NT-sector. The mechanism via which that transfer takes place is an appreciation induced increase in the real product wage measured in terms of T-goods prices (the real traded product wage) and a decrease in the real non-traded product wage. We show it is possible that that combination , if allowed to take place, will lower the real consumption wage; in that case downward real consumption wage rigidity will cause unemployment during the transition to an oil-economy.

NOTES

1) We adopt the convention of using upper case letters for first period variables and lower case letters for second period variables.

2) Ignoring a second order effect $\dfrac{dK_Q}{d\theta}$ $(T_K - r_k) C_N$.

3) The model used is similar to the one used in Neary (1980) and van Wijnbergen (1984b); a full dynamic 2-period version of this model with first period contract-based wage-price rigidity is used in van Wijnbergen (1984c).

4) See van Wijnbergen (1984b) for some minor qualifications.

5) This hinges on our assumption of no direct labour use in oil production and of exogenous labour supply.

6) Use $Q\,R_{LQ} + R_{LT} = W$ to get from (17c) to (17d).

7) This implies that $\Pi_Q Q/\Pi$ is the NT share in consumption, Ψ_N. A similar expression holds for Ψ_T, the T-goods share $(\Psi_T = 1 - \Pi_Q Q/\Pi)$.

8) Furthermore we assume some sort of non-distortionary tax to fund the subsidies so that we can ignore income effects and additional distortions caused by the raising of revenues to finance the subsidies.

9) The analysis in this section follows van Wijnbergen (1984b), where algebraic proofs are presented. We confine outselves here to diagrammatic representations.

10) NT1 also depends on q so that complete graphical analysis is not really possible. A similar remark applies to NT2 concerning S. The algebraic analysis in van Wijnbergen (1984a) takes those interactions into account and shows that the diagrammatic analysis gives the correct conclusions.

can be shown that that will not reverse the result of an increase in S* after an increase in first period oil revenues.

REFERENCES

Balassa, Bela (1964): "The purchasing power doctrine: a reappraisal." Journal of Political Economy, vol. 72, pp. 584-96.

Corden, W.M. (1984), "Booming Sector and Dutch Disease Economics: Survey and Consolidation". Oxford Economics Papers.

Corden, W.M. and P. Neary (1982), "Booming Sector and De-industrialisation in a small open economy", Economic Journal.

Dixit, A. and V. Norman (1980), Theory of Internationa Trade, Cambridge University Press/Nysbet.

Hall, S. and F. Atkinson (1983), Oil and the British Economy, Croom Helm, London.

The Economist (April 9, 1981): "Norway's oil: More Money than it Properly Knows what to do with".

Neary, P. (1980), "Non-Traded goods and the Balance of Trade in Neo-Keynesian Temporary Equilibrium", Quarterly Journal of Economics.

Malinvaud, E. (1977), The Theory of Unemployment Reconsidered, Blackwell.

van Wijnbergen (1984a), "The Dutch Disease: a Disease after all?", Economic Journal.

───── (1984b), "Inflation, Employment and the Dutch Disease in Oil Exporting Countries: a Short run Disequilibrium Analysis", Quarterly Journal of Economics.

───── (1984c), "Macro-economic and Intertemporal Aspects of the Shadow Price of Foreign Exchange", mimeo, University of Warwick.

OIL REVENUES AND THE NORWEGIAN ECONOMY IN THE SEVENTIES

BY

ADNE CAPPELEN, ERIK OFFERDAL AND STEINAR STRØM

ABSTRACT

This paper is concerned with the counterfactual question of how the Norwegian economy might have performed in the 1970's if there had been no prospects of oil and gas in the North Sea. A small macroeconomic model is used to shed light on the following issues:
a) what would have been the macroeconomic impacts on the economy if no investments and production in the oil sector had taken place since the late 1960's given that economic policy remained unchanged?
b) As a result of the problems that would have developedin the situation a), what kind of economic policy might have been pursued and what would the outcome have been?

1. INTRODUCTION

The macroeconomic impacts of oil and gas revenues have been the subject of a number of studies over the last few years. The viewpoint has mainly been a theoretical one, with the emphasis on changes in industry structure or deindustrialization, and the possibilities of recession and unemployment caused by excessive domestic spending of oil revenues. A survey of this work is given by Corden (1984).

The interest in empirical research of the _actual_ impacts of domestic spending of oil revenues seems, however, to have been slight. The purpose of this paper is therefore, by means of an econometric model, to analyse how these revenues and the activities in the oil sector itself affected the Norwegian economy over the period 1966-1983. We shall employ a counterfactual approach, trying to imagine how the Norwegian economy might

O.Bjerkholt & E.Offerdal, eds., Macroeconomic Prospects for a Small Oil Exporting Country. ISBN 90-247-3183-6.
Copyright 1985, Martinus Nijhoff Publishers, Dordrecht.

have developed in a hypothetical situation where no exploration had taken place, and the oil revenues never emerged.

Similar studies have been undertaken by Atkinson et al. (1983), and Barker and Fairclough (1983) of the UK economy. The approach adopted by these authors with regards to policy changes, is, however, a _passive_ one. They ask what would have happened to variables such as the exchange rate, fiscal and monetary instruments if no oil were discovered in the 1960's and the 1970's. Atkinson et al. assume that economic policy would have been no different if UK had no oil, which implies an unchanged volume of public spending, constant tax rates etc. Barker et al. assumes that the monetary policies pursued by Mrs. Thatcher would have been the same irrespective of oil discoveries. In both studies there is an attempt to estimate the effects of oil on the exchange rate. By contrast, we shall raise a rather different question, namely: how would important macroeconomic policy instruments have to be adjusted if Norway had no oil and gas revenues, but with major policy _targets_ unchanged?

Section 2 gives a brief review of the actual development of the Norwegian economy over the period, and section 3 outlines an aggregate macroeconomic model to be used in our counterfactual policy simulations. Section 4 gives the numerical results, and section 5 offers some concluding comments. An appendix describes the model in more detail.

2. NORWAY IN THE SEVENTIES

A substantial exploration activity took place on the Norwegian continental shelf in the period 1965-1975. Oil was found in 1969, and the first barrel of oil was produced in 1971. During this period investments in offshore equipment were rapidly increasing, and reached a level of 15,5 percent of total investments in 1975. Oil and gas revenues started to become an important factor in the Norwegian economy around 1975. By then these revenues amounted to around 3 percent of GDP and almost 7 percent of total export earnings. In the following eight years these figures have grown to nearly 20 and 40 percent respectively. These historical events are illustrated in table 1.

Of special importance is the "extra" revenue obtained in the pro- duction of oil and gas. This pure profit, or economic rent is partly due

37

Table 1: The share of the oil and gas sector in some main macroeconomic
figures

Share of the oil and gas sector in:	1970	-75	-77	-79	-80	-81	-82	-83
GDP	0	2.9	4.5	9.9	15.1	17.1	17.1	18.3
Gross Investments	1.5	15.5	19.2	10.6	9.0	19.3	14.5	24.3
Total Exports	0	6.7	12.5	23.6	33.2	33.8	36.2	37.2

to decreasing returns to scale associated with the utilization of
exhaustible resources and partly due to the cartelization of the oil market
achieved by OPEC. An estimate of this economic rent is given in table 2. A
normal real rate of return on capital of 7 percent is assumed.

Table 2: Economic rent of oil and gas production.

	1976	-77	-78	-79	-80	-81	-82	-83
Rent in billion NOK	3.3	2.8	7.0	13.7	31.9	36.4	40.5	49.6
As percent of GDP	1.8	1.3	3.3	5.7	11.2	11.1	11.4	12.3

However, the full importance of the revenues can not be grasped
from these tables alone. In the wake of the OPEC price hikes in 1973/74
and 1979/80 most of the industrialized world fell into an economic
recession unprecedented since the 1930's. Increasing import expenditures
on oil and dwindling world demand for manufacturing products posed a severe
threat to the balance of payment of most countries within the OECD area.
Not surprisingly, many of these, such as the UK, chose to counter this
development with a restrictive monetary and fiscal policy so as to keep
domestic inflation rates down, trying to keep the competitive edge of their
exposed sectors.

The skyrocketing development of the oil revenues was clearly not
percieved by Norwegian authorities in the early seventies. Still, it is
reasonable to say that the prospect of the coming revenues gave Norway a
scope in conducting demand management policies that had no comparison with
any other OECD country, possibly with the exception of Holland - and it
appeared at a time when it was more needed than ever in postwar times.
Public spending together with investments related to the off-shore activities in the oil sector were financed by borrowing against future oil revenues up to the point where total foreign debt amounted to 45,6 percent of

GDP (1978).

Some consequences of these differences in policies may be seen in table 3. While the growth in GDP in the European OECD-countries fell dramatically off in the late seventies and even became negative in the early eighties, Norway achieved a positive growth rate of the same magnitude as in the preceding decade. For the last 2-4 years (1981-84) growth has been reduced and the rate of unemployment has nearly doubled during these few years. Although an unemployment rate of around 3 percent is low in a current OECD context, it is record high by Norwegian post-war standards.

Table 3: Main Macroeconomic indicators, Norway and OECD.

	Growth in GDP		Inflation		Unemploym.rate	
	Norway	OECD-Eur	Norway	OECD-Eur	Norway	OECD-Eur
1960-73	4.3	4.8	4.7	4.9	1.0	3.0
1974-77	4.9	2.1	9.8	12.3	1.1	4.9
1978-79	4.8	3.3	6.5	10.5	1.3	6.2
1980	4.2	1.3	10.9	14.1	1.3	6.8
1981	0.9	-0.1	13.6	12.2	1.7	8.5
1982	1.0	0.6	11.3	10.1	2.4	9.5
1983	3.2	1.0	8.4	8.2	3.1	10.7

One should expect the expansionary fiscal policy pursued by the Norwegian government to have a substantial effect on the industry structure by driving up wage levels and disrupting the competitive position of the exposed sectors. Although some changes in the disfavour of exposed industries have taken place, they are nowhere near the magnitude sometimes prophesiced by the Dutch Disease literature.

This has two main reasons. In the first place, in conjunction with the expansionary fiscal policy, Norwegian authorities launched an extensive subsidy program towards exposed industries. This program was mainly intended to be a temporary relief while the slump in world markets lasted. Secondly, the rapid growth in the public sector entailed an equally rapid growth in female employment opportunities. The increase in the work participation rate among married women were thus the main drive behind an average annual growth rate in total employment of 1.24 percent in the years 1974-1980. Thus, sectoral redistribution of the labour force as predicted by the Dutch Disease literature was dampened mainly as a consequence of increased labour supply and increased subsidies to exposed industries.

3. SOME COMMENTS ON THE MODEL USED IN THE SIMULATIONS

For the purpose of this paper we have developed an aggregate version,called AMEN (Aggregate Model for Economic policies in Norway), of the short- to medium-term models KVARTS and MODAG, developed by the Central Bureau of Statistics. These models are disaggregate, inputoutput models of a Keynesian type without any explicit monetary sector. In AMEN a few new elements are added mainly related to the functioning of the labour market.

Our model contains one private production sector and one government sector. However, in all definitional equations and material balances we have kept Shipping and Oil-related activities separate and exogenous. This is based on the following considerations. Shipping is a sector that is quite separated from other economic activities in the Norwegian economy. The input-output links to the rest of the economy are very weak. The ship-owners have had very little access to the domestic credit markets and have relied on foreign banks when investing. Furthermore, it is difficult to model investments, exports etc. related to this sector. Since shipping has been quite important to the foreign trade of the Norwegian economy, we would like to avoid this sector to distort our results when modelling the rest of the economy. The oil sector is separated for obvious reasons partly given by the purpose of our paper and partly by the nature of this sector compared to the other sectors.

Since the rest of the economy is lumped into one aggregate sector, we will not be able to study the structural changes between sheltered and exposed sectors which is so predominant in the Dutch Disease literature. Our choice at this point is motivated by two factors. In the first place, our interest lies primarily in macroeconomic aggregates such as unemployment, inflation and the current account. Secondly, econometric experiences from previous modelling work on MODAG and KVARTS indicate empirical support to the following points:

* The sheltered sectors had 30 percent of total exports (excl. oil and shipping) in 1980. Thus, even if export is a small fraction of output in the sheltered sectors it is important as a share of total exports.
* The differences in the determination of export prices between exposed and sheltered sectors, although important, is far from the traditional, simple text-book distinction between price-taking exposed sectors and mark-up pricing in the sheltered sectors.

The model is schematically described in figure 1. The cornerstones of the model are two simultaneous blocks, one for quantity aggregates and one for price indices. We have so far not made any attempt to model the money market; thus interest rates and the exchange rate are kept exogenous. This can be justified by the existence of credit control and rationing on the money markets during the period we study. We have assumed, however, unless otherwise stated, that total nominal credit supply is related to nominal GDP (excl. the oil sector) as long as the nominal rate of interest is constant.

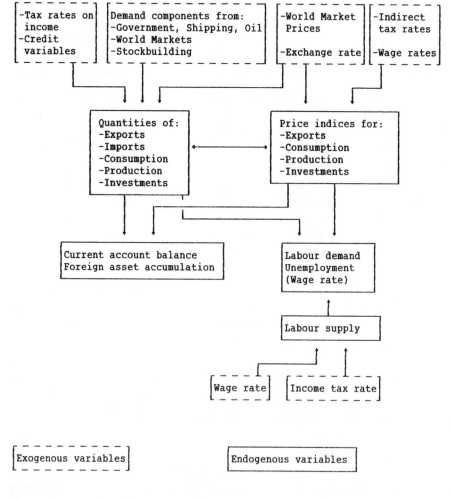

Figure 1. A schematic presentation of the model

In the price block Norway is modelled as a "semi-small" open economy. Thus, the economy is not a price taker in world markets, but is assumed to have some autonomy in setting the prices of their products. The reasoning behind this is an analogue to the well-known Armington hypo-thesis; domestic production for material input and final demand categories are qualitatively distinguishable from internationally traded goods. This product heterogeneity may, at least in the short run, be exploited by Norwegian producers by setting prices different from world market prices. In the model we have chosen the price index of imports to Norway as an indicator of world market prices, and kept this exogeneous. The price of the products from the private sector delivered for purposes other than final demand are thus assumed to be a function of unit labour costs and the import price. Prices of exports, consumption and investments are similarly determined by the product price and the import price.

In the quantity part of the model, exports are determined by an indicator for world market demand, and by export prices relative to world market prices. In a similar fashion, imports are determined by an indicator of domestic demand and domestic product prices relative to world market prices. The indicator of domestic import demand is specified to take care of different import propensities between different demand categories. Pri-vate consumption is a function of real disposable income and credit supplied to households. Private investments is related to growth in production, credit supplied to firms and user cost of capital relative to wages. Private production is related to labour and the capital stock by a Cobb-Douglas production function with slightly increasing returns to scale.

There are two submodels attached to this model. One contains the current account balance and foreign asset accumulation, which is completely recursive to the rest of the model. Some effort is made here to take account of changes in the valuation of the stock of foreign assets due to changes in the exchange rate.

The second submodel concerns the labour market. At this point we have developed two different versions of the model, one in which wages are given exogenously, and one in which wages are determined via a Phillips-curve equation. In the first of these versions the model is quite simple. Labour supply for men and unmarried women are given exogenously, while for married women it is determined by a set of equations relating their deci-cions whether to work or not to the marginal wage rate (=wage rate times one minus the marginal tax rate), income and socio-economic variables. The decision of how many hours to work, given that one works, is assumed to be institutionally given. Labour demand is derived directly from the price/-quantity relations, and unemployment is then determined residually. There are thus no feed-backs from unemplyoment to wages and labour supply and demand in this version of the model. In the second version of the model we have incorporated a hyperbolic Phillips-curve, relating wage increases to increases in the consumer price index, growth in labour productivity and unemployment. This means that the labour market will give feed-backs to production and the current account via the price/quantity equations, and also to labour supply for married women.

A more detailed documentation of the model and the estimated parameters is given in the appendix.

4. NORWAY WITHOUT OIL

Let us now turn to the question of how important macroeconomic variables might have developed if Norway had not discovered oil or gas in the North Sea. That is to say, if production, investment, employment and export revenues from this sector remained at a zero level throughout the seventies and up to 1983. We shall start from the same point of departure as Barker and Fairclough (op. cit.) and assume that the same macroeconomic policies would have been pursued throughout the period. Similarly we also assume that exogenous variables apart from policy instruments would also have been unaffected by the non-appearance of oil revenues. This is analysed in section 4.1, and provides us with a background for section 4.2, where policy instruments are used to reach specified targets for the economy. The first approach is denoted the passive approach (section 4.1) while the second is called a target-instrument approach. We believe this second approach to be the more realistic for two reasons:

* "Full employment" has a long tradition among Norwegian politicians as the supreme macroeconomic target. Thus, there are reasons to believe that "Norway without oil" would have taken strong measures in order to avoid the unemployment rate from reaching a level much above the levels experienced in the postwar period.

* With no oil discoveries and therefore no future oil revenues Norway would have been forced to pay more attention to the development of the current account.

4.1. A PASSIVE APPROACH

The development of GDP, private consumption and private investments in two passive approach scenarios are given in table 4.

Table 4. Percentage deviation from historical paths of GDP, private consumption, private investments and exports with no oil revenues.

	GDP		Consumption		Investments		Exports	
	I	II	I	II	I	II	I	II
1974	-2.1	-2.3	-0.4	-1.5	-0.4	-1.0	0.1	0.6
1975	-8.5	-8.7	-2.2	-3.9	-7.0	-7.4	0.1	0.9
1976	-10.3	-10.6	-2.2	-5.5	-7.0	-11.8	0.1	1.2
1977	-11.9	-12.4	-4.1	-7.2	-20.4	-22.4	0.1	1.7
1978	-16.3	-17.0	-4.7	-9.2	-17.4	-20.4	0.2	2.4
1979	-18.1	-18.6	-4.8	-9.7	-17.2	-21.2	0.4	3.2
1990	-19.8	-20.1	-4.5	-9.8	-13.5	-16.1	0.6	4.0
1981	-20.2	-20.1	-5.0	-10.4	-9.7	-9.5	0.9	4.8
1982	-18.2	-17.9	-4.1	-9.5	-8.3	-5.9	1.2	5.7
1983	-20.8	-20.2	-4.5	-10.3	-4.9	-1.4	1.3	6.4

I: Model without Phillips-curve,wages exogenous.
II: Model with Phillips-curve included.

Our simulations starts in 1966, but up to 1974 none of the variables would have deviated significantly from their historical values. From this point on, however, the development is rather dramatic. By 1980, after the second OPEC price hike, GDP would have stabilized around a level 18-20 percent below the historical one, and consumption would similarly have dropped to a level 5-10 percent below the historical one.   For private investments the major impact of removing the oil sector would have appeared somewhat earlier,around 1977-1978. The explanation to this is fairly simple; in the years prior to this a major investment boom took place in the oil sector, creating a substantial demand both for material inputs to this sector and for on-shore facilities related to oil exploration. Among other things, a large petro-chemical plant were built in 1978-79.

As can be seen from table 4, there are some important differences in the simulation results, depending on whether a Phillips-curve is included or not. This difference becomes even more pronounced when looking at what happens in the labour market. This is illustrated in table 5.

With no Phillips-curve, and therefore no adjustment mechanisms in the labour market, there is only have been a marginal decline in real

Table 5. Percentage deviation from historical paths of real wage, inflation, unemployment rate and labour supply. Deviation in unemployment measured as difference in percentage points.

	Real wage		Inflation		Unemployment rate		Labour supply*	
	I	II	I	II	I	II	I	II
1974	-0.1	-2.1	0.1	-0.2	0.4	0.3	0	-0.7
1975	-0.6	-4.0	0.5	0	2.0	1.9	0	-0.7
1976	-0.8	-5.5	0.3	-0.5	2.8	2.8	0	-1.0
1977	-0.9	-7.2	0.1	-0.9	3.8	3.7	0	-1.4
1978	-0.9	-11.5	0	-1.3	4.2	4.1	0	-2.0
1979	-0.9	-10.4	-0.1	-1.4	4.3	4.1	0	-2.6
1980	-0.8	-11.0	-0.1	-1.5	4.1	3.5	0	-3.2
1981	-0.9	-12.6	0.1	-1.1	4.5	3.5	0	-3.7
1982	-0.7	-13.0	-0.2	-1.5	3.7	2.4	0	-4.2
1983	-0.7	-13.7	0.1	-1.1	4.1	2.3	0	-4.4

I : Model without Phillips-curve, wages exogenous
II: Model with Phillips-curve
*) Labour supply for married women.

wages. This is as should be expected; wages follow their historical
development, and the way the model is constructed the fall in demand has no
influence on the consumer price index which is used as a deflator. The
effects on real wages are mainly due to lower productivity growth as a
result of lower investments and henceforth lower capital stock. Female
labour supply, and thus total labour supply, would then only be marginally
affected. However, the lower demand will give lower production and lower
labour demand and increased unemployment. The unemployment rate would
therefore have been around 4 percentage points higher from 1978 onwards.
The reason why unemployment in 1983 is not higher when GDP decreases by 20
percent is that employment in the oil sector is only 1% of total
employment, while value added in the sector is more than 18 percent of GDP
in 1983.

A Phillips-curve will to some extent function as a built-in
stabilizing mechanism, and this has a dramatic influence on wages. When
doing simulation II we have added two extra restrictions on the model:

* that government transfers in real terms follow their historical
path.

* that an accommodating monetary policy is pursued, keeping interest rates constant.

Compared to its historical level the unemployment rate will still rise in
the years 1975-78 due to the lower demand caused by the removal of the oil

sector. This higher unemployment would now put a downward pressure on
wages; in 1983 they would have been 30 percent lower in nominal terms or 14
percent in real terms. This wage depression would have two consequences,
namely to check the decrease in labour demand, and give a significant
reduction in female labour supply. The unemployment rate would thus
gradually return to its historical path. This lower unemployment level
now explains why GDP would decrease less if the labour market adjusts via a
Phillips-curve, whereas the lower real wage explains the greater decrease
in consumption and smaller decrease in private investment.

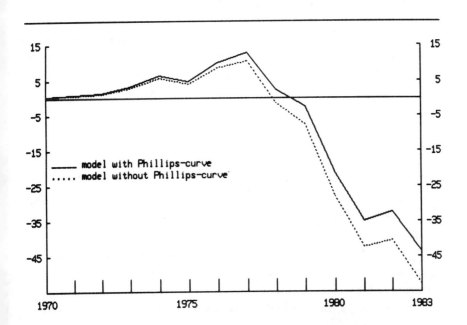

Figure 2.   The impact on the current account (in billion NOK) when the oil
            sector (investment and revenues) is removed. No change in poli-
            cy instruments.

        A final point is the development on the current account when the
oil sector is removed, as illustrated in figure 2. Not surprisingly this
would have given a major improvement on the current account in the period
1972 to 1978, almost irrespective of labour market adjustments. This is due
to substantially lower investment demand in this period, partly because
there would be no investment in off-shore activity which has a very high
import propensity, and partly due to the concurrent decrease in private

investment demand. From 1978 on, however, the importance of export
revenues to the current account becomes readily apparent, an enormous debt
accumulation would now take place and wind up at a level some 160-185
billion NOK above the historical level. As expected the built-in
stabilizing mechanism caused by including a Phillips-curve improves the
current account, as the exposed sectors of the economy benefit from a lower
wage level.

There are several interesting things to note about these scenarios,
most notably perhaps, that they are highly hypothetical ones. Most likely,
if Norway had no oil, wages in the private sector would neither have
followed their historical path with rapid growth in the mid-seventies, nor
have followed the path indicated by the Phillips-curve.

However, it is interesting to note that whichever the case, in the
period 1976-1983 Norway would have had very much the same development in
GDP and unemployment as most other western European countries. The major
effect of the expansionary fiscal policy waged in the mid-seventies would
have been to drive the current account out of control, without ameliorating
the unemployment situation.

4.2. MACROECONOMIC POLICIES FOR NORWAY WITHOUT OIL

In this section we shall study how macroeconomic policies might
have been adjusted if the oil revenues never emerged. We shall assume that
the government has two important policy targets; the unemployment rate and
the current account development. As should be amply illustrated above the
development in these two targets became dramatically different when the oil
investments and revenues were removed, and it therefore does not seem
likely that any of the scenarios outlined above would have been tolerated
by policy makers.

In the following we shall develop two different policy strategies,
to be termed a Restrictive Fiscal Policy (RFP) and Incomes Policy (IP) for
short. In the RFP strategy we assume that the labour market adjusts
according to the Phillips-curve, and that policy makers therefore does not
use incomes policy as an instrument. Neither is the exchange rate used as
an instrument. In this strategy the government places great emphasis on
the current account development, and pursues this policy by fiscal
instruments. The idea behind this is simple; if Norway were not blessed
with oil revenues the government would opt for a restrictive policy that
curtailed demand and thus the pressure on labour markets. This would lower

domestic inflation and improve the competitive edge of the exposed industries. The RFP strategy has obvious similarities with the policy waged in the UK and other continental economies. The incomes policy is in a certain sense the opposite of the one above and might be associated with policies pursued by Scandinavian countries. The background for this is the system of centralized wage settlements in the Scandinavian countries where the government often takes an active part. This was particularly the case in Norway during the seventies. The IP strategy is therefore a strategy where the government uses incomes policy actively to restrain domestic inflation and thus to improve the competitiveness of the economy. This is combined with an expansionary fiscal policy to attain targets on the unemployment rate, i.e. the expansionary policy waged in Norway in the mid-seventies is not changed.

4.2.1 A RESTRICTIVE FISCAL POLICY STRATEGY

We have here assumed that government demand for material inputs, investments and employment is gradually reduced from 1975 onwards compared to the actual development. Total government spending on these three

Table 6. Restrictive Fiscal Policy. Percentage deviation from historical paths of GDP, private con- sumption, exports, real wage and unemployment*. Deviation in unemployment measured as difference in percentage points.

	GDP	Private consumption	Exports	Real wage	Unemployment rate
1974	-2.3	-1.5	0.7	-2.1	0.3
1975	-8.9	-4.0	0.9	-4.1	2.1
1976	-11.1	-5.9	1.2	-5.7	3.2
1977	-13.5	-8.1	1.7	-7.5	4.6
1978	-18.9	-10.8	2.4	-10.1	5.7
1979	-20.6	-11.6	3.3	-11.3	6.0
1980	-22.5	-12.2	4.2	-11.9	6.0
1981	-23.1	-13.3	5.0	-13.7	6.6
1982	-20.7	-12.4	5.8	-14.1	5.3
1983	-24.6	-14.3	6.6	-15.3	6.1

*) The model used is the version with a Phillips-curve included.

categories ends up at a level around 20 percent below the historical level in 1983, but still higher than in 1975. The model used in the RFP strategy exercises is the version with the Phillips-curve included.

Not surprisingly, as shown in table 6, this policy will primarily have demand effects and thus drive GDP further down and unemployment further up when compared with tables 4 and 5. An interesting point is, however, that at this level of unemployment the Phillips-curve apparently has a very flat curvature; this policy gives an increase in unemployment of 3.8 percentage points compared to the passive approach, but only reduces real wages by 1.6 percentage points. This is still enough to give a substantial boost to exports and thus give a marked improvement on the current account. This is illustrated in figure 3. The upper curve in figure 2 is reproduced in figure 3 in order to compare it with the outcome of the RFP strategy. Over the period 1975-1983 the RFP improves the debt situation by a total of NOK 46 billion (compared to Norway without oil and with no changes in policy). This reduction might be considered to be small on the background of the huge debt accumulation which would have taken

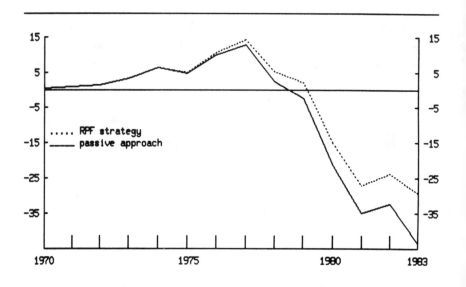

Figure 3. The impact on the current account (in billion NOK) when the oil sector is removed and the RFP strategy is followed from 1975.

place in Norway in the passive approach. Over the period the reduction in debt caused by the RFP strategy is around 30 per cent.

A further reduction however, would have put much strain on the Norwegian economy in terms of an incredibly high rate of unemployment (again, judged by Norwegian standards). As seen from table 6 the RFP strategy

drives the unemployment rate up by 6.1 percentage point in 1983, which
implies a rate of unemployment of 9.7 percent i 1983. A further reduction
in foreign debt would have required further cuts in government demand and
hence, further increases in the rate of unemployment. Thus, there is a
specific trade-off between reduction in foreign debt and increased unemployment, provided that the instruments used are of the RFP type. The
trade-off inherent in the present model (with a Phillips-curve included) is
shown on figure 4. Along the vertical axis we measure foreign debt relative to nominal GDP and along the horizontal axis the unemployment rate in
percent. If no oil were found in the 1970's and no policy changes were
made, the debt ratio would have been close to 0.6 and the rate of unemployment would have been around 6 percent (1983). The RFP strategy brings the
debt ratio down to 0.45 and unemployment up to 9.7 percent. Still, this is

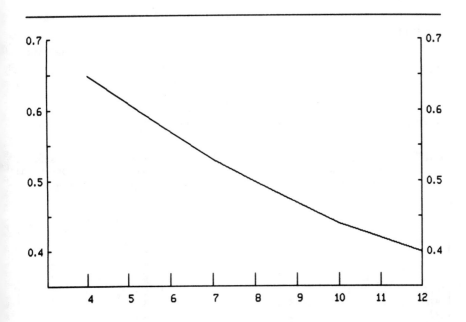

Figure 4. The trade-off between the debt ratio (ordinate) and the rate of
unemployment (abcissa) in 1983 estimated in the model with a
Phillips-curve included.

a high debt ratio, but figure 4 shows that further reduction would have required almost "mass unemployment" by Norwegian standards. The flat trade-
off curve indicates that RFP may not be the best strategy. Better instruments should be considered, which is the purpose of the next section.

4.2.2 INCOMES POLICY COMBINED WITH EXPANSIONARY FISCAL POLICY

In this case the expansionary fiscal policy waged in the 1970's is
kept unchanged, but an incomes policy is introduced from   1974 onwards.
Thus, the model version with exogenous wages is used, and wage rates are
gradually reduced relative to the historical path.   The nominal wage rate
ends up in 1983 at a level 25 percent below the historical level. Government transfers to households are assumed to follow changes in the wage
rates. In addition the exchange rate is increased by 5 percent in 1973 and
1974 and another 10 percent in 1975. Thus the appreciation of the currency
that took place in the mid-seventies is eliminated. Taking into account the
impact on the consumer prices of this change in incomes policy, the annual
growth rate of the real wage is reduced from 1,8 percent to -0,7 percent
from 1973 to 1983.

On the debt issue this policy would score equally to the RPF strategy. However, the IP strategy scores far better than the RFP strategy on
most other indicators. GDP, private consumption and employment are reduced
less than in the RFP-case as can be seen from table 7. Most important,
however, is the fact that the rate of unemployment is reduced compared

Table 7. Incomes Policy. Percentage deviations from historical paths of
GDP, private consumption, exports, real wage, labour supply and
the unemployment rate*. Deviation in unemployment measured as
differ- ence in percentage points.

	GDP	Private consumption	Exports	Real wage	Labour supply	Unemploy- ment
1974	-1.6	-1.8	0.3	-6.0	-0.1	0.0
1975	-8.1	-6.6	1.7	-14.3	-0.5	1.1
1976	-10.1	-10.0	4.8	-17.9	-1.0	1.6
1977	-11.4	-12.1	8.8	-19.5	-1.5	1.9
1978	-15.3	-13.4	12.4	-20.3	-1.9	1.6
1979	-16.1	-12.2	14.5	-18.1	-2.1	1.0
1980	-17.7	-11.7	14.9	-19.6	-2.2	0.2
1981	-18.0	-12.6	14.9	-21.0	-2.3	0.3
1982	-16.3	-12.5	15.1	-23.8	-2.6	-0.6
1983	-19.0	-13.6	15.9	-24.5	-2.8	-0.6

*) The model used is the version without a Phillips-curve

even to Norway with oil. However, the real wage rate is 10 percent lower
than in the RFP-case.

Table 7 reflects both the impact on the economy if there were no
oil sector and the introduction of an incomes policy as described above. If

we compare the figures in table 7 with those in table 5 we see that the isolated impact of an incomes policy is to reduce the unemployment rate by 4-5 percent at the end of the period. More than half of this reduction in the unemployment rate is due to lower labour supply (by married women). In 1983 the participation rate for married women is reduced from around 62 percent to 56 percent due to the substantial reduction in the marginal real wage rate as a result of the incomes policy. Even though the real wage per employee is reduced 10 percent more than in the RFP-scenario, total private consumption is almost equal in the two scenarios due to the higher number of employed persons in the IP-scenario. The lower real wage rate and the devaluation now leads to 10 percent higher exports as compared to the RFP-case. This explains why demand and imports can be higher in the IP-case implying higher employment, without further deterioration of the foreign debt situation compared to the RFP-strategy. The devaluation in the IP-case would have led to a slightly more inflationary development than in the RFP-case.

5. CONCLUSIONS

The Norwegian economy without the oil would have been significantly different from the one we can observe today. The foreign debt situation would have placed severe restrictions on the feasibility of different eco-nomic policies. It would have been difficult to obtain a ratio of foreign debt to nominal GDP of less than 50 percent without either accepting very high unemployment rates or unrealistically low real wages. We could of course have gone further in developing policy-scenarios that would be more "optimal" in some sense than the RFP- and IP-strategies introduced in sec-tion 4.2. We believe, however, that they are quite illustrative with re-gard to the macroeconomic problems Norway would have to cope with if there were no oil sector.

Some readers may perhaps be puzzled by the severity of the adjust-ment problems Norway would face without oil according to this analysis. To some extent our model exaggerate the problems because the shipping sector is treated exogenously in the model. There are many reasons to believe that the reduction in the real wage and/or the devaluations introduced would have lead to increased export of shipping services. However, one should also bear in mind that the structure of Norway's exposed sectors was, and still is, quite unfavourable in a situation which the OECD area has experienced since 1973. The shipping sector is a good example. In

1974 Norway had the world's third largest merchant fleet specializing in tankers that earned one third of our total export revenues. The oil shock of the seventies resulted in an enormous over-capacity of tankers, hitting Norway harder than perhaps any other country in the world. In addition Norway's tradeable sector apart from shipping is concentrated in the production of raw materials and semifinished goods, markets where the growth have been _less_ than in the total OECD market. This is partly reflected in the coefficients of the export equation in the model. A more rigorous treatment of these issues would, however, have demanded the use of a much more disaggregated model. Still we believe that our results indicate some of the macroeconomic adjustment problems Norway would have had to face if there were no oil sector, although the severity of the problems may be somewhat accentuated.

APPENDIX : THE MODEL USED IN THE SIMULATIONS

A. EXPORTS, IMPORTS AND BALANCE OF PAYMENTS

Both the volume of exports (APF) and imports (BPF) (excluding shipping and the oil sector) are determined by demand equations as in other
disaggregated Norwegian models (MODAG, KVARTS). The volume of exports is a
function of relative export prices (the endogenous export price APP
reflecting Norwegian unit costs, divided by the exogenous import price BPP
which is used as an indicator of the world market price), and total imports
to the OECD-area which is used as an indicator of the demand for Norwegian
products (M). The estimated export-equation is (using OLS with Almon-lags):

$$\log APF_t = \text{const} - \underset{(0.081)}{0.371} \left(\log (APP/BPP)_t + \log (APP/BPP)_{t-3}\right)$$

$$- \underset{(0.122)}{0.556} \left(\log(APP/BPP)_{t-1} + \log (APP/BPP)_{t-2}\right) + \underset{(0.053)}{0.882} \log M_t$$

$$R^2 = 0.990; \quad D.W. = 1.55;$$

(The numbers in parentheses are standard deviations of estimated
parameters, R^2 is the multiple correlation coefficient, D.W. is the
Durbin-Watson statistic and SER is Standard Error of Regression). The
long-run price elasticity is -1.85 while the demand elasticity is 0.88;
indicating that Norway has lost market shares on the OECD markets.

Similarly, the volume of imports is determined as a function of the
price of imports (BPP) relative to the GDP deflator for the private sector
excl. shipping and oil (RPP), and an indicator of import demand Z given by

$$Z_t = 0.247 \, (CPF_t + VOF_t) + 0.214 \, (JOF_t + JBF_t + JLOLF_t) + 0.4 \, JLPF_t$$

$$+ 0.65 \, JPF_t + 0.7 \, JSF_t + 0.25 \, (1/3 \, APF_t + 2/3 \, APF_{t-1})$$

CPF is private consumption, VOF is government expenditures on goods
and services (except labour and investment), JOF is government gross
investments, JBF is housing investment, JLPF is increases in stocks, excl.
construction of oil platforms, while JLOLF is stock of oil platforms (work
in progress). JPF is private gross investment and JSF is investment in

shipping. The coefficients are determined by use of a detailed input-output model with data from 1970. The estimated import function is:

$$\log BPF_t = \text{const} + \underset{(0.039)}{1.351} \log Z_t - \underset{(0.105)}{0.313} (\log BPP/RPP)_t$$

$$R^2 = 0.997; \quad D.W. = 1.36;$$

The import function implies a long run income elasticity of approximately 1.4 and a price elasticity of - 0.3 which seems to correspond fairly well to estimates of aggregate import equations for other countries (Thursby and Thursby (1984)).

Exports of oil and shipping services are exogenous in the model. Imports of goods and services to the shipping sector (except investment in shipping which is exogenous and enters the import function) and to the oil sector are also exogenous.

Transfers from abroad are exogenous while transfers to abroad are endogenous, reflecting that these are mainly development aid and determined as a percentage of nominal GDP in Norway. This percentage is exogenously given while nominal GDP is endogenous in the model. Net interest and dividend payments (excluding those related to the oil sector which is endogenous), are determined by the exogenously given "rate of interest" multiplied by the endogenously determined net foreign debt (excl. the oil sector). The model takes into account changes in net foreign debt resulting from changes in the exchange rate.

B. PRODUCER BEHAVIOUR AND PRICE EQUATIONS

The basic idea behind the model is that producers maximize profits assuming monopolistic competition, ie. producers faces downward sloping demand curves both on markets at home and abroad. Value added in the private sector exclusive of oil and shipping in constant 1980-prices (RPF) is related through a Cobb-Douglas production function to the number of hours worked and the capital stock at the beginning of each year. The number of wage-earners working full time (NWPF) and the number of hours worked per wage-earner (HWF) are determined separately, assuming that producers minimize short run labour costs We have assumed the existence of hiring and firing costs and contractual payments for normal working hours. Given the production function:

$$RPF_t = A_t \; NWPF_t^{\gamma} \cdot HWF^{\alpha} \; KPF_{t-1}^{\beta}$$

where KPF is the stock of capital, the demand for full time workers is estimated as:

$$\log NWPF_t - \log NWPF_{t-1} = const + 0.400 (\log RPF_t - \log HWFN_t - \\ (0.101)$$

$$\log NWPF_{t-1}) - 0.108 \log KPF_{t-1} + trend \\ (0.206)$$

$$R^2 = 0.693; \quad D.W. = 2.47 \quad SER = 0.0058$$

where HWFN is normal working hours per full time worker. The implied elasticities of the production function is $\gamma = \alpha = 1$ (restricted) and $\beta = 0.27$ implying increasing returns to scale which is quite common when using time series. Dropping the restriction $\gamma = \alpha = 1$ lead to higher returns to scale and even more imprecise estimates. Assuming only $\gamma = 1$ gave an estimated value of α around 1.5 without changing β very much. The number of hours worked (HWF) is implicitly given by:

$$NWPF_t - NWPF_{t-1} = const (HWF - HWFN) HWF^2$$

and it can be shown from the first order condition for profit maximum that this equation is valid only when $\gamma = \alpha$, which is another reason for restricting the parameters of the production function. From the estimated production function it follows that short run variable (labour) costs are proportional to value added which implies that short run marginal costs are independent of output.

Generally both the export price (APP) and the domestic price (RPP) can be shown (from the first order conditions) to depend on labour unit costs (LUC) and the world market price (equal to the import price BPP). Thus the estimated price equations are:

$$\log RPP_t = const + 0.306 \log LUC_t + 0.153 \log LUC_{t-1} + 0.340 \\ (0.038) \qquad (0.018) \qquad (0.071)$$

$$\log BPP_t + 0.178 \log BPP_{t-1} + 0.065 \log BPP_{t-2} \\ (0.038) \qquad (0.051)$$

$$+ 0.264 \log TIND_t \\ (0.053)$$

$$R^2 = 0.999 \quad D.W. = 1.96 \quad SER = 0.013$$

$$\log APP_t - \log BPP_t = \text{const} + 0.217 \log WP\ (1 + LP)_t$$
$$(0.064)$$

$$- 0.110 \log KPF_{t-1}$$
$$(0.079)$$

$$R^2 = 0.713; \quad D.W. = 1.41 \quad SER = 0.024$$

TIND is the rate of indirect taxation. The export price equation is estimated in a slightly different way. Instead of using labour unit costs we use the wage cost per full time worker (the wage rate WP times social costs $(1 + LP)$) corrected for increased labour productivity due to changes in the capital stock. Given the estimated production function labour unit costs can be written as:

$$LUC_t = \frac{WP_t (1 + LP)\ NWPF\ .\ HWF}{RPF} = WP_t (1 + LP)_t\ A_t^{-1}\ KPF_t^{-\beta}$$

According to this formula and the estimation result from the production function that gave $\beta = 0.27$, the effect of increases in capital stock on APP should have been 0.06 - not 0.11 as estimated. Taking into account that our model is a simple aggregate model we have however not imposed cross equation restrictions of this nature as long as the estimated equations are "reasonably" consistent.

The price index of private non-residential gross investment is determined by:

$$\log JPP_t = \text{const} + 0.715 \log RPP_t + 0.193 \log RPP_{t-1}$$
$$(0.058) \qquad\qquad (0.054)$$

$$R^2 = 0.999 \quad D.W. = 1.90 \quad SER = 0.013$$

Prices of private residential gross investments are given by:

$$\log JBP_t = \text{const} + 0.444 \log LUC_t + 0.222 \log LUC_{t-1}$$
$$(0.036) \qquad\qquad (0.018)$$

$$+ 0.310 \log BPP_t$$
$$(0.066)$$

$$R^2 = 0.999; \quad D.W. = 1.44; \quad SER = 0.017$$

The private consumption deflator is:

$$\log CPP_t = \text{const} + 0.526 \log RPP_t + 0.489 \log CPP_{t-1} + 0.012 \text{ DUM}$$
$$(0.089) \qquad\qquad (0.096) \qquad\qquad (0.007)$$

$$R^2 = 0.999; \quad D.W. = 1.51; \quad SER = 0.011$$

where DUM is a dummy for price-controls. Notice the substantial inertia in the adjustment of consumer prices to other prices in the economy. This is probably due to the prevalence of government regulated prices.

Private non-residential gross investment is determined by a traditional stock adjustment formula. We assume that firms minimize long run factor costs for any given level of value added. The desired capital stock KPF_t^D may then be written as a function of relative factor prices and value added. Define RENTE as the interest rate on loans, relative input prices are then determined by:

$$RFPRI = WP_t(1 + LP)/(JPP \ (RENTE + DPF/KPF \ (-1) \ -(JPP_t - JPP_{t-1}))$$

based on the assumption that depreciation (DPF) is geometric. When depreciation is geometric, tax-rates enter as a multiplicative factor in the user cost of capital (Biørn (1984)). Historically these tax rates have been almost constant and have been dropped for simplification. In the presence of (quadratic) adjustment costs it is optimal for firms only to adjust their capital stock partially to their desired level:

$$KPF_t - KPF_{t-1} = \lambda \ (KPF_t^D - KPF_{t-1}):$$

Due to imperfect capital markets and the existence of credit rationing in Norway during the estimation period, the speed of adjustment is assumed to depend on gross operating surplus (YR) and credit supply to firms (KREDB), both in real terms:

$$\lambda = \lambda_0 + \left[\sum_{i=0}^{T} \alpha_{t-i} \ (KREDB/JPP)_{t-i} + \sum_{i=0}^{T} \beta_{t-i} \ (YR/JPP)_{t-i} \right] /$$

$$(KPF_t^D - KPF_{t-1})$$

We assume that KPF_t^D is always different from KPF_{t-1}. By definition

$$KPF_t - KPF_{t-1} = JPF_t - DPF_t$$

and by substitution we get (assuming $DPF_t = \delta \ KPF_{t-1}$)

$$JPF_t = \lambda_o KPF_t^D - (\lambda_o - \delta)KPF_{t-1} + \sum_{i=o}^{T} \alpha_{t-i} (KREDB/JPP)_{t-1}$$

$$+ \sum_{i=o}^{T} \beta_{t-i} (YR/JPP)_{t-i})$$

The desired capital stock is assumed to be a linear function of lagged values of relative factor prices and output. (This is an approximation since the production function implies that this should have been a log-linear function). The estimation results indicates that gross operating surplus is not significant and was subsequently dropped. The accepted investment equation is:

$$JPF_t = \underset{(0.058)}{0.087} RFPRI_t + \underset{(0.029)}{0.043} RFPRI_{t-1} + \underset{(0.128)}{0.193} RPF_t + \underset{(0.085)}{0.579} RPF_{t-1}$$

$$+ \underset{(0.116)}{0.515} RPF_{t-2} + \underset{(0.095)}{0.245} (KREDB/JPP)_{t-1} + \underset{(0.094)}{0.496} (KREDB/JPP)_{t-2}$$

$$- \underset{(0.055)}{0.422} KPF_{t-1} + trend$$

$R^2 = 0.999;$ D.W. = 2.32;   SER/$\overline{JPF}$ = 2.5%

We were not able to find any economically meaningful equation determining inventory changes ($JLPF_t$). This variable is therefore exogenous in the model.

C.   HOUSEHOLD BEHAVIOUR

Total private consumption (CPF) is determined by

$$CPF_t = const + \underset{(0.084)}{0.677} (Q_t - TDIR_t)/CPP_t + \underset{(0.082)}{0.175}$$

$$(Q_{t-1} - TDIR_{t-1})/CPP_{t-1} + \underset{(0.134)}{0.769} KREDH_t/CPP_t$$

$R^2 = 0.999$ D.W. = 2.08

where TDIR is total direct income taxes, and Q is gross income to households given by:

$$Q = LWH + STO + EH - RR$$

and where LWH is the total wage bill (endogenous), STO is goverment transfers, RR is net interest income paid by households (both exogenous), EH is the part of total operating surplus distributed to households and is determined by

$$EH_t = \underset{(0.042)}{0.422} \; EPL_t + \underset{(0.019)}{0.160} \; (RPF \; RPP)_t - \underset{(0.064)}{0.274} \; (APF \; APP)_t \; trend$$

D.W. = 2.09; $SER/\overline{EH}$ = 3.6%

where EPL is total operating surplus (excl. of Oil and Shipping). The inclusion of nominal value added (excl. of Oil and Shipping) and exports can be justified by the fact that the export sector consists of few self-employed.

Direct taxes on households (TDIR) is determined by a macro tax equation:

$$TDIR_t = \left[TG_t \; Y_{t-1}/N_{t-1} + TM_t \; (Y_t/N_t - Y_{t-1}/N_{t-1}) \right] N_t + TEX_t$$

where TG_t and TM_t is average and marginal tax rates for a representative household/taxpayer. These are given exogenously. Y_t is taxable income, N_t total employment (as a proxy for the number of tax payers) and TEX_t is exogenously given taxes (such as property taxes, fines etc.) Taxable income (Y_t) is equal to gross (nominal) income (Q) minus tax deductions (D_t) which are determined as:

$$D_t = aQ_t + b \; CPP_t$$

where a and b are positive constants. By substitution we eliminate Y_t and D_t, and the estimated tax function is:

$$TDIR_t = \underset{(0.054)}{0.839} \left[TM_t Q_t - (TM_t - TG_t) Q_{t-1} N_t/N_{t-1} \right]$$

$$- \underset{(32181)}{90748} \left[TM_t \; CPP_t - (TM_t - TG_t) \; CPP_{t-1} N_t/N_{t-1} \right]$$

$$+ \underset{(8878)}{24960} \; CPP_t + TEX_t$$

$R^2 = 0.999$;   D.W. = 1.29

The equation explaining residential investment (JBF), which is mainly housing investment by households, is based on a model quite similar to the one determining private investment replacing output with real disposable income, and relative factor prices with user cost of housing capital (BRUKP), where taxes are taken into account, divided by prices of consumption:

$$BRUKP_t = (RENTE_t - (JBP_t - JBP_{t-1}))(1 - TM_t)JBP_t/CPP_t$$

JBP is a price index on investment goods in the housing sector, and KBF is the capital stock in this sector.

The implemented equation is:

$$JBF_t = \text{const} - \underset{(0.041)}{0.101}\ KBF_{t-1} + \underset{(0.061)}{0.167}\ (Q_t - TDIR_t)/JBP_t$$

$$+ \underset{(0.034)}{0.113}\ (Q_{t-1} - TDIR_{t-1})/JBP_{t-1} + \underset{(0.036)}{0.057}$$

$$(Q_{t-2} - TDIR_{t-2})/JBP_{t-2} - \underset{(6453)}{13763} \cdot BRUKP_t - \underset{(2898)}{11197}\ BRUKP_{t-1}$$

$$- \underset{(4240)}{8047}\ BRUKP_{t-2} - \underset{(3645)}{4315}\ BRUKP_{t-3}$$

$$R^2 = 0.983 \qquad D.W. = 1.78 \qquad SER/\overline{JBF} = 3.5\%$$

Credit supply to households were found to have some impact on housing investment, but only with (unreasonably) long lags and was therefore dropped.

Labour supply is exogenous with the exception of labour supply of married women which have increased substantially in the 70's. The work participation rate of married women (YGK) is assumed to depend on a number of sosiodemographic factors in addition to the marginal real wage per hour WP (1 - TM)/(CPP HWFN). The parameters in the equation determining the participation rates is estimated by a logit model using cross section data from 1979. Taking into account the historical change in the marginal real wage rate per hour and changes in sosiodemographic factors, the cross section model gives a prediction of the participation rate over time called YGKTV. This time series was used as prior information when estimating the observed participation rate in the period 1972 to 1983 using labour force statistics. In addition we have included a time trend and the share of government employment in total employment, since almost half of the women are employed in the public sector. YGK is given by:

$$\log YGK_t = 0.230 \log YGKTV_t + 0.345 \log YGKTV_{t-1} + 0.345$$
$$(0.067) \qquad\qquad (0.100)$$

$$\log YGKTV_{t-2} + 0.230 \log YGKTV_{t-3} + 0.647$$
$$(0,137)$$

$$\log (0.3 (NSEL + NWPF) + 0.6 NWOF)/N_t) + trend$$

D.W. = 1.79;   SER = 0.019

NSEL is the number of self-employed and NWOF is the number of government employees. Total labour supply is then:

NTILBUD   =   NTILBUDX + YGK . NGK

where NGK is the (exogenously given) number of married women between 16 and 74 years and NTILBUDX is exogenous labour supply of males and unmarried women.

The rate of unemployment is defined as:

U   =   (1 - AKUN/NTILBUD) 100

where AKUN is the number of employed persons which is related to the number of full time workers NTOT and takes account of an increase in part-time work during the 1970's.

When the model includes a wage equation, determining WP we have:

$$\log WP_t - \log WP_{t-1} = (\log CPP_t - \log CPP_{t-2})/2 + (\log (RPF/NWPF)_t$$

$$- 2 \log (RPF/NWPF)_{t-3})/3 + 0.010/(U_{t-1} - 1.2)$$
$$(0.004)$$

$$-0.019$$
$$(0,009)$$

D.W. = 1.41;   SER = 0.015

Thus, the growth rate in nominal wages depends on the unweighted average of the last two years inflaton rate and the last three years productivity

62

growth rate.   The Phillips-curve part 0.01/(U - 1.2) is specified to capture the effects of unemployment above frictional levels and implies that
unemployment rates above 2.5 percent has very little effect on the wage inflation. The highest unemployment rate observed is 3.3 percent (1983) and
the lowest 1.5 percent.

The estimation method used is usually OLS with or without Almon-
lags. To some extent instrument variables-method has been used to check
whether the simultaneity problem is serious or not. Finally the total
model (without the Phillips-curve) was simulated for the historical period
1966-1982 to test the behaviour of the model as a whole. We believe the
model passed this test rather well. Root Mean Square Error for GDP was
less than 1 percent and the deviations from the historical values of the
current account were moderate. When the Phillips-curve was added we had to
"help" the model a bit with add-factors in the historical simulations. The
Phillips-curve becomes very steep around an unemployment rate of 1.5
percent.   If the model estimated the unemployment rate to be 1.3 percent
instead of 1.5 percent, wages would increase some 6 percent more than
actual figures.   Because the unemployment rate during the 1970's varied
between 1.5-2.0 percent this is not surprising.

REFERENCES

Atkinson, F.J., S.J. Brooks and S. Hall (1983): The Economic Effects of
    North Sea Oil. National Institute Economic Review

Barker T. and I. Fairclough (1983): North Sea Oil and the UK Economy
    1974-1981. Paper presented to the 10th EARIE Conference in Bergen,
    Norway.

Biørn E. (1984): Inflation, Depreciation and the Neutrality of the
    Corporate Income Tax. Scandinavian Journal of Economics 86 (2), pp.
    214-228.

Corden W.M. (1984): Booming Sector and Dutch Disease Economics: Survey and
    Consolidation. Oxford Economic Papers.

Thursby M. and J. Thursby (1984): How Reliable Are Simple, Single Equation
    Specifications of Import Demand? The Review of Economics and
    Statistics, Vol LXVI, No. 1.

7230
Selected W. Europe
OECD

A COMPARATIVE STUDY OF THE MACROECONOMIC PERFORMANCE
OF SOME ENERGY-RICH AND SOME ENERGY-POOR ECONOMIES

BY

BIRGIR BJØRN SIGURJONSSON

ABSTRACT

The paper discusses international differences in macroeconomic performance after the first oil price shock in 1973/74. The five Nordic countries is compared with each other and with USA, United Kingdom, West-Germany and the Netherlands. The discussion focuses on three types of effects. Firstly the direct or terms-of-trade effect. Secondly the indirect effect due to responses to the supply shock in other trading countries. And thirdly, the domestic response, especially the resistance to accept real income cuts.

1. BACKGROUND OF THIS PRESENTATION

The following discussion should be taken as a reflection over a comparative study rather than as a completed research report. I have participated in a research project on the macroeconomic impacts of Nordic oil price shocks during the seventies and studied in particular the case of Iceland (Lindskog and Sigurjonsson (1983)). The Nordic comparisons form the basis for this survey but is extended to include four more countries, USA, United Kingdom, West-Germany and the Netherlands.

2. A BRIEF RECAPITULATION OF THE INTERNATIONAL BACKGROUND

By the end of 1973 and beginning of 1974 the cartel of oil producers, OPEC, succeeded in raising the real price of oil by more than

O.Bjerkholt & E.Offerdal, eds., Macroeconomic Prospects for a Small Oil Exporting Country. ISBN 90-247-3183-6.
Copyright 1985, Martinus Nijhoff Publishers, Dordrecht.

100%. Similarly, the cartel carried out a successful oil price increase in 1979-81. In this context the real oil price is defined as the price of oil deflated by a price index of some important export commodities of the industrial countries (as defined by the UN trade bulletin). So defined, the real price of oil increased by 300% between 1973 and 1981 including exchange rate repercussions.

The success of the unilateral price action of the OPEC countries can up to a certain degree be explained by the size of OPEC as an oil supplier but was also due to the endurance of the cooperation of the cartel, at least in 1973-74. In the late seventies and early eighties the cartel experienced increasing problems in finding agreed compromises on prices and on output restrictions. The problem was enhanced by the increasing number of producers outside the cartel.

It is of major theoretical interest to explain what made these unilateral actions of the cartel possible. In this relation I would like to draw attention to the demand side that made the actions so successful. Let me mention three events: The overvalued US dollar and the collapse of the Bretton Woods Agreement. Secondly, the consequent monetary disorder with an interest rate shock in 1972 and 1973. Thirdly, the large fluctuations of raw materials already fuelling the industrial world with rising input prices after 1970. Also these changes were brought about by cartel arrangements e.g. in the bauxite industry.

By these arguments I simply want to say that the industrial world of 1973-74 already accepted severe monetary distortions with many sudden price changes and rising inflationary tendencies. This was a good climate for the OPEC-cartel to find the market willing to pay a higher oil price.

3. OUTLINES OF THE MACROECONOMIC PERFORMANCE

3.1 STRUCTURAL PRECONDITION

Let us look at some structural differences between the Five Nordic economies and draw a comparison between them and Four important industrial nations; USA, UK, West-Germany (GER) and the Netherlands (HOL).

Size:
The five Nordic countries, Denmark, Finland, Iceland, Norway and Sweden (D, F, I, N and S, respectively) are all small, open economies. Sweden is largest with a national product of 1.6% of the total

OECD-product and the total Nordic value added is around 4% of the total of
OECD.   The US economy is around 35% (1979) and the Four together account
for about 54% of the OECD-product. This is illustrated in table 1.

Table 1: GDP as a share of OECD's GDP

	D	F	I	N	S	US	UK	GER	HOL
1973	0.9	0.6	0.0	0.6	1.6	40.1	5.4	10.5	1.9
1979	1.0	0.6	0.0	0.7	1.6	34.7	6.0	11.1	2.3

(Source: OECD National Accounts)

Openness:

The five Nordic economies are open in a global perspective. The
export share of GNP/GDP in Iceland and Norway exceeds 40% and is around 30%
for the other Nordic economies. The export share of HOL also exceeds 40%,
that of UK and Germany is over 20% but the US economy is very closed with
an export share below 10% of GDP. As can be seen from table 2 the export
shares of all the above mentioned economies, except the US, have increased
during the seventies.

Table 2: Export as a percentage of GNP/GDP

	D	F	I	N	S	US	UK	GER	HOL	OECD
1973	29	26	38	44	28	7	24	22	47	15
1979	30	33	44	45	31	9	29	26	49	19

(Source: OECD Historical Statistics)

Type of export production:

Around 75% of the export commodities of all these economies (except
Iceland) are industrial products. This ratio is only 50% for Norway in
1979, by and large because of the oil and gas industry. Services are
important in most of these economies, especially in Norway because of its
large merchant fleet, and in UK because of financial services overseas. In
1973 the export of these countries was predominantly directed towards EEC,
EFTA and the US. Only a small fraction of the export went to the OPEC area.
In 1979 the export share to the OPEC region had risen sharply. An important
point is the case of Iceland, where raw-fish exports are of equivalent
proportion as the industrial commodities in the other countries.

Table 3: **Export commodity composition as percentage of total**

	D	F	I	N	S	US	OECD
1972:							
SITC 5-8	73	75	21	75	78	72	77
SITC 0, 1, 4	25	5	76	14	3	24	19
1979:							
SITC 5-8	72	75	20	50	81	70	77
SITC 0, 1, 4	24	3	78	8	2	26	16

(Source: United Nations Trade Statistics)

Energy:

In 1973 all these economies relied upon imported energy. Only the US and HOL imported less than 20% of their energy requirements and the UK and Norway less than 50%. In 1973 Denmark imported the whole energy requirements, Finland imported one-third, Sweden and Iceland as well as Germany around 40%, and the rest between 60-90%. In 1979 the situation was changed as can be seen from table 4. Firstly, both Norway and the UK became

Table 4: Domestic energy as a percentage of total energy

	D	F	I	N	S	US	UK	GER	HOL	OECD
1973	0	29	43	66	37	83	52	46	93	65
1979	3	32	50	216	43	81	88	44	107	66

(Source: OECD Energy Balances)

net oil exporters and HOL became a net exporter of energy. Secondly, the oil bill as a percentage of GDP doubled for most of the economies (D, F, I, S, GER and OECD) and even more than tripled for some of the economies (US and HOL), while it decreased for Norway and UK. In fact, the energy balance became positive for Norway in 1976 and for UK in 1980.

In 1973 the share of oil requirements of total energy requirements was about 45-55% except for Denmark, 90%. The share of oil in energy imports exceeded 90% for all the countries. Only the US had considerable

Table 5: Oil requirements as a percentage of total energy

	D	F	I	N	S	US	UK	GER	HOL	OECD
1973	88	59	58	43	60	45	50	57	54	53
1979	76	49	50	39	53	45	43	51	53	51

(Source: OECD Energy Balances)

supply of own oil in 1973 (66% of total oil requirements). In 1979 the situation was different with respect to oil production as both UK and Norway had become important oil producers.

The energy situation of the economies under observation was rather poor in 1973 but had improved in 1979. It is tempting to compare the energy situation of 1973 with that of 1979. Let us draw a somewhat arbitrary borderline and compare energy-rich economies that supply at least 80% of energy requirements by indigenous sources (ER) with the energy-poor (EP) and the Nordic with the Four in the coming comparisons. We may the group the countries as in table 6.

Table 6: Energy supply situation, 1973 and 1979. Eneregy supply from indigenous sources as percentage of total energy requirements.

	Energy supply: 1973	Energy supply: 1979
0-40% 40-80% 80-	Denmark, Finland, Sweden Iceland, Germany, UK, Norway US, HOL	Denmark, Finland Sweden, Germany US, UK, HOL, Norway

The high Nordic oil bill:

The share of net oil import bill in the national product of the Nordic nations in 1973 gives the first impression that the Nordic nations were exceptional energy wasting nations. The net import of oil amounted to around 2% of GDP on the average in the Nordic countries but was much less as a percentage in the Four and in the average of OECD.

Table 7: Net import of oil as a percentage of GNP/GDP

	D	F	I	N	S	US	UK	GER	HOL	OECD
1973	2.3	2.3	2.6	1.3	1.9	0.5	1.8	1.5	0.8	1.0
1979	4.1	5.6	6.4	-3.1	4.9	2.4	0.6	3.2	2.9	2.7

(Source: OECD National Accounts, -: Energy Balances)

The use of energy per unit GDP:

The Nordic countries were energy-thrifty already before the oil crises as compared with the Four and the OECD. The same message appears from the statistics of final energy consumption.

Denmark which was the least energy-intensive among the Nordic economies used roughly a quarter of the US final energy consumption per unit GNP/GDP measured on a common currency basis (Table 8). All of the Nordic nations used less energy in GDP than any of the Four. On the other hand, in 1979 the Four had reduced their energy use per unit of GDP much more than any of the Nordic nations, especially GER and UK, which reached almost the level of energy-intensivity of the Nordic countries.

Table 8: Total energy consumption per unit of GNP/GDP

	D	F	I	N	S	US	UK	GER	HOL	OECD
1973	275	494	412	391	374	988	874	604	794	684
1979	254	488	316	336	322	579	373	278	376	414

(Source: OECD National Accounts; -: Energy Balances)

If the figure for each country in table 8 are seen relative to energy consumption per unit of GDP in OECD, we obtain the picture in figure 1. This illustrates that in relative terms energy consumption between countries have grown gradually more equal from 1973 to 1979.

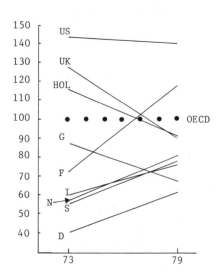

Figure 1. Development of Energy in GDP.

The sectoral use of energy:

For most of the economies, except Iceland and Norway, the share of industry in total energy consumption decreased between 1973 and 1979, while transportation had in some cases increased its share in 1979 relative 1973. In Finland, Norway and Sweden the manufacturing sector is the most energy requiring sector of the economy while Other sectors (services) do play a stronger role in Denmark. In Iceland the fishery fleet is one of the

69

largest consumers of energy together with the aluminium smelter. In the
case of Norway transportation is important, especially the Norwegian
merchant fleet.

3.2 DEVELOPMENT OF MAJOR ECONOMIC AGGREGATES

If we compare the average growth rates before the oil price shock
1973-74, the period 1967-73, with the growth rates after, 1974-81, the
growth rates fell by 50% for most economies, including those we are
studying here, except Norway. Furthermore, the average rates of inflation
doubled.

The oil-price shocks in the seventies can be studied with a closer
look at what happened prior and after the oil price shocks. Look at the
following periods: 1970-73: "prior to 1st shock", 1974-75: the "1rst
shock", 1976-79: "recovery" (for some at least), 1980-81: "2nd shock".
Table 9 illustrates what happened to the growth rates in absolute and
relative terms.

According to table 9 Norway was a special case with improved growth
rate after the 1st oil price shock. And that of Sweden was almost
unchanged. The larger negative number for the relative effect the more
unfavourable change. Denmark together with the US, UK and Germany joined
the club of most recessed economies, but Finland, Iceland and HOL were also

Table 9: The scenario of growth rates

| | THE EP-ECONOMIES | | | | ER-ECONOMIES: | | | | | OECD |
	D	F	I	S	GER	N	US	UK	HOL	
Prior to 1st shock:	3.5	6.0	8.6	3.4	4.5	4.0	3.5	3.4	4.8	4.7
1st shock:										
Absolute	-4.7	-4.6	-6.9	-0.1	-5.0	0.7	-4.2	-4.3	-3.6	-4.4
Relative	-1.3	-0.8	-0.8	-0.0	-1.1	-0.2	-1.2	-1.3	-0.8	-0.9
Recovery										
Rel.terms	0.9	0.4	0.4	0.4	0.9	1.3	1.2	0.7	0.6	0.8
2nd shock:										
Absolute	-3.9	1.0	-1.4	-0.6	-3.1	-2.7	-3.3	-4.5	-3.2	-3.3
Relative	-1.1	0.4	-0.4	-0.5	-0.8	-0.5	-0.8	-1.8	-1.0	-0.8

Note: The 1st shock in "absolute" terms is the difference between the
annual average growth rate 1974-75 and 1970-73. Similarily for the 2nd
shock in absolute terms: (1980-81)-(1976-79). "Relative" terms are found by
dividing by the averages of (1970-73) resp. (1976-79). Recovery in relative
terms is the average of (1976-79)/(1970-73).

severly shocked. In the "recovery" period, 1976-79, the growth rates
improved only for Norway and USA compared with the period prior to the

shock. Finland and Iceland reached less than half of the growth rates
before the shocks. Except for Denmark the Nordic countries were relatively
less shocked during the second shock, especially Finland with its barter
bilateral trade with the USSR.

The inflationary tendencies increased also markedly. Table 10 shows
that rates of inflation doubled for some economies (D, F, N, GER and HOL)
but in most cases more than tripled (I, S, US, UK and OECD average). The
table also expresses clearly the relatively high rates of inflation in the
Nordic countries as compared with the Four countries.

Table 10: A comparison of inflation rates

| | THE EP-ECONOMIES | | | | | THE ER-ECONOMIES: | | | | |
	D	F	I	S	GER	N	US	UK	HOL	OECD
Averages 1967-73	5.8	5.1	9.8	3.6	2.7	4.0	1.7	4.4	3.6	2.7
1974-75/ 1967-73	2.1	3.4	4.7	2.8	2.4	2.7	5.9	4.6	2.8	4.6
1974-81/ 1967-73	2.0	2.5	4.7	3.2	2.0	2.6	5.9	3.7	2.1	4.1

Comparing Nordic and Non-Nordic countries, the content of Tables 9
and 10 can be summarized as in figure 2.

Growth rates

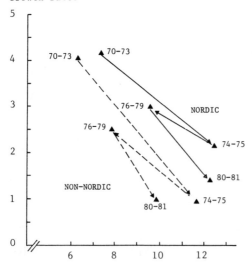

Figure 2. Development of growth rates and inflation in Nordic and Non-
Nordic countries.

Finally, current account position of the economies under observation is given in Table 11 to explain rigidities in demand adjustment after income losses. Before the oil crises, the current account position of the Nordic countries implied general excess demand pressures which were not present in the reference group. In due course after the 1st shock the current account deficit tripled as a percentage of GDP in Finland and Norway and quadrupled in Iceland. Only UK showed rising current account deficit among the Four countries.

Table 11: Current account as a percentage of GDP/GNP. Averages.

	D	F	I	N	S	US	UK	GER	HOL	OECD
1973/70	-2.0	-2.0	-2.7	-2.0	1.1	0.2	0.6	0.6	1.2	0.4
1975/74	-2.3	-6.6	-11.1	-6.7	-0.8	0.7	-2.8	1.9	2.7	-0.4

4. THEORETICAL FRAMEWORK FOR AN ANALYSIS OF OIL PRICE SHOCKS

In an analysis of the influence of sudden oil price increase on the macroeconomic aggregates in oil importing and oil consuming economies it is important to concentrate on three fundamental types of effects:

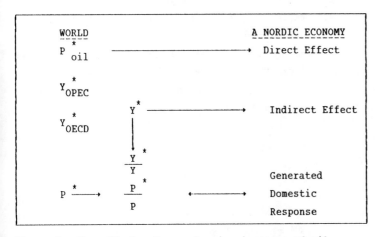

Figure 2:   The effects of a real price increase of oil.

4.1 THE DIRECT EFFECT

The direct effect in the oil importing economy is a variant of what general theory would call a pure terms-of-trade-effect. A rise of the real oil price will, ceteris paribus, imply worsening terms-of-trade of the whole economy. Alternatively, this means that more domestic products in terms of the average domestic product are needed in exchange for foreign products. Thus, a terms-of-trade deterioration due to real oil price rise will mean that less domestic product is left for domestic use, consumption or production, if current account is to stay uanffected.

Oil is almost entirely used in relation with real capital goods. This, of course, is important for the character of substitution possible in due course after an oil price increase. As oil can be both an input in the production process and a consumption good it may cause very different patterns of adjustment. Especially, there may - in the short run - be quite low degrees of substitutability as it takes time to change the functioning and the structure of the existing stock of real capital in use. All factors of production may, however, be interchangeable on the supply side in the long run. In the short run the problem is that planning can be costly and take time to realize.

The aspects of time and persistence of the real price change are extremely important for the reaction pattern and the process of adjustment. The time aspect is complicated. When does the price rise occur - and when is it recognized by the market and by the economic policy makers? Is the real price rise believed to be a short run phenomenon or assumed to be a permanent one? How would such alternatives influence the decision making of the common decision makers on the market and how would it influence the economic policy makers? For the last matter we are almost entirely interested in what type of policy reaction would be taken, to what extent and how fast it would affect the markets.

4.2 THE INDIRECT EFFECT

The indirect effect is based on what happens in other trading countries. In the first place it has to do with the trade with the oil selling/producing country. If the increased real oil price and the corresponding income loss of the oil consuming country will be wholly (and at once) recycled and spent on the export goods of the oil importing economy, the income loss from the direct effect will be largely reversed by this indirect effect and the following multiplicative effects on the domestic economy. The smaller and the slower the real income transfer is spent on the export goods of the oil consuming economy, the bigger the indirect effect. Again, little spending may mean that the supply of international credits increases which in turn may solve the financial problems of the oil importing economies.

In the second place the income losses of the oil importing economy can be reduced due to income policy measures and income response in other trade partners' countries. Although the real oil price rise generally can be regarded as an unique shock for oil consuming countries, it can certainly be argued that the size of the effect may vary between the countries due to differences in foreign trade dependency and the composition of trade partners. The bigger the foreign trade the more probable that the indirect effect becomes large after a real oil price shock due to limited respending of the oil exporting countries and due to contractive effect on international trade.

4.3 THE DOMESTIC RESPONSE

The indirect effect of an oil consuming economy would be cushioned if its trade partners would react with expansive policies to keep their imports unaffected. Likewise, it would influence the economy negatively if it could not reduce its own spending after a real oil price shock. A higher oil price leaves less real incomes for the domestic income earners.

The domestic income earners are regarded as being either capital owners or wage earning labour. It is a well known feature of the Western economies that while the interest rates of capital seem to be largely determined on a global scale the wage rates may vary much from country to country. This implies firstly, that the domestic owners of capital will hardly have to accept more real interest reductions than will capitalists internationally. Thus, the domestic adjustment may depend primarily upon the wage adjustment, i.e. reduction in real wages, corresponding to the real income loss due to the real oil price increase. Secondly, the more similar wage setting pattern in the industrial world, the less probable that labour will accept larger burdens from the oil shocks than any other group of income receivers.

The wage settlements of the oil importing/oil consuming economy are therefore very important for the domestic reaction. Long term wage contracts based on previous more favourable terms of trade may exclude the possibility of fast wage adjustment. A nominal downward rigidity most commonly prolongs the adjustment process, resulting in inflationary tendencies and current account deficits. This may well hurt the export industries if other competing economies adjust faster. Both labour demand and investment good demand will decrease. In some countries wages are linked to prices by wage indexation. This may exclude the possibility of a wage adjustment procedure.

A rigidity in the domestic income adjustment to the income losses has resulted in economic policy responses in most Western economies. The economic policy measures sometimes indicate that the problem is believed to be of short run nature and sometimes the opposite. The most common reaction to the unwillingness of labour to accept the real wage adjustment procedure is to devalue the exchange rate to increase the competitiveness of the export sector. In some countries the fiscal response is preferred either through employment and investment stimulation policies or via tax policies. Whichever is chosen the rate of inflation will rise directly through increased excess demand and indirectly through pressures on the financial markets for financing the increased public activities.

5. EMPIRICAL INDICATORS

5.1 THE DIRECT EFFECT

The direct effect is measured here as: The rate of change of the relative oil price multiplied with the net oil import bill as a percentage of GDP. The rate of change of the relative oil price is calculated in domestic currency units as the rate of change of unit import value of SITC 3 less the rate of change of GDP-deflator.

There are rather big differences in the direct effect on GDP due to the first oil price shock. The main reason is the difference in unit import values of oil. Denmark and Sweden bought their goods on the free markets and were struck by the racing spot markets while Iceland and Finland due to bilateral barter agreements with the USSR received their oil cheaper at the beginning. During the period 1970-74 the Nordic economies (except Iceland) and West-Germany were revaluing their currencies against the US dollar while in the late seventies an increasing strength of the $ increased the direct effect. It should also be noted that the Four, especially the US, had much faster rises in the relative oil price in the first shock than any

Table 11: The direct effect measured as a % of GDP

	The net oil import as % GDP		% change of relative oil price		Direct effect of oil price shock	
	1973	1979	1973/74	1979/81	1973-74	1979-81
Denmark	-2.3	-4.1	162	103	-5.6	-4.8
Finland	-2.3	-5.6	117	80	-3.2	-5.0
Iceland	-2.6	-6.4	134	109	-4.7	-6.7
Norway	-1.3	3.1	132	19	-1.7	1.0
Sweden	-1.9	-4.9	171	79	-5.9	-4.1
"Nordic"	-2.1	-3.6	143	78	-4.2	-4.3
non-Nord.	-1.2	-2.4	218	86	-4.0	-2.6
ER	-1.2	-0.5	208	63	-3.4	-1.2
EP	-2.1	-4.8	151	96	-4.7	-5.0

of the Nordic economies. On the average this was also true in the second
shock. But the net import bill of oil is comparatively much smaller in the
Four than in the Nordic economies although this difference did decrease in
1979.

5.2 THE INDIRECT EFFECT

The Nordic nations are mainly producers of industrial export
commodities and the export is mainly headed for the EEC, EFTA and the US
market. An indirect effect is generated by temporarily lowered incomes and
output in the trade partner's economy, partly due to direct effect and
partly due to domestic response in that country. Generally, the Direct
effect was smaller 1979-81 than 1973-74 in the OECD-region. The OECD
average growth rate and the trade with industrial commodities was not very
much affected in the latter crisis as perhaps in the first. In this context
one may also notice that the economic policies shifted in many countries
from rather expansive to contractive economic policy. The rising US $ and
the global increase in interest rates did put strong pressures on most
economies in this respect. This possibly affected the global demand in the
favour of those who are strong payers and, perhaps, in favour of industrial
goods rather than food. In general the Nordic nations except Norway have
followed the general export pattern of the OECD.

The market shares in the OPEC region increased drastically during
the seventies. This indicates increased respending of the OPEC in the
Nordic region. However, there has been a certain slowdown in the respending
after 1979-80 compared to 1973-75. Both Finland and Iceland do have

bilateral trade agreements with the USSR. Rising oil prices of exported Russian oil induced increased export of Finnish and Icelandic goods to the Soviet Union (Iceland left this barter trade in 1976). In the Finnish case the export share directed to the CCE's increased from 14.5% to 24.2% 1973 to 1975. For Iceland it went from 8.7% to 16.7% for the same period.

The relative smaller direct effect of 1979-81 than 1973-74 plus more restrictive economic policies were the main reasons for the fact that the indirect effects were more beneficiary in 1979-81 than 1973-74.

5.3 THE DOMESTIC RESPONSE

The direct and indirect effects are external factors indicating new rules of allocation and distribution for the small open economies. The domestic response on the other hand measures the domestic reaction pattern to such changes in external conditions.

It was argued above that the wage response may be the most important reaction. In Denmark, Iceland and the Netherlands wage indexation have been the main rule. In Denmark energy prices was taken out of the index in 1980. Partly, this was also done in Iceland 1979. When prices rise due to oil price increases wages react - sometimes with delay. In Finland, Norway and Sweden wage indexation was abandoned several years ago but from time to time wage settlements have had provisions for revisions if prices increase faster than at a given rate. In Finland and West-Germany wage indexation is not legal.

Differences in domestic response have been important for several economies. OECD's analysis of the competitive positions of the member economies shows splendidly how countries with high-cost profiles lose export market shares. Norwegian export industry exemplifies well how high domestic cost economies lose market shares abroad while Swedish industry shows the opposite, the case of cost adjustment and stable market share. One could measure such "terms of trade loss" in terms of GDP.

In the countries where the wage response has been great - perhaps due to a wage indexation mechanism - exchange rate depreciation has become characteristic for the economic policy response after or as a part of an unsuccessful incomes policy.

REFERENCES

Lindskog D. and B. B. Sigurjonsson (1983): Oil Price Distortions and
    Economic Development. Stockholm University, Research paper No. 5

PART TWO:

THE WORLD OIL AND GAS MARKET

MODELLING THE CRUDE OIL MARKET.   OIL PRICES IN THE LONG TERM

BY

LORENTS LORENTSEN AND KJELL ROLAND

ABSTRACT

Those concerned with investment appraisals and energy policy decisions need to take a view about the longer term prospects of the price of oil. The development of world oil prices will be affected by uncertain economic factors and also by political choices. Attempts to forecast a single path for the oil price have not proved to be very useful. The paper outlines a very open model, where the model user can easily impose on the model different assumptions about oil supply and demand in order to indicate a range of feasible projections for oil prices.

1. INTRODUCTION

The current level of oil and gas production in Norway amounts to 1/6 of GDP, 1/6 of government revenues and 1/3 of exports. Remaining reserves are estimated to be at least 100 times the current annual level of depletion. Being oil rich also means that Norway is quite vulnerable to changes in the international oil price. Experience shows that forecasting the oil price is a tricky task, what everybody believed last year might seem quite unrealistic today. The Norwegian government has a decisive influence on Norwegian oil and gas depletion and oil money spending and consequently needs to take a view about the oil price development. This single international price appears as the joker in assessments of government revenues, export earnings, profitability of large new investment projects, energy programmes and in calculations of domestic and international economic development. The Norwegian Ministry of Oil and Energy is responsible for the official oil price forecasts. The model presented in this paper is developed by the Research Department of the

O.Bjerkholt & E.Offerdal, eds., Macroeconomic Prospects for a Small Oil Exporting Country. ISBN 90-247-3183-6.
Copyright 1985, Martinus Nijhoff Publishers, Dordrecht.

Norwegian Central Bureau of Statistics and is intended to serve as a supplementary tool to the Ministry's more pragmatic forecasting efforts.

2. MODELLING THE CRUDE OIL MARKET

The great demand for oil price forecasts, from governments and companies, has resulted in an extensive literature discussing possible behavioral and structural relationships capable of describing this jerky market. On the supply side, much of the attention has been focused on the inner life of OPEC: is it a cartel or not, is it a cartel with a competitive fringe, how strong is the tension between high and low absorbers, are the depletion policies derived from myopic cash requirements or from long term optimization schemes etc. Another issue is the response to price changes from producers outside OPEC. Increased oil prices have motivated exploration and production in high cost areas, proven reserves are higher today than 10 years ago. A third issue is the supply of alternative energy. Consumers need energy, not necessarily oil. Coal and nuclear power are competitive at today's oil prices, and many argue that the unit cost of producing oil from coal, tar sand and shale is the ultimate ceiling to oil prices. This ceiling has been moving, though, and is now estimated in the range of 40-60 dollars per barrel, reflecting high and risky investments and environmental problems. In the short run oil prices might well overshoot the unit costs of these alternatives, since there are long lead times from investments to marketing of backstop substitutes. On the other hand, once developed, the unit costs of substitutes might set "lower limits" for oil product prices, protected by governments.

On the demand side, there are two categories of models: Structural models which deduce oil demand from capital demand, energy/capital ratios and capacity utilization ratios and reduced form models which straightforwardly define demand functions with terms for real prices and incomes, price- and incomeelasticities. Some models include lagged oil prices, expected oil prices and prices and price elasticities for alternative energy. Crude oil demand is normally not derived directly, but deduced from demand for oil products. The events the last two-three years have shown that even the demand side of the oil and energy markets are not easy to model. OECD oil and energy consumption have fallen since 1979, although there have been some economic growth and real energy prices have been stable or falling in some areas.

There is a lot of political actions and regulations in the oil and energy markets, actions taken to protect the interest of producers, consumers and the in-betweeners, oil companies, refining industries and distributers. Actions include government regulation of imports and stock-building for security reasons, barter agreements, regulation of domestic demand to cut import bills, protection of domestic energy programmes, supply of Soviet oil and gas etc. in addition to price or quantity regulations by OPEC. Apart from speculators, probably nobody is interested in abrupt oil price movements. Sharp downward movements imply undesired signals to investors in substitutes and conservation and might make do-mestic energy production unprofitable. Even a breakdown of OPEC might not be in the long run interest of consumers, since a few, big and well organi-zed Middle East producers might then appear with an exceptionally strong grip of the market 10-15 years ahead.

3. THE WOM MODEL

3.1. MODEL FRAMEWORK

The above reasonings are fragments of controversial and partly con-tradictory hypotheses, there is evidently no single consistent model following. The model we have constructed is intended to be used within an administrative process. Our approach has therefore been to establish a very simple, open model, where the model user will have to provide the an-swer to some of the basic behavioural and political uncertainty described above. The model is regarded as a framework to reason within and around, not as a black-box providing The Answer.

WOM (World Oil Market) is an annual model, where the world oil market is defined as the market for oil outside the centrally planned economies, (CPE). The chosen level of regional aggregation of the world oil market is a compromise between several, partly conflicting concerns. It is essential for maintenance of an operational model to have access to reliable and consistent data that are currently updated. One should avoid aggregating over units with different economic structure and development, and the level of aggregation should make it possible to study actions from the most important agents, but at the same time the number of input and output variables should be kept low to avoid unnecessary strain on the model user. On the demand side we have chosen the following disaggregation:

- USA (D_{USA})
- The rest of OECD (D_{ROECD})
- Developing countries (D_{LDC})
- Changes in stocks (L)

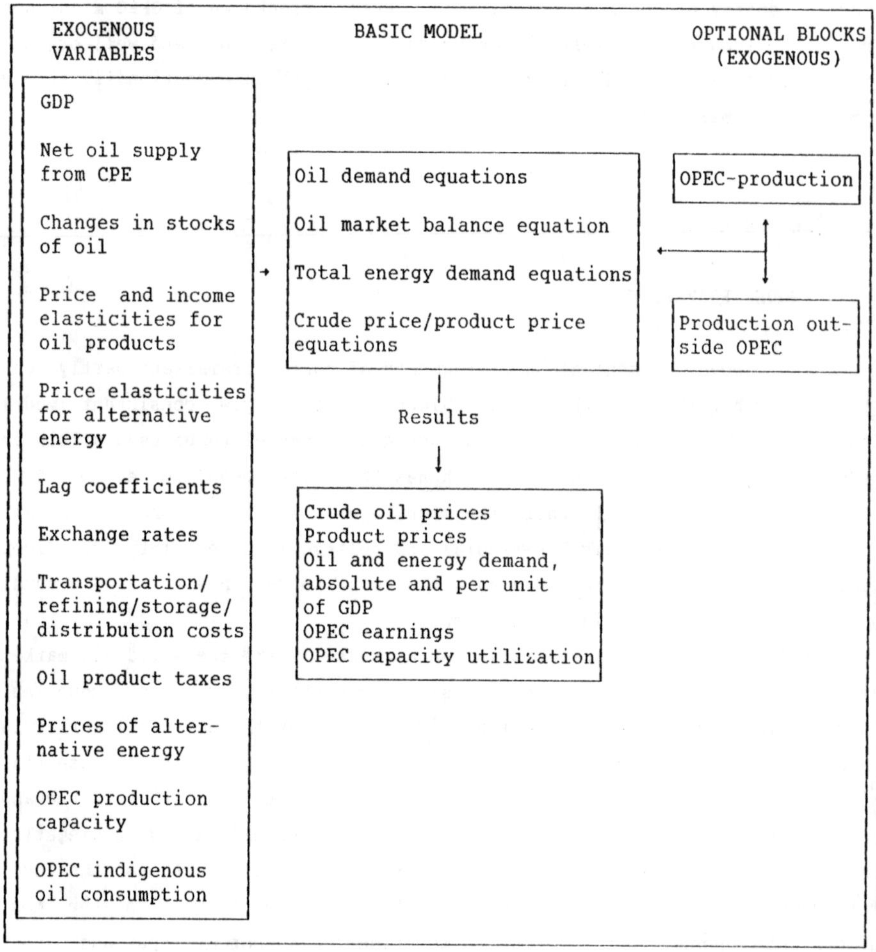

EXOGENOUS VARIABLES	BASIC MODEL	OPTIONAL BLOCKS (EXOGENOUS)
GDP Net oil supply from CPE Changes in stocks of oil Price and income elasticities for oil products Price elasticities for alternative energy Lag coefficients Exchange rates Transportation/ refining/storage/ distribution costs Oil product taxes Prices of alternative energy OPEC production capacity OPEC indigenous oil consumption	Oil demand equations Oil market balance equation Total energy demand equations Crude price/product price equations Results Crude oil prices Product prices Oil and energy demand, absolute and per unit of GDP OPEC earnings OPEC capacity utilization	OPEC-production Production outside OPEC

Figure 1. Model structure

In the simplest version of the model, total supply of oil is exogenous. From a strict modelling point of view, a disaggregation of supply is
then without interest. If the supply agents are supposed to react differently, it might still facilitate the reasoning of the model user to
disaggregate supply. In our attempts to model supply we have chosen to
disaggregate the supply side as follows:

- OPEC (S_{OPEC})
- Other market economy producers (S_{OME})
- Excess supply from CPE-countries (S_{CPE})

As illustrated in Fig. 1, the basic block of the model consists of
demand equations for three regions (USA, the rest of OECD and LDCs) and a
balance equation where the demand of the three regions equal supply from
OPEC, supply from other market economy producers, net supply from CPE and
changes in stocks. The demand from each region is determined as functions
of GDP, current and lagged real prices of oil products and alternative
energy, price and income elasticities, transportation/ refining/storage/-
distributions costs, taxes on oil products and exchange rates. For given
oil supply these equations, solved simultaneously give the crude price and
regional oil consumption. As an alternative to exogenously given oil
supply the model includes optional blocks of equations determining
production in OPEC and outside OPEC as lagged responses to price changes.
The model also includes calculations of product prices, total energy
consumption, oil and total energy consumption per unit of GDP, oil incomes
and capacity utilization in OPEC.

The basic model is estimated by standard FIML-methods on 1970-1982
data to give parameter assessments, cfr. Table 1, but all parameters are
exogenous to the model.

3.2. THE BASIC MODEL

The basic model, or simultaneous block of the simplest version of
the model consists of a balance equation and demand equations for the three
specified regions:

(1) $\quad S_{OPEC} + S_{OME} + S_{CPE} - D_{USA} - D_{ROECD} - D_{LDC} - L = 0$

(2-4) $\quad D_i = (a_i e^{s_i \tau}) X_i^{b_i} P_i^{e_i} Q_i^{h_i} [P_i^*] [Q_i^*]$

where

$$P_i^* = P_{i,-1}^{f_i}\ P_{i,-2}^{f_i g_i}\ P_{i,-3}^{f_i g_i^2}\ P_{i,-4}^{f_i g_i^3}$$

$$Q_i^* = Q_{i,-1}^{m_i}\ Q_{i,-2}^{m_i n_i}\ Q_{i,-3}^{m_i n_i^2}\ Q_{i,-4}^{m_i n_i^3}$$

(5) $\quad P_i = (l_i PV_i + (1-l_i)C_i)T_i$

$\quad\quad i = $ USA, ROECD, LDC

(1) states that supply of oil from OPEC, the rest of the market economies and excess supply from the CPE countries must equal demand from the three demand regions including changes in stocks. (2-4) specify demand from each region as functions of GDP (X_i), oil product prices (P_i) and prices of alternative energy (Q_i). The a_i is a constant term (which equals oil consumption per unit of GDP in the base year if the oil market is in "long term equilibrium"). The trend $\exp(s_i \tau)$ is introduced to account for conservation effects of innovations and improved working methods that are not captured by the estimated price and income elasticities. The coefficients b_i, e_i and h_i are income elasticity and short term (one year) price elasticities. The P_i^* and Q_i^* terms defines long term effects of price changes, where the changes in prices of oil products and alternative energy are assumed to effect oil consumption 4 subsequent years.

The index for the purchaser price of oil products for each region (P_i) is defined in (5) as a weighted sum of the local price of crude (PV_i), costs of transportation/refining/storage/distribution (C_i) and indirect taxes (T_i). P is the crude oil price measured in US dollars and V_i the local exchange rate against US dollars. All price and cost indices are normalized to 1 in the base year. The reason for using the oil product prices and not crude prices as explanatory variables in the demand functions should be obvious. Consumers substitute oil products for other secondary energy, and the price of products - which is a sum of costs of several services in addition to the cost of crude - is the relevant

variable when consumers optimize their energy use. Note also, that even if
the price elasticities for oil products are constant, the price
elasticities for crude oil is dependent on the level of the crude prices.
If the crude oil price increases, its share of the product price will
ceteris paribus increase, and the elasticity of demand with respect to the
crude price will also increase. Hence, a 10 per cent increase in crude
prices today will clearly affect demand more than a 10 per cent increase
did in 1972.

Several different formulations of the basic model have been estimated
by standard FIML-methods on time series available for the period 1960-1982.
Shortly reported, we introduce dummies in the elasticities to distinguish
between pre-1973 and post-1973. There was a shift, but it might as well
have been dated to 1971 or 1974. Second, we excluded the data for the
1960s, they clearly belong to a different structural period and they
influenced estimated coefficients too much. Third, we tried to capture the
lag structure with free estimation and by estimating Koyck-type lags with
different lags for different demand areas. The result we finally accepted
was a compromise, where the first year effects were freely estimated and
the remaining effects were estimated as a four year Koyck-lag, as indicated
in figure 2. The full set of results is displayed in table 1. The main
conclusion from this estimating excercise is that different model formula-

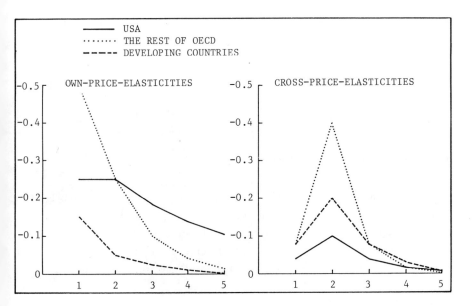

Figure 2. Lag structure, price elasticities.

tions simply give different results, and there is no robust method to choose one formulation as superior to the others. Subjective intuition and judgement have led to the estimates which are reported. These estimates are regarded as one possible set of coefficients, but in the forecasting model they can all be changed exogenously.

Table   1.   Estimated price and income elasticities and lag-coefficients by demand regions

	USA	ROECD	LDC
Direct price elasticity			
first year (e_i)	-0.25	-0.50	-0.15
second year (f_i)	-0.25	-0.25	-0.05
lag coefficient (g_i)	0.75	0.40	0.50
long term elasticity, defined as:			
$e_i + \sum_{t=1}^{4} f_i g_i^{t-1}$	-0.94	-0.91	-0.25
Cross price elasticity			
first year (h_i)	0.04	0.08	0.08
second year (m_i)	0.10	0.40	0.20
lag coefficient (n_i)	0.40	0.20	0.40
long term elasticity, defined as:			
$h_i + \sum_{t=1}^{4} m_i n_i^{t-1}$	0.20	0.58	0.39
Income elasticity	0.70	0.80	1.00

3.3.   OPTIONAL BLOCKS, THE SUPPLY OF OIL

Oil supply is difficult to model due to long lead times between investments and new capacity and extensive political/government inter-ference with production decisions, both within and outside OPEC. The supply blocks for OPEC and non-OPEC described below are estimated or assessed separately from the demand side of the model. These two supply

blocks are optional, i.e. the model can either be solved with totally
exogenous supply or with endogenous supply from OPEC, non-OPEC or both.

OPEC supply

The OPEC supply block is a simple reaction function. The function is
based on the assumption that the organization will meet downward market
pressure with reduced production to stabilize prices, whereas upward market
pressure at low capacity utilization results mainly in increased production
and then - after a certain capacity utilization is reached - mainly in
increased prices. This behaviour is consistent with the observation that
Saudi-Arabia is a central player within OPEC with the aim of stabilizing
prices. In a soft market Saudi-Arabia's power as a swing producer within
OPEC is strong, production can easily be regulated within the capacity
range of 11 mmbd, which also means that Saudi-Arabia can put pressure
on other OPEC members. In a tight market, production in each OPEC country
tends to be based on unilateral decisions, and Saudi-Arabia's influence as
a market stabilizer clearly reduced (given her production capacity). A
simple way of introducing this behaviour in the model, as for example done
by Chao and Manne (1983), is by postulating the following reaction
function:

$$(6) \quad P = \gamma_1 + \frac{\gamma_2}{K_{OPEC} - S_{OPEC}}$$

where

P — world oil price
K_{OPEC} — OPEC production capacity (time dependent variable)
S_{OPEC} — OPEC production
γ_1, γ_2 — coefficients

With the values of γ_1 and γ_2 chosen in the model, the oil price levels
out at around $25, measured in 1982 dollars, whereas the price rises steep-
ly when OPEC production supercede 80 per cent of capacity, as illustrated
in figure 3.

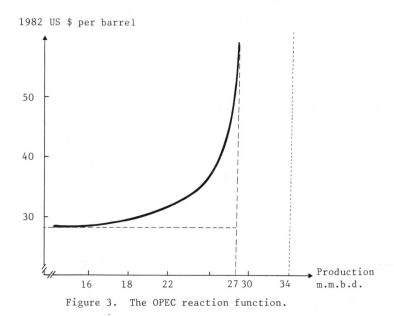

1982 US $ per barrel

Figure 3.   The OPEC reaction function.

Non-OPEC supply:

Outside OPEC, there is a great number of different suppliers, both national oil companies, multinationals and small independent companies. A reasonable hypothesis is therefore that supply is a relatively stable function of present, lagged and expected future crude prices. In addition the resource base and costs involved in exploration and development is likely to play a significant role.

One fairly simple way of modelling this part of the crude oil market is demonstrated by F.P. Weyant and M. Kline (1982). The approach below is a modified version of the Weyant and Kline model. Three essential assumptions are made:

(i) A constant fraction of known recoverable reserves is produced each year:

(7) $S_{OME} = k\ R_{OME}$

S_{OME} - production in year t

R_{OME} - economically recoverable reserves

k   - coefficient

(ii) The fraction of the undiscovered oil-in-place that is discovered in a particular year depends on the price of oil in that year

(8-9) $Z_{OME} = d(P)U_{OME} = (\alpha + \beta P)U_{OME}$

where

Z_{OME} - discovery in year t, addition to proven reserves

$d(P)$ - fraction of the remaining resource base discovered in year t

U_{OME} - remaining, undiscovered (physically given) resource base in year t

α, β - coefficients

Thus, at constant prices, the addition to proven reserves is an exponentially declining function over time. In the model the coefficients α and β are calibrated such that the discovery rate $d(P)$ is 0.03 at todays oil price, the discovery rate is more than doubled if the oil price is doubled, and the discovery rate is zero at $10 per barrel, as indicated in figure 4.

Undiscovered oil-in-place thus evolves according to the accounting equation:

(10) $U_{OME} = U_{OME,-1} - Z_{OME,-1}$

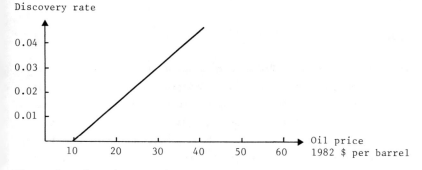

Figure 4. Oil price and discovery rate.

(iii) The optimal recovery factor for the already discovered (remaining proven) oil reserves depends on the price of oil, but only one-tenth of the adjustment from the current to the optimal recovery factor occurs each year.

(11) $f = 0.9f_{-1} + 0.1f^{opt}(P)$

(12) $f^{opt}(P) = \gamma + \delta P$

where

f - actual recovery factor in year t
$f^{opt}(P)$ - optimal recovery factor at price P
γ, δ - coefficients

Then the equation (13) determines economically recoverable reserves in year t as a price dependent fraction of remaining proven reserves:

(13) $R_{OME} = fY_{OME}$

(14) $Y_{OME} = Y_{OME,-1} + Z_{OME,-1} - S_{OME,-1}$

where

Y_{OME} - remaining proven reserves in year t.

Equation (12) is calibrated such that the optimal recovery factor is 0.3 at todays oil prices. If the oil price doubles, the recovery rate increases to 0.5, which is probably a reasonable upper limit with known technology.

Combining (7), (11), (12) and (13) yields:

(15) $S_{OME} = k(0.1f_{-1} + 0.9(\gamma+\delta P))Y_{OME}$

(15) explains current non-OPEC output of oil as a lagged response to the oil price and remaining proven reserves. Equations (15) and (9) explaining additions to proven reserves as a response to the oil price and remaining oil in place, together with the accounting equations (10) and (14) comprise the non-OPEC model. The model thus is highly aggregated and transparent, but it still permits investigation of the effects of alternative assumptions about the values of some key variables and their responses to

price changes.

The first assumption (i) relating production proportionally to known recoverable reserves is consistent with data over the last two decades. The assumptions that the rate of discovery and the recovery factor are depending on the crude oil price is probably uncontroversial. The functional forms and the lag structure are not. As in Weyant and Kline (1982) all relations are assumed linear and the parameters are partly based on the EMF-5 study. This means that outside a price range of - say 15 to 75 dollars - the non-OPEC model will not yield reasonable results.

3.4. SUPPORT CALCULATIONS

The simultaneous model gives the real price of crude oil, oil consumption (and production) and price indices for oil products by region. To facilitate the analysis of the total energy picture, and also to establish some key tables and figures for the oil and energy market, some support calculations are hooked onto the the basic model. Total energy consumption (measured in mtoe) by region is forecasted by Cobb-Douglas demand functions with Koyck-lags:

$$(16) \quad E_i = A_i X_i^{\beta_i} M_i^{\gamma_i} \cdot (E_{i,-1})^{\lambda_i}$$

where

$$(17) \quad M_i = n_i P_i + (1-n_i)Q_i$$

$$(18) \quad R_i = \frac{D_{i,-1}}{E_{i,-1}} \qquad i=USA,ROECD,LDC$$

where

E_i - total energy consumption, region i, measured in mtoe.
X_i - GDP, region i
M_i - price index for total energy, region i
P_i - price index for petroleum products, region i
Q_i - price index for other energy, region i
$A_i, \beta_i, \gamma_i, \lambda_i, n_i$ - coefficients

The information necessary to assess future price indices for total energy, M_i in (16), is drawn from the basic model where P_i - is endogenous and Q_i exogenous. The energy weights R_i are lagged with one year in (17) to avoid unnecessary simultaneity. The estimates of the coefficients β_i, λ_i and γ_i, are based on the study by Lugo and Idemudia (1982). Information on total energy consumption by region in 1982 determines A_i.   The estimates give long run income elasticities for total energy close to 1 and long run price elasticities around -0.3 for USA, ROECD and around -0.1 for LDCs.

Oil and total energy consumption per unit of GDP by region, relative energy prices in local currencies, OPEC's net dollar earnings and capacity utilization in OPEC are also calculated - to give checkpoints for the realism of the model results.

4. RECENT MARKET DEVELOPMENTS

Even with the advantage of hindsight it is hardly possible to decompose precisely why the oil and energy consumption per unit of GDP have been reduced the last 3-4 years. The explanation might simply be delayed responses to the 1973 and 1979 price hikes.   The 1979 jump lifted oil product prices over prices of alternative energy in most countries. The potential for substitution of oil against coal and nuclear power has been estimated by United Nations (1983) to be 20 per cent of todays oil consumption at current prices and known techniques.   Since all energy prices have increased steeply in real terms the last 10 years, there exists a potential for substitution of energy against other input factors, not only for interfuel substitution. High energy prices have also changed the composition of final demand towards commodities with low energy contents. Deregulations of oil and gas prices in the world's largest energy consuming country, USA, might have influenced the oil market balance as much as OPEC regulations, and have made a large share of the oil market more price sensitive than before. There might yet be significant gains to harvest from substitution, and the oil/GDP ratio will probably continue to fall in most areas even at stable prices. This indicates that one should be careful to use parameters estimated from long time series when forecasting the likely development of the energy market from now on.

Some other recent changes in the structure of the oil market are probably also worth noticing:

Suppliers outside OPEC have responded quite strongly to the price changes in the 1970s. Western production outside OPEC was around 17 mmbd in 1972 and 23 mmbd in 1982. In a stagnating total market, OPEC's market share of traded oil have been considerably reduced. "Unreliable" OPEC has been forced into the role of a swing producer.

The power of vertically integrated multinational oil companies is substantially reduced the last ten years. National oil companies have been established and grown strong both within and outside OPEC, independent refineries and distribution companies have been established and the in-betweeners, the traders and speculators, have grown in numbers and influence. During the same period, an increasing share of oil is traded on the spot market. Earlier, stockpiling by a few strong multinationals was used as buffer against unforseen market changes. In the years after 1979, stock movements seem to have had a destabilizing effect, with many inde-pendent agents overreacting to market signals. This development, towards many agents operating in the spot market, might make the oil market volatile also in the years to come - and might in periods put strain on OPEC as a swing producer.

There has been a lot of dispute over the role and power of OPEC. What seems to be a fact is that OPEC, in the recent soft market, has become a more effective cartel than before. In March 1983 the organization for the first time in its history lowered the nominal oil price, and at the same time managed to agree on quotas, limiting production to 17.5 mmbd, down from 28 mmbd two years earlier. So far the member countries seem to have been loyal to the quota arrangements. The first steps were also taken to start cooperation with important non-OPEC producers, in particular Mexico and the UK. These recent events seem to strengthen the belief that OPEC has the ability to be a flexible instrument. In a tight market the organization only needs to coordinate more loosely the actions of individual members and the role is more of an informative and indicative nature. In a soft market, faced with the harsh consequences of uncoordinated actions, the member countries seem to be willing to accept a shift of power towards OPEC as a decisive organization - where Saudi-Arabia plays a leading role.

Looking ahead, at least two factors might undermine the strength of OPEC. First, the present quotas have lead to current account deficits and belt-tightening policies in most OPEC-countries. Some member countries may think theyhave good reasons to cheat on the quotas, but if one breaks out, the house of cards may fall down. Second, the quota agreement is for crude, but many OPEC-countries have increased their exports of oil products and petrochemicals in recent years. If these products are exported in addition to crude, the quota agreements are of course no longer efficient. The efforts of OPEC have so far stabilized the market, but there still exists a glut, and even if economic growth keeps up with the most optimistic forecasts, OPEC production is likely to be well below capacity for some years to come.

5. OIL PRICES IN THE LONG TERM

5.1. A FEASIBLE OIL PRICE RANGE UP TO YEAR 2000

With cartel-like OPEC on the supply side and regulations on the demand side, equilibrium in the oil market might be obtained at many levels of production/consumption and crude oil prices. To predict one single path for the oil price has so far not proved to be very useful to those who need oil price assessments to calculate incomes or profitability of investments.

Below we have calculated a range of possible price developments up to year 2000, arrived at by combining the following sets of exogenous assumptions:

-   High economic growth, 3 per cent annual increase of GDP in industrialized countries and 5 per cent in LDCs, corresponding to the average growth in the 1960s and 1970s. Low economic growth, 1.5 and 2.5 per cent, respectively, corresponding to the average growth the last ten years.

-   High conservation, 0.5 decrease per year in oil consumption per unit of GDP independent of income and price effects, as a result of energy saving innovations and improved working methods. Low conservation with no saving effects.

-   High real prices of alternative energy, alternative prices increase by 2 per cent annually from 1985. Stable real prices of alternative energy. Low real prices of alternative energy, alternative prices decrease by 2 per cent annualy from 1985.

The calculations are made by the simultaneous WOM-model, with the OPEC reaction function and lagged production responses from non-OPEC producers - as described in section 4. The effects of the exogenous changes through this model are fairly transparent: Economic growth (ceteris paribus) means higher oil demand, but less than proportionately since income elasticities are less than 1. The economic growth in LDCs are quite important to the model results since their income elasticity is estimated close to unity. The development of prices of alternative energy is essential to the energy substitution effects which are estimated to be high in the USA and the rest of OECD (Table 1). Again, the development in the LDCs is important to the results, since their price responsiveness is estimated to be low. The effects of conservation, reducing oil consumptions per unit of GDP, are obvious. (The chosen assessment of 0.5 per cent is on the other hand disputable.) To interpret the results of the calculations it is important to notice that also the supply-side of the model tends to dampen price movements. If the crude prices increase, the non-OPEC supply will gradually increase. If crude prices decrease, OPEC supply will be reduced immediately and non-OPEC supply after some years.

The calculated crude oil prices in the year 2000 are displayed in Table 2 and the full pricerange in Figure 2. The calculated prices in year 2000 vary from 32 to 59 dollars per barrel, measured in 1982-prices.

We have chosen scenario III with low economic growth, stable real alternative price and low conservation as a reference scenario, from which we give some further details: Although the average economic growth is assumed to be low in this scenario, GDP in industrialized countries is 30 per cent higher and in LDCs more than 50 per cent higher in 2000 than in 1982. Oil demand is therefore increasing, and the crude oil price is creeping upwards especially through the 1990s, reaching 38 US dollars in 2000. Most of the increased demand is met by OPEC production which is calculated to approximately 27 mmbd or around 80 per cent of OPECcapacity in year 2000. Starting from today's 50-55 per cent capacity utilization, the model (through equation (6)) explains that OPEC benefit from the increased demand mainly by increased production. Production responses outside OPEC are moderate in this scenario, but the price increase after 1990 induce some increases in production in the late 1990s, and non-OPEC production is estimated to be 1.5 mmbd over today's level in the year 2000.

Although the crude oil price is increasing by 26 per cent over the period 1982-2000, product prices only increase by 10-12 per cent. (The costs of transportation, refining, storage, distribution and taxes are assumed to develop according to the general level of inflation.) Since the real price of alternative energy is assumed to be stable, the relative prices of oil products also increase with 10-12 per cent, which leads to a substitution away from oil. Thus, as an effect of both incomes and price changes, oil products per unit of GDP is estimated to fall by 20-22 per cent in the industrialized countries over the period 1982-2000. For LDCs the oil/GDP ratio is only reduced by 4 per cent over the same period. The absolute level of oil consumption is increasing in all areas, with moderate 10 per cent or less in the USA and the rest of OECD, but close to 50 per cent in LDCs. The reference scenario - together with the other low growth scenarios (Table 2, Figure 5) indicate that the crude oil price might be kept more or less at today's level if alternative prices are kept low and energy saving techniques are introduced at a moderate pace. If, on the other hand, alternative prices increase rapidly and energy saving techniques are introduced slowly, even low GDP growth rates at 1.5-2.5 per cent per year might create a tight oil market in the 1990's. Looking at the results of the high growth scenarios, the conclusion is clear: It is necessary to combine high growth with low alternative prices, fuel switching and high conservation if major increases in oil prices should be avoided after 1990. Up to 1990 the price movements are moderate for all scenarios.

Table 2. Estimated crude oil prices in year 2000 under different assumptions of economic growth, conservartion and alternative energy prices. 1982 US dollar per barrel.

	Low alt. price. High conservation	Low alt. price. Low conservation	Stable alt. price Low conservation	High alt. price. High conservation	High alt. price. Low conservation
	I	II	III	IV	V
Low economic growth	32	34	38	39	43
	VI	VII	VIII	IX	X
High economic growth	39	44	51	53	59

1982 US $ per barrel

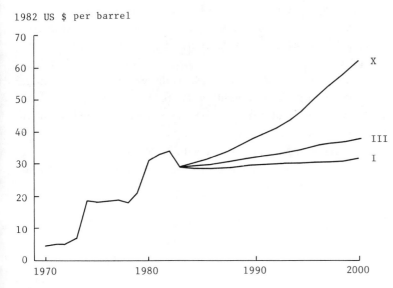

Figure 5.   Crude oil prices, 1982 dollars per barrel. Actual prices
             1970-1980. A feasible price range 1983-2000.

5.2 The effects of a tax increase on US oil products - and a depreciation of US dollars

The calculations in section 5.1 show the effects on model results of uniform and stylized changes in exogenous variables. The oil market is, of course, also greatly affected by unilateral actions and events that immediately might seem to influence only segments of the market.   To illucidate such effects in the model we have calculated the effects on the oil market of a 20 per cent tax increase on US oil products, and the effects of a 20 per cent depreciation of US dollars.

The tax scenario is calculated by increasing the indirect tax levied on US oil products by 10 per cent in 1985 and another 10 per cent in 1986, whereafter the tax rate is kept constant until the year 2000. The immediate effect is a 20 per cent price increase on US oil products, the level still being below the European average. The price increase reduces US oil consumption by around 10 per cent by 1987 and by 15 per cent by 1990 compared to the reference scenario. The repercussions are, shortly, that the crude oil price falls, consumption outside the US market increases, but not enough to compensate for the US reduction. Both OPEC and non-OPEC production are reduced. The net price effect is a reduction of the crude oil price by roughly 1.5 dollars in 2000 compared to the reference scenario. Production outside OPEC is reduced by 1 mmbd as compared to the reference scenario. If this reduction is distributed among producers proportionally to 1983 production levels, the following situation would emerge: The US import bill would, as a response to 20 per cent ad valorem tax levied on petroleum products, be reduced by $32 billion in year 2000. Even the rest of OECD would gain slightly despite increased consumption and reduced domestic production.

The depreciation scenario is calculated by reducing the value of dollar against OECD and LDC currencies by 10 per cent in 1985 and another 10 per cent in 1986. The immediate effect is a reduction of oil product prices by 8-9 per cent (measured in local currencies) in the rest of OECD and the LDCs. Oil consumption outside the US increases, especially in the rest of OECD. Increased consumption triggers an oil price increase measured in dollars; OPEC and non-OPEC producers expand production. The net price effect in the model is an increase of the oil price by around 1-1.5 US dollars per barrel. Oil consumption in the US market is reduced. The effect of the dollar depreciation on the oil market as a whole is thus partly offset by the increase in the dollar-price of oil. The income distribution effects between regions might though be significant. The depreciation of US dollars might be especially beneficial to the oil importing (dollar-indebted) LDCs; their import volume of oil is only marginally increased and the price of the dollar reduced by 20 per cent.

REFERENCES

Aperjis, D. (1982): The oil market in the 1980s. Ballinger, Cambridge.

Chao, H.P. and A. Manne (1983): Oil Stockpiles and Import Reductions: A Dynamic Programming Approach. Operations Research, Vol. 31, No. 4. July-August.

Daly, G. & al. (1983): The future of OPEC: Price level and cartel stability. The Energy Journal, January.

Jacoby, H.D. & al. (1983): World oil prices and economic growth in the 1990s. The Energy Journal, May.

Johany, A.D. (1980): The myth of the OPEC cartel. John Wiley & Sons Ltd.

Fesharaki, F. and S.L. Hoffmann (1983): Determinants of OPEC supplies.

Physical, economic and political factors. Resource Systems Institute. East West Centre, Honolulu, Hawaii.

Kouris, George (1981): Elasticities - science or fiction? _Energy Economics, April._

Lorentsen, L. and K. Roland (1984): The World Oil Market (WOM) Model. An assessment of the crude oil market through 2000. Sixth annual North American conference of IAEE, San Fransisco, November 5-7.

Lugo, L. and T. Idemudia (1982): Energy indicators. Documentation section of _OPEC review, Vol. VI, no. 4._

Mitchell, J. (1982): Anatomy of an oil crisis. _Zeitschrift für Energiwissenschaft, June._

Penrose,E. (1983): Decade of price stability within OPEC's grasp. _Petroleum Intelligence Weekly, August._

UK Interdepartmental Group (1982): Oil prices in the long term. Mimeographed report, London, December.

United Nations (1983): An efficient energy future. Prospects for Europe and North America. _Butterworths & Ann Arbor, London._

Weyant, J.P. & M. Kline(1982): OPEC and the oil glut: Outlook for oil expor- ting revenues during the 1980s and 1990s. _OPEC review, Vol. VI, no. 4._

NORWAY'S EXPORT OF NATURAL GAS TO THE EUROPEAN GAS MARKET.
POLICY ISSUES AND MODEL TOOLS

BY

LORENTS LORENTSEN AND KJELL ROLAND

ABSTRACT

This paper outlines a recently startet research project with the aim of
analysing the demand for natural gas and gas trade in Western Europe with
special attention paid to the role of Norway as a gas supplier. It
reviews plans of a natural gas demand model and a gas trade model for the
European gas market. The models suggested in this paper will be made
operational through 1984 and 1985, and are intended to serve research
purposes as well as administrative use. The project is also a contribution
to IIASA's international gas study.

1. MAIN NORWEGIAN NATURAL GAS POLICY ISSUES

Total gas use in Western-Europe was in 1982 approximately 210 bcm,
out of which Norway supplied 25 bcm. European gas contracts already signed
will, if they are serviced, cover Europe's demand up to at least the early
1990's. Gas supplies after 1990 are not restricted by the resource base,
there are sufficient reserves in the USSR, Algeria, the Middle East and
Norway to cover Europe's need for gas - even if demand should grow rapidly.
The questions to be settled now are who should deliver how much gas at what
time and at what terms in the 1990s and beyond. The answers of course will
depend on costs and prices of gas, but European consumers will also consider security, diversification and other commercial and political issues
linked to energy supplies. From Norway's point of view, the following,

O.Bjerkholt & E.Offerdal, eds., Macroeconomic Prospects for a
Small Oil Exporting Country. ISBN 90-247-3183-6.
Copyright 1985, Martinus Nijhoff Publishers, Dordrecht.

partly overlapping and simultaneous policy issues seem to be important:

*   THE LEVEL OF PETROLEUM PRODUCTION

Today the petroleum sector accounts for 20 per cent of Norway's GDP. The production level is approximately 60 mtoe. per year, of which 40-45 per cent is gas. The influence from the petroleum sector to the rest of the economy is significant, directly through the use of human and capital resources and indirectly through the domestic spending of oil revenues. Concern over dependency of uncertain oil revenues has constrained Norwegian willingness to expand the oil sector. A theoretically feasible solution to the problem, which is presently debated, is the introduction of a buffer fund between uncertain and unstable oil incomes and more stable and controlled oil money spendings. Norwegian policies up to now have been to expand moderately, but to keep production below the ceiling of 90 mtoe. per year.

* OIL OR GAS ?

Norway has relatively huge resources of both oil and gas. Depending on market prospects - particularly the expected relative price between oil and gas - Norway might decide to produce oil or gas or both. Given a total production target in toe. per year, a favourable (expected) relative price for crude would over time imply increased production of crude and reduced production of gas. Relaxing the total production target, an alternative to low volumes of gas at high prices might be high volumes of gas at lower prices. In addition to prices paid, a Norwegian export strategy will have to take into account the institutional settings of the market; regulations and tax policies pursued by importers.

* FIELD DEVELOPMENT STRATEGY

Having decided on total production over a planning horizon, a detailed field by field development plan has to be work out. This include decisions on which fields to develop at what time, the best mix of associated and non-associated gas and so forth. Important in this respect is to make sure existing infrastructure (pipelines, processing equipment, etc.)

is efficiently used. Of more interest from our perspective, is the step-wise increasing nature of the Norwegian supply curve. Because each field or even each phase of a field is large in comparison to the market, consider-able problems exist in ensuring that the market can absorb new projects. As an example, the first phase of the TROLL development is assumed to produce 15 bcm per year, likewise is the second phase projected to produce 15 bcm. This imply that not only the natural gas price and total level of consump-tion will influence the optimal export policy, the growth rate of consump-tion may be of equal importance.

In the long term it might be possible to smoothen the steps in the supply curve by introducing new technology which allows for a more flexible production. Also, development of a spot market for natural gas could make it possible to boost consumption in periods by trading in this market at a lower price than in the market for long term contracts.

* RISK-SHARING

Due to the long term nature of natural gas projects (20-30 years), the volatile nature of energy markets and extensive governmental inter-ference in these markets, investors in development and production face high risks on their investments. So far, the risk has been shared between pro-ducers and consumers (i.e. gas companies in importing countries as well as final consumers) by the contractual terms agreed upon. Important measures being take-or-pay clauses, minimum load factors and escalation of prices in accordance with a basket of competing crude oils. Considerably higher capital costs for Norwegian producers than for most other suppliers of the European market makes it important to ensure that Norwegian export projects are guaranteed high load-factors. More precise, if the market is soft for whatever reason, an important Norwegian goal would be to make sure that production in the North Sea is the last one shut down.

In addition to traditional policy measures (i.e. contractual arrangements) aimed at a reasonable split of risk between producers and consumers, others may be worthwhile studying. One possibility could be to involve buyers on the ownership side in production and/or transportation.

* DIVERSIFICATION AND TIMING OF SUPPLIES TO DIFFERENT MARKETS

A detailed study of the sectoral composition and development of de-

mand and of alternative supplies to different European countries is
necessary to determine what is the optimal exported volume to which country
at what time. Sectoral composition of the market largely determines season-
ally variations in load-factors. In markets where the load-factor changes
drastically it may be optimal to invest in storage capacity, for instance
in empty gas reservoirs. The price may vary between markets and countries
for several reasons. It may in some cases be possible to extract monopoly
profits by discriminating between buyers. More important is probably the
fact that the natural gas price in certain countries is regulated for deliveries to some or all consumers . This of course implies different net
pay-back for deliveries in different markets.

Several approaches exist to come to grip with the questions raised
above. In this paper we shall concentrate on the rather aggregated and
long term problems of a market strategy including the optimal diversification and timing of supplies to different markets. The field specific
development plan and the problem of risk-sharing will only be touched upon
occasionally. The approach chosen is:

- first, to give a brief overview of the present status of the
  European gas market, displayed by energy statistics and a gas trade
  matrix between supply and demand regions.

- second, to establish demand functions for gas dependent on incomes,
  gas prices and prices of substitutes in each region and sector
  (residential, commercial, industrial, electricity production). This
  demand system can be used to analyse different gas market
  developments dependent on different assessments of economic growth
  and energy prices. Norway's concern over diversification and
  timing of different markets and countries, or more aggregated by
  looking at oil and gas developments, might be analysed by looking
  at demand in the UK and continental Europe separately over time.
  Different developments in market segments, premium and industrial
  markets, is of interest when deciding load capacity and flexibility
  of pipeline systems

- third to establish a gas trade model with supply and demand
  functions by region and transportation costs associated with each
  (potential) trade flow. This model can be used to illucidate
  the cost minimizing or "optimal solution" of gas trade in Europe -

given the present status of the European energy market and common goals of a future best solution. By introducing upper and lower bounds on deliveries in this model, it can also be used to analyse the effects (costs or premiums) of political actions or disruptions, as compared to the "optimal solution". The model might also be used to analyse Norway's role as a gas supplier - seen from Norway's more narrow perspective: when and to which market should Norway sell to maximize over time the incomes from her gas sales (intertemporal optimization). The model framework might also be used to illucidate game theoretical aspects of gas trade.

2. PRESENT STATUS OF THE EUROPEAN GAS MARKET

Tables 1-3 give a brief statistical survey of the European natural gas market in 1982, summing up estimates of reserves, production, consumption and trade by country.

In broad terms the European supply-demand pattern is rather transparent. The heavy gas consumers are the rich, densely populated countries of continental Europe - FRG, BeNeLux, Italy and France - in addition to the UK. Together these countries consumed more than 90 per cent of the Western European total of 211.8 bcm in 1982. Continental Europe's consumption (ca. 160 bcm) was covered by the Netherlands (production 67.8 bcm, net exports 32.2 bcm), production in other countries on the continent (ca. 40 bcm), Norway (13.6 bcm) and by imports from USSR (27.5 bcm) and Algeria (8.7 bcm). UK-consumption (49 bcm) was covered from two sources; indigenous production (38.3 bcm) and imports from Norway (10.7 bcm). Western Europe's proven gas reserves are concentrated in the Netherlands, Norway and the UK. Hypothetically, Europe's proven reserves (4 324 bcm) might cover present consumption (211.8 bcm) for about 20 years.

In detail, the European gas market is more complicated than revealed by tables 1-3. Most of the trade agreements are bilateral and not only based on "pure economics" but also influenced by political con- sideration over security, diversification, self sufficiency etc. For instance:

- Dutch production and exports are influenced by consideration over conservation and future self-sufficiency. Netherlands own resources might cover indigenous consumption for 40 years with no

Table 1. Estimated proven natural gas reserves, per cent of world's proven reserves, production and reserves-to-production ratios by country.

	Proven reserves 1.1. 1983 (bcm)	% of world reserves	Production (net) 1982 (bcm)	Reserves/ Production
Austria	10	-	1.3	
Denmark	152	0.2	-	
France	73	0.1	6.6	
FRG	176	0.2	16.8	
Ireland	38	-	1.9	
Italy	172	0.2	14.6	
Jugoslavia	82	0.1	2.3	
Netherlands	1.515	1.8	67.9	22
Norway	1.440	1.7	25.3	57
Spain	18	-	-	
Turkey	15	-	-	
UK	633	0.7	38.3	17
Total Western Europe	4.324	5.0	174.9	25
USSR	34.500	39.8	500.8	69
Algeria	3.195	3.7	26.0	123

(Sources : Cedigaz (9183) and J. P. Stern (1983).)

Table 2.   Estimated (net) production, imports, exports and consumption of natural gas by country, 1982 (bcm).

	Net production	Imports	Exports	Consumption
Austria	1.3	2.8	-	4.1
Belgium	-	8.7	-	8.7
Denmark	-	0.1	-	0.1
Finland	-	0.7	-	0.7
France	6.6	19.8	-	26.3
FRG	16.8	32.1	1.5	47.4
Ireland	1.9	-	-	1.9
Italy	14.6	13.5	-	28.1
Jugoslavia	2.3	2.7	-	4.9
Luxembourg	-	0.4	-	0.4
Netherlands	67.9	2.7	34.9	35.7
Norway	25.3	-	24.3	1.0
Spain	-	2.2	-	2.2
Switzerland	-	1.3	-	1.3
UK	38.3	10.7	-	49.0
Total Western Europe	174.9	(97.6)	(60.7)	211.8
USSR	500.8	2.5	57.9	445.4
Algeria	26.0	-	11.0	15.0

(Source: Cedigaz (1983)).

Table 3. Western-European gas trade 1982 (bcm)

Importing region	Exporting region							Import from outside W. Europe
	FRG	Nether-lands	Norway	Σ	USSR	Algeria	Libya	
Austria	–	–	–	–	2.8	–	–	2.8
Bel-gium	–	6.6	1.8	8.4	–	0.3	–	0.3
Den-mark	0.1	–	–	0.1	–	–	–	
Fin-land	–	–	–	–	0.7	–	–	0.7
France	1.1	5.9	2.2	9.2	3.7	6.9	–	10.6
FRG	–	15.8	6.8	22.6	9.5	–	–	9.5
Italy	–	5.3	–	5.3	8.1	–	–	8.1
Jugo-slavia	–	–	–	–	2.7	–	–	2.7
Luxem-bourg	–	0.4	–	0.4	–	–	–	
Nether-lands	–	–	2.7	2.7	–	–	–	
Spain	–	–	–	–	–	1.4	0.8	2.2
Switzer-land	0.4	0.9	–	1.3	–	–	–	–
UK	–	–	10.7	10.7	–	0	–	–
Σ	1.5	34.9	24.3	60.7	27.5	8.7	0.8	37.0

(Source: Cedigaz (1983))

exports, but perhaps only for 20 years with today's export level.

- Norway's production and export of gas are decided simultaneously with oil production and is constrained by concern over the total magnitude of the oil sector in the domestic economy.

- France is (for historical reasons) a significant buyer of Algerian gas. On the other hand, Algeria might service France's present gas consumption for 100 years or more.

- Concern over energy-supply-security has constrained USSR gas exports to Western Europe.

The present status of the Western-European gas market is therefore not a result of a "common energy cost minimization scheme". Concerning the future development of the market, the localization of the resource base put some limits on possible solutions, but there are still many interesting options, to explore.

3. A EUROPEAN GAS DEMAND MODEL

A variety of different approaches have been used to model energy demand, depending on the sector which has been analysed, the energy (supply) situation of the country in question and not least - the availability of data. Basically all models belong to one of two classes (cfr. Bohi (1981)): reduced form demand models or structural demand models. In reduced form models the demand for a specific fuel is defined and estimated as a function of the fuel's own price, the price of substitutes, the income or activity level and other relevant variables. The demand for fuel i may be expressed as:

$$(1) \quad Z_i = Z_i (P, Y, X)$$

where P is prices of fuels, Y is income or activity level and X denotes other relevant variables.

Reduced form models are often not based on specified economic relations describing the behavioural process by which adjustments in stocks of energyconsuming capital take place. They are usually justified by rather vague analogies to static demand theory. The most common way to deal with the dynamics of the adjustment process is to introduce some kind of lagged adjustment hypotesis, for instance the Koyck model (Koyck (1954)). A slightly different lagged adjustment model is suggested by Houthakker and Taylor (1970). A third model is the polynomial lag scheme based on Almon (1965).

In addition to the lack of any explicit economic optimizing behaviour, these models have been critized along several lines. The lag structure imposes in some cases severe ex ante restrictions on the estimated coefficients (Koyck lag). The choice of lag-structure often is ad hoc implying that the method mainly is a matter of choosing the results that fit data, rather than using data to test hypothesis deduced from economic theory. This objection to lagged adjustment models is stressed by the fact that empirical use of these models reveals extreme sensitivity in results as respons to variations to model specification. Consequently, the accumulated response to changes in exogenous assessments seem somewhat arbitrary.

An alternative approach to reduced form models is the structural demand models where relations describing the underlying behavioural process are explicitly defined and estimated. The most common approach is to define the energy use as functions of different vintages of (consumer or producer) capital, where the changes in capital stocks and capacity utilization depend on relative factor prices, activity levels etc. Another approach is to model explicitly energy demand and supply in macroeconomic models, where the behavioural relations of consumers and producers include energy decisions like in Hudson and Jorgenson (1974) or in the Norwegian MSG-4 model. (Longva, Lorentsen and Olsen (1984)).

Essential in the dynamic model of Balestra (1967) is the distinction between "captive" and "free" demand (called "new" demand by Balestra) for natural gas. The distinction is based on the recognition that energy demand is closely connected to the stock of energy using equipment. The part of total demand which is locked in to existing stock of capital is called captive. Free demand, on the other hand, is the sum of three parts. Replacement demand originating from renewal of the existing capital stock (depreciation), expansion demand which is net growth in demand from the preceding period and changes in demand as response to decisions by consumers to change the short-run utilization rate of existing appliances.

Balestra assumes that the utilization rate is constant. This is somewhat justified by the fact that he is studying the residential/commercial market for natural gas, where natural gas is mainly used for space-heating and variations in the utilization rate predominantly is due to variations in temperature. Furthermore, he uses degree day adjusted gas consumption data. The assumption of a constant utilization rate makes it possible to by-pass the problem of getting data on the gas-consuming capital stock. Balestra finally arrives at the following equation:

(2) $E_t = f(P_t, Y_t, H_t, t) + (1-\delta) E_{t-1}$

where:

$f()$ - the free demand function,

E_t - demand for natural gas

Y_t - real income pr. household

P_t - relative prices of fuels and other inputs,

H_t - household variable,

δ - the rate of economic depreciation,

t - time

To allow for empirical estimation, one needs to specify the functional form of the free demand function f().

Balestra used a linear specification of the demand function for free demand. This approach has been further elaborated by Berndt and Watkins (1977) in a model constructed for the residential/commercial sector. They assume a mixed additive-multiplicative model, using loglinear relationships and adding present and lagged consumption. A parameter (degree-days: the product of the number of degrees below 65 ^{0}F and the number of days) indicating the climatical conditions, is introduced. The reason for doing so instead of using weather adjusted gas consumption, is that the authors do not find apriori arguments supporting the assumption that there is a unitary elasticity between temperature and temperature sensitive gas consumption. This assumption might of course influence the estimated elasticities.

$$(3) \qquad E_t = D_t^{\alpha_1} \left[\alpha_2 + P_t^{\alpha_3} H_t^{*\alpha_4} Y_t^{*\alpha_5} \right]$$

where:

$$H_t^* = H_t - (1-r)H_{t-1}$$

$$Y_t^* = Y_t - (1-r)Y_{t-1}$$

D_t - the ratio of degree days in year t to average

H_t - number of households

P_t - fuel prices

r - the rate of depreciation on fuel consuming equipment.

Y_t - real income per household

The most serious objection to the Balestra model is the assumption about constant rate of utilization. This rate varies for two principally different reasons: technical efficiency of the gas consuming equipment is improved over time and relative prices determine the optimal utilization of the capital stock in the short run. A more complete optimization model, of course, would endogenously determine the rate of utilization.

A more theoretical satisfactory basis for (2) is provided by

Berndt, Morrison and Watkins (1981). They show that the Balestra equation could be generated from an explicit dynamic model where costs of adjustment of quasi-fixed factors are taken into account.

In all models considered so far, the adjustment process in the market for the one good studied, is independent of disequilibrium in connected markets. For example, adjustments in optimal level of natural gas consuming capital equipment as response to changes in natural gas prices obviously depends on the adjustment of other fuel consuming stocks of capital. In short, disequilibrium in one factor market should not be isolated, but the general disequilibrium should be taken explicitly into account.

This criticism might be dealt with by the introduction of interrelated disequilibrium as done by Nadiri and Rosen (1973). This is a generalized adjustment scheme where disequilibrium in one market for a quasi-fixed input affects demand for another factor. This model is not justified as another ad hoc approach to the adjustment process, but as an approximation to the solution of a dynamic optimization problem. It is shown in Berndt, Morrison and Watkins (1981) that the solution to a dynamic optimization model coincide with the generalized adjustment scheme provided that the restricted cost function is quadratic and the discount rate is stable over time.

Models based on the theory of duality between prices and quantities in the demand start out with the notion of a restricted variable cost function (Samuelson, (1953) and Lau (1976)). Technological constraints, in particular the fact that some inputs are quasi-fixed, is embodied in the restricted variable cost function. The firms (households) minimize variable costs subject to these short-run constraints. Applying Shephard's lemma, the cost-minimizing demand for a certain (variable) input factor is equal to the partial derivative of the restricted variable cost function with respect to this factor's price:

(4) $\qquad E_i \quad = \quad \dfrac{\partial G(P,Y,X)}{\partial P_i}$

$\qquad$ G() - restricted variable cost function

$\qquad$ P - prices of variable inputs

$\qquad$ Y - income / activity level

$\qquad$ X - quasi-fixed input factors.

If a functional form of the restricted variable cost function is specified, the short-run demand function for natural gas might be estimated from (4). These short-run demand functions depend not only on prices on variable inputs, but is conditional on the quantities of quasifixed inputs (and output). This approach generates both short and long term elasticities of demand and allows for an economically meaningful measure of capacity utilization. This model has one major short-coming. It does not provide information about the time lag from an exogenous shock until long run equilibrium is re-established. This reflects the basically static nature of the model.

One of the attractive properties of this model is the possibility to take into account supply contraints in one or several markets. The commonly used assumption about infinitely elastic supply curves is not necessarily a reasonable approximation for the European gas market. In Fuss (1981) it is shown that by replacing market prices by the appropriate shadow prices, the duality between cost and production is retained.

More advanced models are based on dynamic optimization where the cost of adjustment of quasi-fixed factors are included, Lau (1976). In these models, the firm minimizes the present value of the future stream of costs subject to the fact that the firm initially owns a stock of quasi-fixed factors and that adjustment in these state variables is costly. This model, given certain assumptions, "degenerates" to the general adjustment scheme (Nadiri and Rosen (1973)) or to the Balestra (1967) model.

The structural models are normally superior to the reduced form models in clarity and theoretical content. Reduced form models can often only be derived from structural models by making questionable simplifications and assumptions. On the other hand, reduced form models demand less data and they are often simpler to use as forecasting tools than structural models, (and the quality of energy forecasts are of course only partly dependent on the model formulation.)

When modelling the European gas market, it seems reasonable to include both a regional and a sectoral dimension. UK and continental Europe are two separate gas markets. For continental Europe, it seems appropriate to disaggregate further to five or six regions. A sectoral breakdown within each region is important for several reasons. The growth potential for gas and the substitution possibilities for gas against other types of energy are clearly different within the residential/commercial, industry and electricity generating sectors. Energy policies also seem to be drawn along sectoral lines. Both the regional and sectoral dimensions of estimated gas demand are of interest when analysing different transportation solutions, load capacity etc. in the gas trade model. Thus, within each demand region, three sectors will be represented: the residential/commercial, the industrial and the power generating sector.

When it comes to the choice between structural and reduced form models, few a priori criteria exists.

Our decision to base our model of West European natural gas demand on a structural formulated demand scheme are based on the following reasoning. Most recent projections of future demand of natural gas in Western Europe projects natural gas share of total energy consumption to stay constant or change only slightly. In addition, total energy consumption is expected to grow moderately, see Manne and Schrattenholzer (1984) or Roland (1984). This implies low growth rates in gas demand and no significant market penetration. The predominant part of total demand in such a market is in the short/medium term captive demand, which underlines the importance of the interrelationship between natural gas demand and the stocks of gas consuming appliances.

Thus, we have so far decided to experiment with both a Balestra-type model (3) and a model based on the restricted variable cost function (4). With several specifications of the free demand function and the restricted variable cost function. Finally, different solutions for different regions and sectors might be chosen.

4. A EUROPEAN GAS TRADE MODEL

This section outlines a model describing the European natural gas market. The model is basically a "transportation" model based on the GMT (Gas Trade Model) developed by Beltramo et. al (1984), but important references are also made to Mathiesen and Lont (1983), Boucher and Smeers (1984) and Rogner et. al. (1984). The main structure of the model suggested here, is shown in figure 1. The model describes trade flows between six supply regions (Algeria, Netherlands, Norway, UK, USSR and Others) and seven consuming regions (BeLux-countries, France, FRG, Netherlands, Scandinavia, UK and finally Austria, Switzerland and Italy lumped together).

Within each supply region, several producing activities takes place.

Supply side		Demand side	
Activity	Country/region	Country/region	Sector

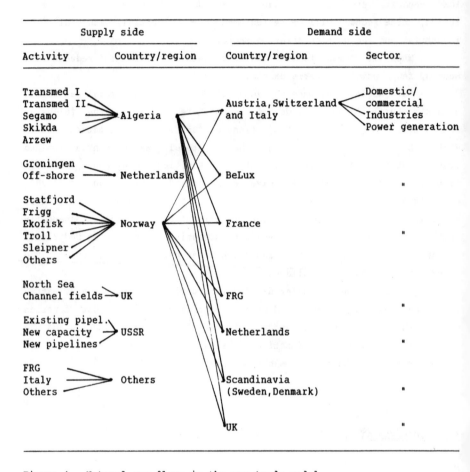

Figure 1. Natural gas flows in the gas trade model

To allow for flexibility, the model includes the option to represent each supply region by a set of production activities or simply as one aggregated supply function. When analyzing the policy options discussed in section 1, a detailed representation of each supply region is in general not necessary, with the exception of Norway who needs a more careful attention in our analysis.

On the demand side, the different patterns of consumption in different sectors of the economy necessitates dissaggregation within each demand region. Consequently, three sectors are specified; the domestic/-commercial sectors, the industrial sector and the power generation. All three sectors are represented by one single node. This implies that transportation costs, cif. prices etc. are identical for sectors within each region. The parameter assessment of demand functions in each sector will be based on the econometrically estimated demand model described in section 3.

Except for the supply and demand variables that enter nonlinearly into the objective function, the model is a straightforward "transportation" model. The primal variables are nonnegative, and are defined as follows:

x_{ij} = quantity transported from supply region i to demand region j

y_i = total quantity supplied by region i

y_{ih} = total quantity supplied by activity h in region i

z_j = total quantity demanded by region j

z_{jk} = total quantity demanded by sector k in region j.

Economic policy or technical constraints may affect one or more of these variables. E.g., there may be pipeline capacity limits which impose upper bounds on the transportation variables x_{ij}. There may be producibility constraints on the production variables y_i. Some of the demands may be predetermined by controlled prices and/or fuel-use allocation rules. And some of the supplies may be determined by export controls. Each of these conditions may be described as an upper or a lower bound on an individual variable. In addition, there are the following supply and demand constraints for all regions i and j:

(5) $\sum_j x_{ij} \leqslant y_i$ (supply constraint, region i)

(6) $\sum_i x_{ij} \geqslant z_j$ (demand constraint, region j)

A simple way of representing the demand side in the trade model, is to deduce from the demand model regional demand functions with constant elasticity of demand with respect to the gas price. Thus, omitting the subscripts for demand region and sector, these willingness-to-pay functions are of the following format at each point in time:

(7) $g(z) = az^b$

where the exponent b is the reciprocal of the price elasticity of demand. On the supply side, two different functional forms have been employed by Mathiesen and Lont (1983) and Beltramo et al (1984). In Manne's model, the regional marginal cost function is assumed to be of the form:

$$(8) \qquad f(y) \quad = \quad \alpha + \frac{\beta}{\gamma - y} \qquad \qquad \text{where } \alpha, \beta \text{ and } \gamma \text{ are positive constants.}$$

In this way, the elasticity of supply may be high at low production levels, but approaches zero as production approaches the producibility limit γ. Also, by setting $\beta = 0$, marginal costs remain constant up to whatever upper bound is imposed upon y, the production level (a reverse L-shaped supply curve).

The marginal cost curve chosen by Mathiesen is the following one:

$$(9) \qquad f(y) \quad = \quad \alpha \, (\gamma - y)^{\beta} \, , \qquad \qquad \alpha > 0, \ \beta < 0 \ \text{ for } y < \gamma \ .$$

The parameter β determines the curvature. The smaller the absolute value of β, the closer the curve comes to the reverse L-shape.

Transportation costs are in this version of the model assumed constant per unit transported.

The model outlined here, is a model of interrelated gas markets. In some regions, prices may be free to move so as to equilibriate supplies and demands. In others, there may be disequilibria associated with controls over prices and/or quantities traded. Under perfect competition, the overall system may be described in partial equilibrium terms - as though it were operating so as to maximize the sum of producers' and consumers' benefits less the costs of production and transportation - subject to constraints on the prices and quantities traded. With a slight modification of the maximand, the market solution for a monopolist can be obtained in a similar way as the solution to a certain optimization problem. In the European gas market, it is of significant interest to study monopolistic behaviour such as the Nash-Cournot game strategy or the leader-follower relationship described by Stackelberg. In Mathiesen (1983) it is shown that the solution to these market equilibria can be obtained by solving a sequence of linear complementarity problems. This approach is based on the first order necessary conditions of an equilibrium. This method for solving the model seems more flexible than those used for similar optimization models, and is the one to be applied.

119

5. USE OF THE MODELS

As outlined in section 3 and 5, we plan to develop two different
models. The gas demand model, mainly consisting of an econometrically
estimated demand scheme, is designed to shed light on the following type of
problems: What are the quantitative importance of interfuel substitution
in different sectors? Which are the competing fuels and what are the income and price elasticities involved? Since natural gas consumption is
closely connected to the capital stock in each particular sector, what are
the short and long term reaction to changes in prices and how long does the
adjustment process take?

The demand model might be used to make projections of consumption
given prices and incomes. In the short and medium term, this kind of projections do allow for consistency checks. Given the existing contract
structure including prices and minimum take clauses, is the market balanced and at what time is supplies under new contracts required? What would
the Norwegian market share in different markets be, and at what time will
the market be ready to absorb deliveries from new projects in the North Sea
or elsewhere?

In the natural gas trade model, both supply, demand and transport
of natural gas is represented. One way of solving this model is by maximizing the sum of consumer's and producer's surplus. This is equivalent to
deriving the competitive equilibrium of the natural gas market.

One might question the relevance of a competitive equilibrium in a
market characterized by a small number of participants. However, even if
such a market will differ from a competitive market, it may be useful to
derive the competitive equilibrium solution because of it's well-known properties and as a benchmark.

In Beltramo (1984) a static equilibrium is derived. A natural extension would be to derive an intertemporal competitive equilibrium. This
imply that market participants are "clairvoyant" as opposed to "myopic"
when the model is solved for a sequence of independent static equilibriums
(e.g. static expectations).   To solve the intertemporal version of the
model, we would have to exogenously specify (i) a time horizon, (ii) maximum accumulated extraction til the time horizon in each producing activity
or region, (iii) a discount rate, and (iv) time paths for all exogenous
variables (e.g. oil prices, economic growth).

Whether using the intertemporal or the static version of the model,
one would be interested in tracing out effects of changing the values

chosen for exogenous variables and constraints. Obvious examples are effects of increased interfuel substitution in particular markets (e.g. under boiler use, electric power production) or changes in the assumed economic growth, reserves, alternative energy prices etc. One would also study the effect of changing political constraints on e.g. the amount of gas delivered from USSR to Western Europe, or capacity constraints on transportation between various regions (e.g. connecting UK to the continental pipeline grid).

An alternative to deriving a complete competitive equilibrium (static or intertemporal) is to specify the development of the price of natural gas exogenously, and minimize the discounted costs of producing and transporting the corresponding gas demand. This procedure may be used to derive other equilibria than the competitive one. To arrive at an equilibrium which one regards as "reasonable" taking political and negotiation aspects into consideration, one might have to run several iterations. If e.g. for the initial gas price development one arrives at marginal production plus extraction costs in excess of this price, one can recalculate with a higher gas price.

So far, we have discussed uses of the model which treat Norway symmetrically with other regions included in the model. Obviously, Norwegian policy makers might be interested in using the model in a way which gives Norway a more central role.

The European gas market apparently is not a competitive market. On demand side, relatively few buyers exists; in most countries the purchasing of gas is nationalized or at least partly nationalized by means of distribution companies exercising a considerable amount of monopoly power. In addition, a handful of multinational oil companies have property rights in the same distribution companies in several countries where private ownership exists. On the supply side, negotiations on prices and quantities are controlled by the government or government owned companies. This implies that relatively few agents interact. A Nash game theoretic approach thus seem appropriate.

The model could be used to solve for an intertemporal Nash equilibrium involving three (or more) players: UK, Continental Europe and Norway. Other suppliers may be netted out: demand for Norwegian gas being net demand after subtraction of imports from USSR, Algeria etc, or they may be explicitly included as players in the game. In addition to constraints on accumulated gas extraction over the time horizon chosen, one could have lower and upper bounds on production in each period and/or contraints on how fast the extraction rate could change, on transportation capacity

between different regions etc. The solution to such an optimization problem would indicate when and to whom Norway should export natural gas.

REFERENCES

Almon, S. (1965): The distributed lag between capital appropriations and expenditures. Econometrica vol. 33, no. 1, pp. 178-196.

Balestra, P. (1967): The demand for natural gas in the US: A dynamic approach for the residential and commercial market. Amsterdam, North-Holland.

Beltramo, M.A, A.S. Manne and J.P. Weyant (1984): A North American Gas Trade Model: GTM. International Energy Project. Stanford University, September 1984.

Berndt, E.R., C.J. Morrison and G.C. Watkins (1981): Dynamic models of energy demand: An assessment and comparison, in: Berndt, E.R. and B.C. Field, ed: Modelling and measuring natural resource substitution. MIT Press.

Berndt, E.R. and G.C. Watkins (1977): Demand for natural gas: residential and commercial markets in Ontario and British Colombia. Canadian Journal of Economics, E, pp. 97-111.

Bohi, Douglas R. (1981): Analyzing demand behavior. A study of energy elasticities. The John Hopkins University Press, Baltimore and London.

Boucher, J. and Y. Smeers (1984): Gas trade in the European Community during the seventies. A model analysis. Mimea, Universitè Catholique de Louvain.

Cedigaz (1983): Le gas naturel dans le monde en 1982. Cedigaz Rueil Malmaison, France, Juin 1983.

Fuss, M.A. (1981): The derived demand for energy in the presence of supply constraints. Reprint series no. 151. Institute for policy analysis. University of Toronto.

Houthakker, H.S. and L.D. Taylor (1970): Consumer demand in the US: Analysis and projections. Cambridge, Mass., Harvard University Press.

Hudson, E.A. and D. Jorgenson (1974): The US energy policy and economic growth 1975-2000. Bell Journal of Economics, vol. 5.

Koyck, L.M. (1954): Distributed lags and investment analysis. Amsterdam, North- Holland.

Lau, L.J. (1976): A caracterization of the normalized restricted profit function. J. of Econ. Theory 12, Febr., pp. 131-163.

Longva, S., L. Lorentsen and Ø. Olsen (1984): The multi-sectoral growth model MSG-4; Formal structure and empirical characteristics. Article from Central Bureau of Statistics, Oslo.

Manne, A.S. and L. Schrattenholzer (1984): A summary of 1983 poll responses. Appendix C. Frequency distribution of responses for Western
Europe (unpbl.).

Mathiesen, L (1983): Computational experience in solving equilibrium models
by a sequence of linear complementarity problems. Technical report SOL
83-1, Stanford University.

Mathiesen, L. and A. Lont (1983): Modelling Market Equilibria: An application to the World Steel Market. Working paper MU 04, Norwegian
School of Economics and Business Administration.

Nadiri, M.I. and S. Rosen (1973): A disequilibrium model of demand for factors of production. New York.

Rogner, H-H., S. Messner and M. Strubegger (1984): European Gas Trade: A
Quantitative Approach. WP-84-44, IIASA, July.

Roland, (1984): Natural gas supply and demand in Western Europe, 1990 and
2000. International Energy Project. Stanford University, February 1984.

Samuelson, P.A. (1953): Prices of factors and goods in general equilibrium.
Rev. of Econ. Stud. 21 October, pp. 1-20.

Statoil (1983): The pricing of natural gas. Statoil background paper no.
15, June 1983.

Stern, Jonathan P. (1983): International Gas Trade in Europe. The Policies
of Exporting and Importing Countries. Heinemann Education Books, London
1983.

Valais, M & al. (1982): L'industrie du gaz dans le Monde. Editons Technip,
Paris 1982.

MEASURING THE CONSEQUENCES OF THE TAKE OR PAY CLAUSES IN NATURAL GAS CONSUMING COUNTRIES

BY

JACQUELINE BOUCHER AND YVES SMEERS[1]

ABSTRACT

Imports of natural gas are subject to more or less rigid take or pay clauses in which the buyer promises to lift a certain amount of natural gas or to pay for it. This arrangement implies large risks on the buyer by committing him to buy fixed quantities of a product over a long horizon without prior knowledge of the price. Because of the uncertainty on the future price of natural gas, the take or pay clause is bound to induce surpluses or shortages of natural gas in the importing countries. The paper first casts the problem of choosing the optimal mix of gas imports in a statistical decision analysis context. Applying this approach requires an analysis of how the economy is able to cope with committed quantities that are short or in excess of the demand that materializes at the market prices. This is examined using a multitemporal equilibrium model which accounts for the substitution of gas with oil products in the main industries and in the power sector. Other substitutions with capital, labour, electrical energy and other material are also allowed in the industrial sectors. The analysis is presented in the context of the Belgian situation but with artificial data.

1. INTRODUCTION

Most gas contracts imply take or pay clauses. The buyer, without any guarantee on the prices, commits himself to lift a prespecified quantity of gas or to pay for it. This clause, while protecting the investments of the producer, shifts most of the risks to the buyer who may not be able to resell the committed quantities at the prevailing price. Careful planning cannot completely eliminate the risks implied by the take or pay clause. Because demand depends on future relative prices which are by nature uncertain, any commitment to lift fixed quantities of gas is

O.Bjerkholt & E.Offerdal, eds., Macroeconomic Prospects for a Small Oil Exporting Country. ISBN 90-247-3183-6.
Copyright 1985, Martinus Nijhoff Publishers, Dordrecht.

bound to lead to surpluses or shortages. The problem is thus one of decision under uncertainty where actions are taken, not to meet well identified gas needs, but to balance expected losses due to gas bubbles or shortages.

The purpose of this paper is to describe a methodology for dealing with the problems raised by the take or pay clause and to illustrate by some examples how it can be applied. The problem, which is cast in the general context of statistical decision analysis, is methodologically stated in section 2.

The next part indicates how the different branches of the decision tree defined in section 2 can be valuated. We rely, for this purpose, on a multitemporal general equilibrium model simulating the evolution of the economy and allowing for substitution between different production factors. Shifts between oil and natural gas are represented in several industrial sectors and in power generation. The model also allows for different behavioural constraints on the gas importing company which may be restricted to financial equilibrium or allowed to run heavy deficits. A general equilibrium model is not the most natural tool for tackling the problem, our model could however be constructed relatively easily from tools already developed in Belgium (Guillaume (1978), Bossier et al (1978))(see below). The approach is also a natural extension of previous studies (SPPS (1978), (1983a)) which makes the analysis more easily receivable in practice.

The paper is meant to be methodological and the numerical simu-lations are presented only for illustrating the different points of the approach; the figures, although realistic, have been disguised so as to make the results unsuitable for direct applications.

2. METHODOLOGICAL CONSIDERATIONS AND PROBLEM STATEMENT

Gas supplies may exhibit various degrees of flexibility; we formalize the problem by considering two types of contracts. The first class requires fixed annual liftings and are usually the fact of Algeria and Norway. Dutch contracts usually exhibit more flexibility and typify the second class of contractual arrangements that we consider. Lifting can be chosen between a lower and an upper bound; a global amount is however committed and must be lifted over some horizon. We shall not consider here the possibility of renegotiating the contract to adapt the committed quantities to changing demand. Our objective is limited to an evaluation of the economic consequences of the take or pay clause but can, however, provide the basis of an evaluation of the relevance af a renegotiation.

The price of natural gas can depend on both the sources (Guillaume (1978) and the type of contracts, the more flexible suppliers charging normally more, at least in principle, for their deliveries. We shall adopt here a simplified view and suppose that the price of gas can only depend on the type of contract. We also make the following assumptions:

(1) gas contracts cannot be renegotiated to reduce the committed quantities. New quantities can be added in a five year horizon;

(2) any quantitiy in each contractual category can be committed at the prevailing price of that category. In the first category the quantities are fixed annual amounts; in the second category, they are averages and define a certain interval. We shall consider as a typical situation the one adopted to represent Dutch contracts in Bossier et al (1978), and suppose that liftings can be up or down by 10 per cent with respect to the average quantity;

(3) the decision maker has selected a certain number of scenarios to which he attributes a certain probability. The scenarios define the external environment and consist of prices, foreign demand , etc. The mix of gas contracts should be "optimal" with respect to this multiple environment.

These assumptions are only introduced for simplifying the presentation and none of them is really essential to the methodology. The most drastic one with respect to a general analysis of the problem is probably the third one; we indeed assume a set of scenarios rooted at a single origin node (the situation in 1980). This is the simplest decision tree than can be thought of in this context; it is depicted in figure 1 with three scenarios retained in recent studies by official Belgian agencies that will be used in this paper SPPS (1983b), (1983c), (1983a). We consider the choice of the decision maker in year 1980; contracts typically span a twenty year period (see Valais et al (1982)), and we have assumed that it takes a period of five years between the basic agreement and the first suppliers. Taking the Belgian situation as an example, this would correspond to assuming that the agreement for the Norwegian and Algerian new gas supplies coming on line in 1985 and 1986 were reached in 1980. Assuming as indicated before that these contracts cover a twenty year horizon, their effect will be felt until 2005; because the take or pay clause of existing contracts is only felt in 1985 and 1990 (see below) we limit our analysis to a relatively short term horizon (1980 to 1995); in order to avoid end effects over the period of interest, we extend, for computational purposes, the horizon up to year 2025 but do not use the result of the six last periods.

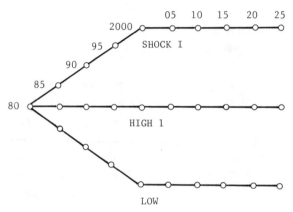

Figure 1.   Illustration of the decision tree.

The analysis can thus be conducted as follows. Suppose that a certain mix of first and second class contracts has been decided in 1980; simulate the evolution of the economy over the horizon 1985-2005 starting from the common origin 1980.   Value each scenario by an appropriate index (for instance the discounted sum of private consumption). Select the contract mix that leads to the highest expected value of the index.

Because of space limitation we shall not conduct the whole analysis here but instead concentrate on a set of methodological issues that we illustrate with numerical results. The interested reader is reported to a companion paper (forthcoming) for a more complete treatment.

This is simple statistical decision analysis and, besides our simplifying assumptions, there is probably not much to object to it.   We shall conclude this section by a few words of introduction to the model used for capturing the macroeconomic effects of gas surpluses or shortages. Natural gas is used by the final consumer in industrial sectors and power generation. While private consumption typically exhibits little short term flexibility for switching fuel, industry and the power generation sector generally have a capacity of bifuel boilers that allows them to easily switch from oil to gas and vice versa. Surpluses and shortages can be dealt with using that flexibility, by inducing or restricting the consumption of natural gas. There are obviously different approaches for doing so which may have drastically different economic effects. One possibility is to press the power sector to absorb most of the surpluses (Financial Times (1984)). An other more balanced approach is to allocate the discrepancy so as to minimize the cost over the whole economy; this corresponds to allowing the domestic price to move up or down in order to clear the market. The gas company whether public or private, may be prevented from doing so because of budgetary reasons; the take or pay clause will then force it, in case of gas surplus, to raise its price so as to transfer to the less elastic customers the burden of too small a demand. Other approaches are still possible with, for instance, different prices for different types of consumers.

We shall in this paper only consider two situations; in one of them, the gas company is allowed to modify the domestic price so as to clear the market; in the second case it is restricted to break even and hence must raise its price in face of decreased demand. The next section briefly describes the model used and how these different behaviours been taken into account.

3. MODELING CONSIDERATIONS

3.1. THE SIMULATION MODEL

We consider, for conducting the analysis, a dynamic input output model of the economy which explicitly accounts for the substitution of natural gas with other fuels and factors in both the industrial and the power generation sector. More specifically our model relies on a 24 sector description of the economy; each sector produces a single commodity and final consumption is described by six aggregate commodities that appear in a multitemporal utility function with leisure. The industrial sectors and the final consumer constitute the main final users of natural gas in the economy. 14 of the sectors are described by fixed technologies only allowing for zero elasticity of substitution between natural gas and other fuels; the 10 main energy users which represent the bulk of gas consumption in industry are more satisfactorily accounted for. Each of them is described by a translog demand system (Capital, Labour, Electricity, Materials, Other energy factors); inside the Other energy factors we allow for substitution between oil and natural gas through a Cobb-Douglas production function. No substitution is currently permitted between coal and the mix oil/gas; this is obviously an approximation, but it appears justified by surveys of industrial behaviour in Belgium (SPPS (1983d)). The final consumer is a main user of natural gas but it does not allow for much short term substitutions; we accordingly represent the consumption for space heating by a fixed technology which reflects projection of a larger share of natural gas in the future. The maximisation of the multitemporal utility function derives the system which is of a classic type. Commodity balance equations describe the supply and consumption of goods in the economy; national productions and imports supply the intermediate demand, investments, final consumption and exports. The activities of the sector are bounded by or equal to the available capacity which is the result of existing and new investments; capacity decays at a constant rate. We shall not elaborate much here on the utility function; because it involves leisure, the employed worker can select the number of hours that he is willing to supply with respect to the additional consumption that he can gain in return. This trade-off determines the price of labor in the model. Because it can be an important consumer in case of gas bubbles, the power generation sector has received a particular attention. The model includes a rather refined description of the sector with five types of power plants (nuclear, coal, bifuel and trifuel plants, gas turbines) and a disaggregation of the annual electricity demand in four demand segments; the main features of the expansion of the power generation system and, in particular the possibility of substituting to natural gas in case of gas surplus, are captured in that representation. In contrast with the capacities of the other sectors, electrical equipment are represented with a fixed technical life as in usual capacity expansion models.

The balance of payment is the main constraint of the model and we proceed to discuss it now. Let (p_m, p_G) be the price in BF (Belgian Francs) of all imported commodities with p_G denoting the gas component of that vector; we consider a demand curve p_z (z) of the exports of the country. The balance of payment is specified as

$$ p_m \, m + p_G \, g - \int_0^z p_z(\xi) \, d\xi. $$

This formulation is not very satisfactory from an economic point of view, while we rely on the small country assumption and suppose a competitive market for representing the imports, we admit that the country can discriminate among its customers for exports. This representation of the model has been adopted in several case studies in Belgium (SPPS (1978), SPPS (1983a)). Although somewhat strange, this formulation can be considered as a first approximation of the real problem which presents significant computational advantages. A more refined treatment that avoids the classical drawbacks of input-output models would indeed require the model to be stated as a general equilibrium problem several consumers; in this context, the model can be completely handled by optimization which implies drastic simplifications.

3.2. MODELING SURPLUSES AND SHORTAGES

As indicated before we consider two types of contracts that basically differ by their flexibility. Contractual arrangements made in 1980 carry over up to 2005; new commitments can be made later in the horizon for the years from 1990 on. The assumptions stated in the preceeding sections led us to consider the following constraints for the supply of gas in year 1985 and later:

- Gas is committed between a lower and a upper bound in year 1985. The lower bound results from the amount specified in the contracts of the first type and the lower value in the contract of the second type; the upper one is determined in an analogous way.

- Gas is committed above some lower bound from 1990 on. This lower bound is determined from past decision as for the year 1985. In contrast with 1985, there exists no upper bound from 1990 on because we suppose that new contracts can be obtained at the prevailing price.

It should be noted that we neglect to model the effect of the signature of new contracts in 1985 and after on the evolution of the lower bound. Although such constraints should, in principle, be included in the model, they have been neglected here because they appear to be always satisfied in practice.

The national gas company, jointly owned by the state and the private sector, is regulated. It is required to remain in financial equilibrium and can discriminate between its different consumers in order to do so. We shall consider here two simplified behaviours for describing

its pricing policy; these correspond to different regulatory assumptions
and are introduced here as extreme cases. The first approach is dictated
by considerations of efficiency. The company is allowed to clear the
market by lowering the domestic price. This corresponds to the most
efficient approach (it minimizes the overall cost of the surplus) but puts
the com- pany in the red. This situation is depicted in figure 2. The
domestic gas market is represented by the overall demand curve and the
supply curve of the national gas company acting under the take or pay
clause and willing to clear the market.

Let l and u be respectively the lower and upper bounds on the
commitments, p^i is the import price (we assume in this discussion a single
price whatever the contract) and p^d the full unit cost to the company;
p^d is equal to p^i plus some unit distribution cost r, the latter assumed
constant as a simplification. Because of the take or pay clause the
company has to pay p^i to the gas supplier whatever the quantity sold on
the domestic market. We assume, in this first case, that the company
chooses to take its minimal contractual quantity and is prepared to
uniformly lower the domestic price so as to clear the market. Figure 2
depicts three demand curves (DC_1, DC_2, DC_3), that correspond to different
incomes and other domestic prices (these are endogenous in our model). If
the demand curve is DC_1, the equilibrium of the domestic market is attained
at a price p_1^e and the company incurs a deficit of $(p^d - p_1^e)l$; when the
demand curve is DC_2, it breaks even with a domestic price equal to p_2^e; the
demand curve DC_3 corresponds to a shortage and brings a profit $(p_3^e - p^d)u$ to
the company.

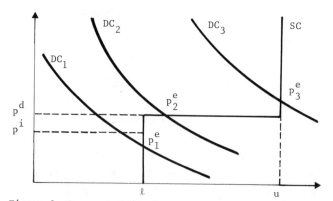

Figure 2. Gas market if the gas company can be in deficit.

This type of behaviour is dealt with in our model in the following way. Let S be the allowed trade deficit (see SPPS (1983b)) for assumption on that deficit), let p_1^i and p_2^i be the international price in constant BF (see below for a discussion of that problem) of the gas from the two types of contracts and g_1, g_2 be the quantities imported from both types of contracts. The balance of payment is stated as

$$P_m m + p_1^i g_1 + p_2^i g_2 - \int_0^z p_z(\xi) d\xi \leqslant S$$

$$g_1 \geqslant 1$$

The second behaviour of the gas company is closer to current practice; in case of a glut, the company is allowed to discriminate between its customers. Increasing the price for low elasticity users and reducing it for high elasticity users will make it possible to meet the budgetary constraint imposed by the take or pay clause. However, regulation imposes rather tight constraints on the maximal discrimination that the company can be allowed into and it may be appropriate in this first exercise to consider the no discrimination case as a first approximation of the problem. Assuming that the full unit cost is equal to p plus some markup r, the company may now be forced to increase p so as to cover the fixed charges implied by the take or pay clauses. Let x be the quantity sold, we have for p^d

$$p^d = p + r$$

where
$$px = p^i 1 \qquad \text{if } x \leqslant 1$$

$$p = p^i \qquad \text{if } u > x > 1$$

$$p \geqslant p^i \qquad \text{when } x = u.$$

The first condition expresses the fact that domestic prices must be increased in order to cover the import costs in case of a low demand; the firm breaks even by charging the import cost and a markup when demand is between the upper and lower bound. As in the first case, demand is rationed at a higher price when it is too high. The situation is depicted in figure 3. The supply curve SC is here identical to the average cost curve. Although moving along SC will generate inefficiencies, it is this policy

132

which is enforced by imposing financial equilibrium to the gas company.
From a numerical point of view, one should also note that SC is decreasing
below 1 which may lead to multiple equilibria. This requires some special
attention as we discuss now.

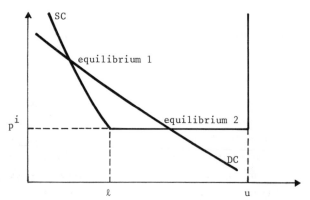

Figure 3. Market equilibrium when the gas company is
restricted to break even $(r = 0)$.

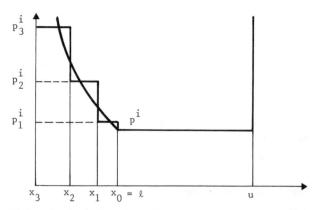

Figure 4. Approximation of the supply curve when the
gas company is restricted to break even.

In order to handle multiple equilibria, we consider a piece-wise constant approximation of the downward supply curve (see figure 4); we assume that the approximation is sufficiently refined for the product $p_j^i x$ to remain close to $p^i 1$ in each segment (x_{j-1}, x_j). In a given segment, the balance of payment constraint is written as:

$$p_m m + p_j^i x - \int_0^z p_z(\xi)d\xi < S$$

when $\quad x \in [x_j, x_{j-1}]$

Needless to say it is the equilibrium with highest imports which is of interest. In order to deal with the difficulty, we proceed by some enumerative approach. The problem is first solved with a balance of payment constraint which amounts to assuming that imports fall between 1 and u. If the lower bound on imports is binding in some periods, a new problem is constructed with a modified balance of payments where imports are assumed to lie in the next lower segment. The procedure stops when the problem generates a solution with all imports of gas between the specified bounds.

3.3. ADDITIONAL CONSIDERATIONS ABOUT THE BALANCE OF PAYMENTS

As indicated before we measure the effect of an assumption on the mix of gas contracts by the discounted sum of private consumption over the horizon 1985-2005. This comparison between contract mixes is only valid when all other conditions remain identical; although we have control in the model over most parameters that determine the evolution of the economy, we cannot specify a priori the dual variable of the trade balance constraint which expresses the exchange rate of the Belgian franc with foreign currencies. More specifically, if S designates the trade deficit in some year and μ is the dual variable of the trade balance constraint in that year, a comparison between two mixes of contracts is only valid, at least in principle, if S is invariant. We shall neglect that question in this first analysis and assume that the field of variation of the gas commitments is not great enough to generate evolutions of the economy that could lead to different exhange rates.

4. NUMERICAL RESULTS

This section provides some numerical illustrations of considerations made in the preceding section.   The general economic environment
governing the simulation model can be described by the following price
assumptions (in US $/GJ)(table 1).

Table 1: Assumption of price evolution (US $/GJ).

	1982	1985	1990	1995	after 1995
Crude Oil	5.44	5.16	6.25	6.87	2% / year
Natural Gas	4.275	4.873	5.13	5.685	2% / year
Coal	1.76	1.76	1.98	2.09	1% / year

The realism of the version of the model used in the study can be
assessed from the comparison between computed and observed (SPPS (1983d))
final consumption of energy as depicted in table 2.

Table 2: Comparison of Observed and Computed Final Consumption
          in 1980 (in 10^3 TJ).

	Coal	Coke	Oil	Electricity	Natural gas	Total
Computed	78	196	612.4	154.2	267	1307
Observed	85.3	138.5	711	156.2	304.9	1395.9

It is clear from these results that the model is not tuned to
reflect the conditions that prevailed in 1980; results should thus not be
considered as an analysis of the exact situation currently existing in
Belgium, but more as an illustration of phenomena that are likely to occur
in a similar environment. It may be useful in that context to compare our
evolution of the demand of natural gas to the one recently given in (SPPS
(1983d)) under similar assumptions (table 3).

Table 3: Comparison of Forecast of Future Demand of Natural Gas
          (in 10^3 TJ)

	Our Evaluation	SPPS
1980	267	306
1985	259	238
1990	297.3	237.5

While our starting point is lower than SPPS (1983d) our figures are higher in 1985 and 1990. Our discussion of the surpluses that are likely to prevail in 1985 and 1990 would thus be even more relevant in official scenarios such as SPPS (1983d). The evolution of the final consumption of natural gas (industry (energy and non energy uses) and private consumption) and of the lifting by the power sector are given in table 4.

The decrease of the final consumption is mainly due to the collapse of the steel industry from 1985 on. The drastic reduction of the

Table 4: Evolution of the Power Generation and Final Consumption of Natural Gas (in 10^3 TJ).

	1980	1985	1990	1995
Final Consumption Observed Value	267 304.9	259	297.3	305.6
Power Generation Observed Value	44.91 66.4	1.09	1.27	1.42

lifting of the power sector is a direct consequence of the arrival of new nuclear plants and the conversion to coal of bifuel oil-gas fired boilers. In contrast with this depressed demand, total committments for gas imports in 1985 and 1990 are taken as in table 5. These figures are adapted from CCE (1983) after eliminating the possibilities of amending the terms of the contracts and considering that the Dutch supplies have been significantly reduced in 1995 (again these are realistic but not real assumptions). Needless to say amounts of that order were negotiated when demand was buoyant (the expected growth of gas demand was still expected to lie between 2.1 and 3.2 per cent per year in 1980 (CCE (1980)) and could hardly be justified now.

Table 5: Assumed Contractual Commitments in 1985 and 1990 (in 10^3 TJ).

1985		1990
[355	384]	≯413

Consider now the situation where the national gas company has decided to lift the minimal committed quantity and to clear the market by lowering the domestic price. The evolution of the power generation and final consumption are given in table 6.

Table 6: Evolution of the Power Generation and Final Consumption
          of Natural Gas under the Take or Pay Clause (in 10^3 TJ).

	1980	1985	1990	1995
Final Consumption Observed Value	269.7 304.9	348.6	331.5	312.6
Power Generation Observed Value	49.03 66.4	6.9889	81.28	1.49

As specified in the contracts, the economy is now lifting the
minimal amount committed in 1985 and 1990. In contrast with other studies
(SPPS (1983b)) or recommendations (SPPS (1983c)), this is equally done by
allocating the excess gas between the power generation and final demands.
This phenomenon is illustrated in table 7; the difference of allocations
between 1985 and 1990 results from the exogenous scrapping of coal capacity
in the power sector in 1990; when sufficient coal and nuclear capacity
exists (which often results from recent decisions) the excess gas is mainly
diverted to the final consumption.

Table 7: Allocation of the Excess Gas under the Take or Pay
          Clause (in 10^3 TJ).

		1985	1990
Final Consumption ←	without take or pay	259.1	297.3
	with take or pay	348.6	331.5
Power Generation ←	without take or pay	1.09	1.27
	with take or pay	6.89	81.28

It is interesting to look at how this induced consumption can be
achieved. Table 8 gives the gas price and its structure in 1985 and 1990
with and without the take or pay clause.

The contribution of the imports to the overall price is taken as
one for facilitating the comparisons. It can be seen that the gas company
needs to lower the domestic price by 60 percent if it wants to clear the
market.

We now turn to the situation where the gas company wants to break
even. We recall that this is achieved by raising the price and shifting

Table 8: Comparison of the Price Structure of Natural Gas with and without the Take or Pay Clause

| | 1985 | | 1990 | | Observed 82 prices (adapted from Comitè de Contrôle) |
	without take or pay	with take or pay	without take or pay	with take or pay	
Imports	1	1	1	1	1
Added Value	.04	.05	.18	.20	.11
Other Inputs and Subsidies	.09	-.60	.10	-.77	
Final Price	1.13	.45	1.28	.43	1.11

all the cost of undelivered gas to the least elastic customers. Needless to say this approach still reduces the contributions of the power sector for handling the gas surpluses. The evolution of the demand for natural gas is given in table 9.

Table 9: Demand for Natural Gas when the Gas Company wants to Break Even (in 10^3 TJ).

	1980	1985	1990	1995	2000
Final Consumption Observed Value	267.9 304.9	250.8	282.8	308.4	317.6
Power Sector Observed Value	46.25 66.4	1.09	1.24	1.54	1.38

As could be expected the price increase can only result in a reduction of the lifting of natural gas by the power sector. Table 10 summarizes the evolution of the total consumption of natural gas in the three cases considered here (no take or pay, take or pay without breaking even and take or pay with a break even constraint).

Table 10: Evolution of Total Natural Gas Consumption in the Three Cases (in 10^3 TJ).

	1980	1985	1990
Observed Value	371.3		
No Take or Pay	311.9	260.1	298.6
Take or Pay without Break Even	318.7	355.5	412.8
Take or Pay with Break Even	314.2	251.9	284.

The difference of consumption between the two take or pay cases is clearly due to the requirement (in the first case) of minimal consumption. It is interesting to note how the price rise induced by the take or pay clause entails an additional drop of consumption with respect to the reference case.

Table 11: Structure of Domestic Prices under the Break Even Constraint.

	1985	1990	Observed 1982 prices
Imports	1.36	1.5	1
Added values	.02	.19	.11
Other inputs and subsidies	.1	.13	
Final price	1.48	1.82	1.11

Table 11 gives the new price structure when the national gas company must break even. The contribution to import indicators that because of the reduction of demand, the unitary price paid for imports is raised by the order of 30 and 50 percent in 1985 and 1990.

NOTES

1) This research has been conducted with the financial help of the Belgian Department for Science Policy. All errors and shortcomings are ours. A preliminary version appears in: Risks and Benefits of Energy Systems. International Atomic Energy Agency, Vienna 1984.

REFERENCES

Bossier, F. and D. Duwein, (1978): "Etude de la demande d'energie globale dans le contexte d'une analyse structurelle approfondie des secteurs de la demande intermediaire belge", Recherches Economiques de Louvain, 44(2).

Boucher, J. and Y. Smeers, "Planning for Gas Surplus and Shortages: An Analysis of the Take or Pay Clause, in preparation.

Boucher, J. and Y. Smeers, (1985):"Gas Trade in the European Community during the Seventies", to appear in Energy Economics.

Commission des Communautés Européennes, (1980): "L'approvisionnement de la Communauté en gaz naturel et ses perspectives", Office des publications officielles des Communautés Européennes, Luxembourg.

Commission des Communautés Européennes, Direction Generale Science, Recherche et Développement, (1983): "Scenarios a l'horizon 2000, projections énergétiques pour les pays de la Communauté Européenne - 1983 -", COD. XII/1075/83.

Financial Times, (1984(1): "Pressure Grows for Danish Coal-to-Gas Switch", European Energy Report, 159.

Guillaume, Y.,(1978): "Modélisation de système energetique belge. Presentation des principaux axes de recherche et d'un premier modèle d'essai", Cahiers Economiques de Bruxelles, 78.

SPPS, (1978): "Modèle central et modèles de demande finale", Services de Programmation de la Politique Scientifique, rue de la Science, Bruxelles.

SPPS, (1983a) "Modèlisation des interactions économie-énergie", Services de Programmation de la Politique Scientifique, rue de la Science, Bruxelles.

SPPS, (1983b): "Analyse du système énergétique belge", Synthèse au 1er juin 1983 des travaux réalisés dans le cadre du Programme National R-D Energie, Services de Programmation de la Politique Scientifique, rue de la Science, Bruxelles.

SPPS, (1983c): "Eléments pour une comptabilité macro-économique de l'énergie", Services de Programmation de la Politique Scientifique, rue de la Science, Bruxelles.

SPPS, (1983d): "Utilisation du charbon en Belgique: Possibilités et obstacles", Programme National R-D Energie, Services de Programmation de la Politique Scientifique, rue de la Science, Bruxelles.

Valais, M., Boisserpe, P. and J.L. Gadon, (1982): "The World Gas Industry", ED. Technip, Paris.

PART THREE:

PRODUCTION, PROFITABILITY AND TAXES

COST STRUCTURE AND PROFITABILITY OF NORTH-SEA OIL AND GAS FIELDS

BY

LORENTS LORENTSEN, KJELL ROLAND AND ASBJØRN AAHEIM

ABSTRACT

The amount of economically depletable oil and gas reserves on the Norwegian Continental Shelf is highly dependent upon future oil prices and extraction costs. The paper gives a ranking of known fields according to per unit costs. The ranking is based on individual anticipated cost and production profiles available from Wood & MacKenzie. Incomes and "oil-rents" by field are also calculated under different assumptions of prices and costs. Finally, an attempt is made to estimate cost functions and production profiles, dependent on field specific key parameters as size of reservoir, water depth, number of wells etc.

1. INTRODUCTION

Per unit costs and profitability undoubtedly vary from one oil or gas field to another. Available cost estimates are not easy to compare though; they refer to different time periods, fields on stream are calculated with or without sunk costs, transportation costs are included or excluded, different inflation rates and discount rates are applied and even the seemingly simple concept of "a barrel of oil" is not a clear-cut concept, unless physically specified and time-tagged. In sections 2-3 below Norwegian and U.K. North Sea oil and gas fields are ranked according to three different cost concepts, the amount of high and low cost reserves are displayed in a Salter-diagram, and the robustness of profitability is checked against two different price paths.

It is a commonly held view that each field is a unique phenomenon, that the information one can draw from one field can not be applied to

O.Bjerkholt & E.Offerdal, eds., Macroeconomic Prospects for a Small Oil Exporting Country. ISBN 90-247-3183-6.
Copyright 1985, Martinus Nijhoff Publishers, Dordrecht.

deduce or predict cost figures or production profiles for a different field. This assumption is scrutinized in section 4 and set up against the hypothesis that costs and production profiles vary systematically between fields as functions of a small number of key parameters.

Cost structure and profitability are here analysed for field level, i.e at a micro level. The aim is to establish forecasting and check-point routines to be used in a macroeconomic context. The project, of which this paper is a result, aims at improving existing macroeconomic planning models applied by administrative bodies within the Norwegian government in analysing questions related to petroleum activities.

The data used in this paper are provided by the British consultant firm Wood & MacKenzie (W & M), and give information for individual fields on recoverable reserves, time table for development and production, financial profiles for capital and operating costs in addition to geo-technical and other field specific information. The data source comprises information on all Norwegian and British fields on stream and in addition some fields where development is initiated.

Costs are divided into capital costs and operating costs. The costs of platforms, installations and platform equipment are capital costs. Operating costs are costs connected with field operation i.e. wages, material input and repairs. Both capital and operating costs are divided into costs at wellhead and transportation costs.

Transportation costs include pipelines, buoys, terminal facilities, tariffs etc.

The capital costs of transportation are given by W & M. The operating costs of transportation are separated from total operating costs only at peak production. The ratio at peak production is used to allocate total operating costs between transportation and other operating costs for all years.

Table 1 displays key figures by field, Norwegian and British North Sea fields are grouped separately according to the amount of recoverable reserves.

- On average the size of Norwegian fields are three times the size of British fields. Most of the British fields are medium sized or small.
- The water depth varies from 45 meters at Beatrice to 186 meters at Magnus. On average the water depth on the Norwegian side is a little less than on the British side, 112 and 125 meters respectively.

Table 2.1. Key figures by field.

	Reserves (million t.o.e.)	Oil-reserve ratio	Water depth	Production wells	Injection-wells	Platforms	Peak-production (million t.o.e.)	Production start up
Norwegian oil- and gas fields:								
Statfjord [1]	500.3	84%	145	83	43	3	32.6	1979
Ekofisk	418.7	49%	73	191	9	17(+ tank)	37.2	1971
Frigg [1]	226.5	0	105	48	0	6	17.3	1977
Gullfaks*	134.6	90%	180	68	12	2	10.9	1987
Valhall	53.0	60%	70	22	2	3(4)	5.6	1982
Heimdal*	36.4	7%	120	12	0	1	3.1	1986
Odin*	22.7	0	100	12	0	1	3.7	1984
N-Ø Frigg	8.5	0	102	8	0	1	3.1	1984
Average	175.0	-	112	56	8.25	4.25	14.1	
Total	1 400.7	56%	-	444	66	34	-	
U.K. oil and gas fields:								
Brent	312.2	75%	140	88	66	4	26.1	1976
Forties	270.5	100%	128	88	18	4	24.7	1975
Bery	143.3	81%	115	44	17	2	9.0	1976
Ninian	144.9	100%	135	65	44	3	15.1	1978
Cormorant	86.9	98%	155	58	18	2	9.3	1979
Piper	86.0	98%	145	26	10	1	13.1	1976
Magnus	79.5	96%	186	15	5	1	6.7	1983
Thistle	60.5	97%	162	48	12	1	5.9	1978
Fulmar	57.4	98%	80	30	12	1	7.9	1982
Claymore	57.2	100%	114	31	15	1	4.3	1977
Murchison [1]	52.5	96%	156	15	12	1	4.5	1980
Alwyn*	52.3	49%	126	32	8	2	7.5	1987
N-W Hutton	42.8	92%	144	30	10	1	5.3	1983
Brae	42.6	90%	112	29	17	1	5.3	1983
Dunlin	40.5	100%	151	41	7	1	5.4	1978
Hutton*	35.5	100%	147	21	11	1	4.0	1984
Maureen*	22.7	100%	96	17	7	1	3.3	1984
Beatrice	15.5	100%	45	30	14	2	2.1	1981
Tartan	14.9	95%	145	20	13	1	2.0	1981
Montrose	11.6	100%	91	19	4	1	1.3	1976
Argyll	9.7	100%	79		0	1	1.1	1975
Heather	9.7	100%	145	26	10	1	1.5	1978
Auk	7.7	100%	85	10	0	1	2.3	1976
Buchan	6.9	100%	119	8	0	1	2.1	1981
Average	69.3	-	125	34	13.75	1.48	7.1	
Total	1 663.3	91%	-	791	330	34	-	
Total North Sea								
Average	95.8	-	122	39	12.38	2.13	8.8	
Total	3 064.0	75%	-	1 235	396	68	-	

* Fields not yet on stream.
1) Norwegian shares of Statfjord, Frigg and Murchison are 84.093%, 60.82% and 16.25% respectively.

- With the exception of North Alwyn, the British fields are mainly
oilfields (gas-fields in the Channel are excluded), while gas
accounts for nearly half of the Norwegian reserves.
- Injection is more common on the UK-side than on the Norwegian,
partly due to the difference in geology. Both water and gas are
injected. Water injection is applied to maintain pressure in the
reservoir.

Injection of associated gas is often used to store the gas.

2. COST STRUCTURE

From a macroeconomic viewpoint, the costs of producing oil are of
interest in several contexts. First, costs are vital to the questions of
profitability, which is not only a question of whether a project is
profitable or not, but also whether it is more profitable than alternative
(oil or non-oil) projects, both to the society and to the oil companies.
Second, costs to one economic agent are income to another, through the tax
system or through input deliveries.

In this and the next section of the paper we are concerned with
social costs and profitability of the oil sector, rather than the questions
of income sharing between the oil companies, the government and the
supplying sectors. The calculations of social costs and profitability are
clearly different from calculations made by an oil company, due not only to
different discount rates and the tax system, but also due to different
assessments of oil prices and costs. For North Sea fields, the signs of
different ways of calculating profitability would in most cases be the
same, but for marginal fields even a well designed taxation system might
not be sufficient to make them coincide.

Oil production involves long time lags between investments and production, a considerable amount of the costs accrues before incomes. Different choices of social discount rates and of future oil and gas prices will
thus not only affect the absolute values of costs and rent, but will affect
new and old fields differently.

Our analysis includes fields that are initiated or on stream.
Capital equipment already installed on a field is not always mobile and may
be considered as sunk cost. We have therefore calculated both the total

lifetime rent and the remaining rent (incomes minus costs from now on) of each field.

We shall introduce three alternative ways of defining average unit costs of producing oil from the North Sea. All three definitions include development and operating costs over the expected lifetime of the field. Exploration (successful or abortive), administrative costs which cannot be attributed to individual fields, and of course payments of royalties and taxes, are excluded.

All attributable costs are expressed in real terms by inflating actual historical costs using the wholesale price indices for the two countries, and by deflating anticipated current future costs on the assumption that the W&M data are obtained in domestic currency and not in US$. A 7 per cent discount rate is normally applied by the Norwegian Ministry of Finance when calculating net present value of investments projects. Despite awareness of the theoretical shortcomings of this procedure (see Lind et al (1982)), a 3 per cent risk premium have been added in this paper. Thus, a 10 per cent real discount rate is used to calculate the present value of costs. The present value of costs for a field is then divided by different denominators to yield the three different per unit cost concepts in table 2.

i) The first column of table 2 relates costs to each $ of income. The lifetime profile of incomes are first expressed in 1983 US $ and then discounted by 10 per cent to yield the present value of incomes. (For incomes prior to 1984 actual income figures are used, for anticipated future income the real price of oil is expected to be constant). The real lifetime cost ratio for the field is then defined as the present value of costs divided by the present value of incomes from production.

ii) The second column of table 2 relates costs to a 1983 barrel of oil. The lifetime profile of production measured in physical terms as barrels of oil is discounted (similar to incomes in i) to get the present value of production. The real lifetime cost per 1983-barrel of oil is then defined as the present value of costs divided by the present value of production measured in 1983-barrels. The rationale for discounting the number of barrels is the same as for discounting incomes; a barrel of oil today is not equivalent to a barrel of oil in 1975 or 1990 and the opportunity cost of capital is reflected by the 10 per cent discount rate. This cost concept is preferred elsewhere in this paper since it has the property of relating costs and production to one specific point in time.

iii)   The third column of table 2 relates costs to a barrel of oil of
unspecified vintage. The annual production (actual or expected) measured
in barrels is simply added together to give the total number of barrels the
field is expected to produce.   The real lifetime cost per unspecified
barrel is then defined as the present value of costs divided by the total
number of barrels.

According to definition ii) above, the average cost of Norwegian
fields on stream by 1983 is US $ 11.52 per barrel, varying from $ 9.09 to $
23.27.   The corresponding figures for British fields are $ 12.87, varying
from $ 6.82 to $ 35.61. For fields under development, the average cost of
Norwegian fields are $ 23.00 and $ 21.36 for British fields. These figures
can be interpreted as the constant real oil price (over the whole life of
the field) which would be necessary to cover the costs, including a 10 per
cent return to capital. Since the cost figures exclude royalties and
taxes, the economic rent per barrel from the field, whether it accrues to
the companies or the government, would be the difference between the
average real oil price and these costs.

Table 3 breaks down costs per 1983 barrel into 4 cost categories;
capital and operating costs at wellhead, capital and operating costs of
transportation.   Although the differences between average costs on the
Norwegian and UK side are small, capital costs at wellhead are lower on the
Norwegian side but operating costs are higher. Few and large Norwegian
fields compared to many small UK-fields might explain the cost
differentials in capital costs.

The results in table 2 and 3 are sensitive to the magnitude of
the discount rate. At 15 per cent discount rate, per barrel costs on four
fields are above $30, (according to definition (ii)). Fourteen fields fall
in between $20 and $30, but Piper, Forties and Fulmar are still below $10.
The ranking of fields is almost unaffected if the discount rate is
increased from 10 to 15 per cent.

Figure 1 displays the cost figures for each field in a Salter-
diagram where the size of each field (i.e. recoverable reserves) is
visualized by the size of the rectangle.

The diagram indicates a significant correlation between the amount
of reserves and costs per barrel. With the exceptions of Gullfaks and
Ninian, costs per barrel are below $15 for all "giants". Piper, Fulmar and

Murchison are small/medium sized low cost fields, where the costs per barrel are $12 or less. Most of the fields in figure 1 are highly profitable at todays oil prices and would give a positive lifetime rent

Table 2. Real cost per dollar of income and per barrel. 1983 prices.

	i) Costs per $ of income	ii) Costs per 1983 barrel	iii) Costs per un- spec. barrel
Statfjord 1)	0.31	9.09	4.65
Ekofisk	0.40	10.43	9.99
Frigg 1)	0.52	11.66	10.34
Gullfaks	0.80	23.82	8.48
Valhall	0.59	16.11	9.81
Heimdal	1.23	28.55	12.99
Ula	0.63	18.32	9.17
Odin	0.81	17.66	11.18
N-Ø Frigg	1.04	23.27	17.25
Average, Norwegian fields	0.54	11.50	8.03
Brent	0.49	14.08	10.34
Forties	0.28	7.97	9.15
Beryl	0.46	13.52	10.79
Ninian	0.53	16.80	13.59
Brae	0.67	19.77	9.04
Piper	0.24	6.82	7.81
Cormorant	0.53	15.62	11.05
Magnus	0.51	14.81	7.74
Fulmar	0.28	8.33	5.85
Claymore	0.47	14.16	12.64
Thistle	0.56	16.87	16.28
Alwyn North	0.71	18.76	9.06
Murchison 1)	0.38	11.70	9.10
Dunlin	0.54	16.44	16.67
N-W Hutton	0.40	11.52	7.49
Hutton	0.80	23.66	13.07
Maureen	0.77	22.59	14.84
Clyde	0.83	24.87	10.66
Beatrice	0.98	29.31	22.25
Montrose	0.71	20.14	23.15
Buchan	0.63	19.44	17.60
Heather	1.06	32.82	32.12
Tartan	1.19	35.61	28.72
Argyll	0.67	17.64	24.03
Balmoral	0.82	23.90	12.91
Auk	0.74	18.79	28.69
Highlander	0.52	15.17	9.57
Duncan	0.70	20.48	16.02
Average, UK fields .	0.53	13.31	11.03
Average North Sea ..	0.54	12.57	9.69

1) Cfr. note 1) table 1.

Table 3. Real costs per 1983 barrel by cost category

	Capital costs		Operation costs 2)	
	Wellhead	Transport	Wellhead	Transport
Statfjord 1)	5.13	0.37	1.21	2.37
Ekofisk	3.97	2.82	1.94	1.71
Frigg 1)	6.07	3.35	1.15	1.09
Gullfaks	13.19	1.12	5.28	4.23
Valhall	7.63	0.53	1.39	6.55
Heimdal	11.56	1.43	3.19	12.38
Ula	10.27	0.83	1.75	5.47
Odin	7.52	0.62	2.50	7.01
N-Ø Frigg	14.43	1.02	3.49	4.32
Average, Norwegian fields	5.43	2.04	2.28	1.76
Brent	7.15	3.62	1.30	2.00
Forties	4.76	1.50	1.06	0.65
Beryl	7.43	1.24	2.51	2.34
Ninian	8.90	3.61	2.71	1.59
Brae	12.93	1.30	1.64	3.91
Piper	2.86	1.95	1.05	0.96
Cormorant	8.61	2.27	2.93	1.81
Magnus	8.10	2.97	2.24	1.50
Fulmar	4.61	1.47	1.54	0.72
Claymore	6.72	3.44	2.45	1.56
Thistle	9.83	2.89	2.58	1.57
Alwyn North	9.56	3.07	1.98	4.15
Murchison 1)	6.05	2.14	2.15	1.36
Dunlin	10.60	2.55	2.08	1.22
N-W Hutton	6.29	2.23	1.76	1.24
Hutton	16.20	2.12	1.51	3.83
Maureen	16.28	0.65	3.39	2.26
Clyde	16.03	1.00	5.01	2.82
Beatrice	15.75	5.69	5.50	2.36
Montrose	11.24	1.45	3.48	3.98
Buchan	12.35	2.11	2.18	2.81
Heather	18.61	6.12	5.33	2.75
Tartan	18.72	2.85	5.51	8.52
Argyll	6.77	2.75	5.60	2.52
Balmoral	14.68	1.07	2.18	5.98
Auk	10.45	1.52	3.58	3.24
Highlander	7.05	0.91	2.34	4.88
Duncan	9.14	1.23	6.80	3.31
Average, UK fields .	7.32	2.41	1.66	1.92
Average North Sea ..	6.55	2.26	1.91	1.85

1) Cfr. note 1) table 1.
2) W&M divides total average operating costs into transportation and other
   operating costs only at peak production. The ratio at peak production
   is used to allocate total operation costs between transportation and
   other operating costs for all years.

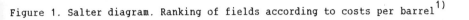

Figure 1. Salter diagram. Ranking of fields according to costs per barrel[1]

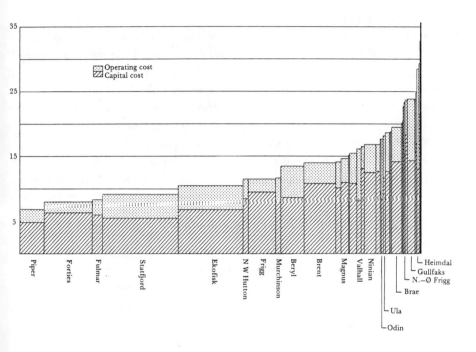

[1] The vertical axis measures the wellhead costs per 1982 barrel according to definition ii.

even if oil prices were substantially lower than today. The figure also indicates that for many fields where capital costs are ex post expenditure, the remaining economic rent would be positive even at oil prices well below $10. Such low oil prices would, though, be disastrous to the profitability of new fields, and to the incomes from North Sea oil production. (Note that figure 1 should not be used to draw definite conclusions about cut-off decisions of fields on stream. The costs displayed in figure 1, are the costs which accrue if production continues as estimated by W&M. Cut-off decisions are more likely to be taken comparing current costs against current incomes, as discussed briefly in section 4.

3. PROFITABILITY

The profitability of future oil production is dependent on the development of the oil price, of exploration, development and operating costs and the opportunity cost of capital. In table 4 net present value of each North Sea field is calculated under two different assumptions of price development. In the "standard scenario" the real price of North Sea oil is expected to stay at US $ 29 per barrel from 1983 until 1990, whereafter the real price is assumed to increase at a rate of 1.5 per cent annually. Gas prices are assumed to develop parallel to oil prices.

In the "collapse scenario" the price of oil is assumed to fall to $ 25 in 1984 and stay at this nominal level until the year 2000 whereafter the real price is kept constant. This implies a real oil price below US$10 in year 2000 measured in 1983-dollars.

The figures in table 4 are derived by calculating the present value of fields with a discount factor of 10 per cent. Table 4 displays total present value of fields and the present value of the remaining economic rent by field for fields on stream. Looking at Norwegian fields, the difference in present value of income amounts to $ 34 000 mill. between the two scenarios, or a difference of approximately $ 8 000 per capita.

Another way of looking at profitability is to consider capital expenditures as sunk costs and calculate at what combinations of future prices and operating costs fields on stream will be closed down. Figure 2 compares the current operating costs per barrel and the current price of oil for the two price scenarios for 4 Norwegian and 4 British fields.

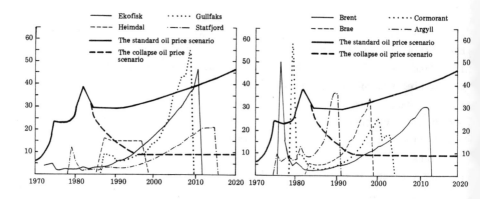

Figure 2. Operation expenditure (1982 $ per barrel).

Table 4. Total and remaining net present value. Million 1983-dollar[1]

Field	The standard oil price scenario		The collapse oil price scenario	
	Total net present value	Remaining net present value	Total net present value	Remaining net present value
Statfjord 2)	40 365	41 805	22 010	23 449
Ekofisk	49 145	21 452	41 570	13 877
Frigg 2)	13 421	13 273	9 859	9 711
Gullfaks	1 895	2 133	-2 874	-2 637
Valhall	2 361	3 853	689	2 181
Heimdal	-523	-419	-1 517	-1 413
Ula	955	955	-100	-100
Odin	301	732	-171	261
N-Ø Frigg	-32	196	-171	57
Total, Norwegian fields	108 443	84 399	74 128	49 536
Brent	25 056	30 249	15 989	21 182
Forties	46 851	17 274	43 233	13 655
Beryl	9 882	7 666	6 836	4 620
Ninian	13 066	9 765	9 781	6 479
Brae	2 435	4 192	-308	1 449
Piper	21 206	7 651	19 726	6 172
Cormorant	5 758	7 748	3 215	5 205
Magnus	4 790	7 650	1 461	4 321
Fulmar	7 423	8 324	5 077	5 977
Claymore	5 813	4 068	4 580	2 835
Thistle	5 348	3 986	4 337	2 975
Alwyn North	1 364	1 517	-592	-439
Murchison 2)	5 502	5 148	4 168	3 814
Dunlin	4 337	2 439	3 688	1 790
N-W Hutton	3 322	4 625	1 840	3 143
Hutton	657	2 163	-511	995
Maureen	768	2 340	-143	1 429
Clyde	324	350	-572	-546
Beatrice	60	1 376	-488	830
Montrose	795	401	646	252
Buchan	771	1 182	549	960
Heather	-156	600	-340	417
Tartan	-363	696	-673	386
Argyll	777	340	711	274
Balmoral	191	191	-202	-202
Auk	641	38	629	26
Highlander	263	263	95	95
Duncan	171	195	58	82
Total, UK fields	167 572	132 435	126 619	89 362
Total North Sea	276 014	216 835	200 747	138 898

1) Fields are excluded from sums and subsums from the point in time when they give negative quasi-rent.
2) Cfr. note 1) table 1.

4. ESTIMATES OF COST FUNCTIONS AND PRODUCTION PROFILES

Off-shore petroleum production is characterized i.a. by the
following: The production is extremely capital intensive and there are
long time lags between investments and production. Second, production is
highly dependent upon geo-physical conditions, and only to some extent
dependent on the amount of factor inputs such as capital and labour. Figure
3 depicts the lifetime investment and production profiles of a standard
North Sea oil field.

The   production of oil or gas from a specific field in year t could
be expressed as a function of several different kinds of capital accumulated prior to t, several kinds of labour and material inputs in year t, in
addition to field characteristics as size of the field, water depth, field
complexity etc.   The production function would not be of the smooth neo-
classical type. With known techniques there are only a few ways of
developing an off-shore field. It would therefore be more adequate to
define the ex ante production function as a set of alternative development
schemes, where substitution possibilities are limited. Once a development
scheme has been chosen, the substitution possibilities would be almost
none, except that new development activities might be added for instance by
introducing enhanced recovery methods.

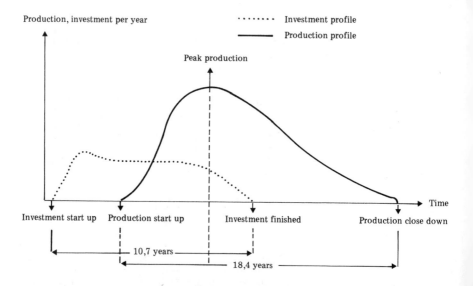

Figure   3.   Investment   and production profiles of a standard North Sea oil
field

The ex ante planning problem for an oil company is to choose the development scheme that maximizes total net discounted income from the project, given technical constraints, expected price profiles for outputs and inputs and also the tax system. In the following, we have assumed that project decisions are independent. This might be justifiable for some projects, but less convincing for fields where transport and processing equipments are shared. We have neglected the distorting effects of taxes, and assumed price expectations and discount rates to be common to decision makers. Labour and material inputs are assumed to be dependent on capacity and production. We have simplified further by distinguishing between only two types of capital. The production structure for one project (described in more detail in the appendix) is approximated as:

$$(1) \quad X_t = \text{Min} \left[F_{1t}(K_1, S, H, Q), F_2(K_2, S, H, Q) \right]$$

$$(2) \quad C_t = C_t(X_t, K_2)$$

where

C_t = operation costs in year t

X_t = production measured as m^3 per year in year t

S = resource base

H = water depth

Q = parameter describing the complexity of the field

K_1 = accumulated investments of type 1 at the time of production start up

K_2 = accumulated investments of type 2, at the time of production start up

$F_{1t}(.)$ = intertemporal profile function, dependent on capital type 1 and field specific parameters

$F_2(.)$ = production function describing processing capacity, dependent on capital type 2 and field specific parameters

According to (1) production will either be limited by K_1 or K_2 or both. The idea is that the amount of K_1 will determine the potential production profile or total economically recoverable reserves from the field, given S, H and Q. One might associate K_1 with the number of wells, gathering pipelines and the basic mechanical structure of the production plat-

form(s) -shafts, deck, drilling tower, etc. In short, K_1 is the capital
equipment determining the rate of recovery (and thereby economically recoverable reserves) and the facilities necessary to bring the oil to the
seabed. Increased K_1 will increase the integral below the production curve
in figure 3, at the cost of increasing the integral below the investment
curve. It is furthermore assumed that the functional forms of the production profile will not be changed if K_1 changes as illustrated in figure
4. Capital type 2 should, on the other hand, be associated with processing and handling equipment installed on the platform(s), including flowtanks, equipment to separate gas, water and sand from the crude oil as well
as storage tanks, pumping equipment or loading equipment if the crude is

..... potential production profile
with $K_1 = K_1^*$

...... production profile if
K_2 is large enough to
capture potential peak
production (K_2^*)

——— potential production profile
with $K_1^{**} > K_1^*$

——— production profile if K_2
is too small to capture
potential peak production:
(K_2^{**})

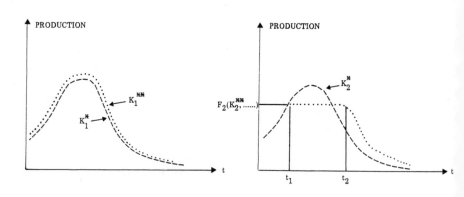

Figure 4. Production profiles and capital equipment.

loaded on tankers offshore. K_2 is necessary to exploit some or all of the potential production determined by K_1 at each point in time. This implies that K_2 has to be of a certain amount to be able to produce the peak production made available by K_1. If K_2 is too small to produce potential peak production, determined by K_1, some of the production will be postponed as illustrated in figure 4.

K_i constitutes the physical accumulated or undiscounted, fixed price value - of capital type i at the time of production start up T. For both categories of capital, we assume that no depreciation occurs and that the capital stock outlive the project.

$$(3) \quad K_i \quad = \quad \int_{t=0}^{T} I_{1t} dt \quad , \qquad i = 1,2$$

In addition to this concept defining production capacity, we need an expression of the present value of each type of capital at the time of investment start up, defined as:

$$(4) \quad \tilde{K}_i \quad = \quad \int_{t=0}^{T} q_{it} I_{it} e^{-rt} dt \quad , \qquad i = 1,2$$

I_{it} = investment of type i in year t, measured in fixed prices, i=1,2

q_{it} = real price of investment type i in year t, $\quad$ i = 1,2

q_{it} is assumed to be dependent on the level of I_{it}:

$$(5) \quad q_{it} \quad = \quad q_{it} (I_t), \qquad i = 1,2$$

$$(6) \quad \frac{\delta q_{it}}{\delta I_{it}} \geqslant 0$$

(6) indicates that the supply curves for capital goods are elastic; if investment deliveries increase (over a certain minimum in one specific year), prices will increase.

In the intertemporal optimization problem described in more detail in the appendix, K_1 and K_2 define capital which is installed at the time of production start up, T. We then need to define a third category of capital, installed after time T, (cfr. figure 3 which shows that investments do not stop at T). This third category consists of dwelling platforms, repair equipment etc. This type of equipment is mobile and might be hired at an early stage of production, so that production start up is not delayed.

In our setting the investment decision is an intertemporal optimization problem where the field operator should choose K_1 and K_2, the investment period T and the investment profiles $I_{i,t}$ (t=1,2,...,T, i=1,2) with the associated production profile - that maximizes net discounted incomes over the lifetime of the project, i.e.

$$\underset{K_i, I_{i,t}, T}{\text{Max:W}} \quad = \quad \int_T^{\infty} (P_t X_t - C_t)e^{-rt} - \tilde{K}_1 - \tilde{K}_2 \quad , \qquad i = 1,2$$

$$\text{s.t.} \qquad \dot{K}_{it} = I_{it}$$

$$K_{io} = 0, \quad (K_{it} = K_{iT} = K_i, \quad t > T,)$$

constrained by (1) - (5).

P_t = price per barrel of crude oil and or natural gas in year t.

From the 1. order conditions of this maximization problem (see appendix for details) it follows that investments at each point in time, total accumulated capital stock of K_1 and K_2, the investment period - and future production, will be functions of the field specific characteristics S, H and Q, output prices, input prices and the discount rate. It then follows that total discounted costs, and discounted costs per 1983 barrel, (CBBL), as defined in section 2 will be dependent on the same variables, i.e.

$$\text{CBBL} \quad = \quad f (S, H, Q, \text{all prices})$$

In estimating the CBBL on project (or field) data, we assume all real prices and discount rates, identical between investors and constant over time. Trial and error on several specifications of the CBBL function has lead to the following modifications:

- There seems to be increasing returns to scale with respect to K_2. Operators tend to invest in K_2, so as to make sure potential peak production is captured. Hence, we have included K_2 (or the proxy peak production XPEAK) as an explanatory variable in the CBBL function.

- Although T in a certain sense is optimized, simple calculations of increases in discounted income by reducing the investment period indicate that oil-companies might have been willing to pay large premiums to contracters who could reduce T. (If Statfjord could be developed 2 years faster than planned, net present value might be increased by $ 7-8000 millions if prices develop as in the standard scenario of section 3. This is more than total estimated lifetime costs.)

    T seems to be limited by lack of capacity and organizational/-institutional factors, which then represents an additional constraint on the maximization problem. Hence also T is included in the CBBL function.

- As a proxy for the complexity of a field (Q) we have chosen the number of production and injection wells. This variable should then capture how costs per barrel are influenced by physical conditions - other than the size of the field and water depth. The approach is convenient, but clearly not theoretically satisfactory since the number of wells is endogenous to the decision maker.

The cost function

From the above reasonings a relevant cost function should include the following explanatory variables: peak-production, in situ resources, water depth, time from investment start up to production start up and the number of wells. The estimated cost function is a pseudo function since it is not deduced from pure theoretic reasonings, but include ad hoc elements and partly endogenous proxies as right hand side variables. Further, the function is estimated on synthetic (not directly observed) data.

We have chosen a log-linear functional form since the right hand side explanatory variables are more likely to have a multiplicative than an additive effect on costs. The log-linear form captures non-linearities and is easy to estimate. Straightforward OLS-estimation gave:

$$(7) \quad \ln \text{CBBL} \quad = \quad 1.938 - 0.419 \ln \text{XPEAK} - 0.164 \text{ RESS} - 0.249 \text{ DEPTH}$$
$$(5.67) \quad (3.37) \qquad\qquad (1.43) \qquad\quad (1.64)$$

$$+ \ 0.335 \ln \text{TIME} + 0.454 \ln \text{WELLS}$$
$$(3.25) \qquad\qquad (3.69)$$

RSQ   = 0.67, t-statistics in brackets

CBBL   - wellhead costs per 1983 barrel of oil (cfr. columns 1 and 2 in table 3.2)

XPEAK   - peak production measured in mill. t.o.e. per year

RESS   - in-situ resources - million t.o.e.

DEPTH   - dummy variable for water depth, and equal to 1 if depth is greater than 125 meters.

TIME   - time from investment start up to production start up

WELLS   - number of production and injection wells

(7) indicates that costs decrease with peak production, increase with the time from investment to production start up and with the number of wells (proxy for the complexity of the field). On the other hand, the coefficients for water depth and in-situ resources are not significantly different from zero. Regarding water depth this result is somewhat surprising, but the explanation might simply be that our sample fields - where water depth varies from 45 to 186 meters - are developed by common technologies irrespective of differences in water depth.

A priori one would expect per barrel costs to decrease with the size of the field for two reasons: increasing returns to scale and duration of the production period. We have argued earlier that XPEAK is a good proxy for the increasing returns to scale effect, and the estimates of (7) seems to support this hypothesis. We would then have expected that the second effect - that a large field produces longer than a small field and the capital equipment is depreciated over a longer period - to be captured by the in-situ resource variable. When the coefficient for in situ-resources is insignificant the reason might be that RESS and XPEAK are intercorrelated, and hence the duration effect is picked up by XPEAK. The reason for the insignificant coefficient might also be due to data manipulation; with a discount rate of 10 per cent the additional production tails of large fields vanish. (Note also that there are effects

161

which tend to make the resource coefficient positive: Since the bulk of investments accrue before production start-up the average time-lag between investments and income is larger for big fields than for small ones).

Omitting the two insignificant variables RESS and DEPTH from (7), and reestimating yields:

(8)   ln CBBL = 1.798 - 0.536 ln XPEAK + 0.315 ln TIME + 0.313 ln WELLS
            (6.23) (6.42)   (3.18)   (3.17)

RSQ = 0.63, t-statistics in brackets.

The estimated coefficients of (8) seem reasonable, well behaved and significant.

The discrepancy between per barrel costs calculated by W&M data and estimated by equation (8) is shown in table 5.   The discrepancy between calculated and estimated costs vary considerably from field to field, as one would expect since physical conditions are only represented by two variables in equation (8). Still, 27 out of 37 fields are within a 25 per cent margin. The greatest outlier is the Highlander field. This field is quite dependent on Tartan installations. These installation costs are in W&M allocated to the Tartan field. This might explain why Highlander is calculated to be cheap, but estimated to be expensive. This example points to a basic weakness of simple approaches to cost estimates for petroleum fields; the interdependency of fields.

We have therefore estimated the cost function on data where interrelated fields are aggregated, to see if better results are obtained. In four areas there are interconnections between fields. The Ekofisk field is already aggregated in the previous estimation. The other three areas are the Frigg area (Frigg, N-Ø Frigg and Odin) on the Norwegian side and Tartan/Highlander and Argyll/Duncan on the British side. Aggregating data for these fields and reestimating gives the cost function:

(9)   ln CBBL = 1.696 - 0.590 ln XPEAK + 0.369 ln WELLS + 0.328 ln TIME
            (4.68) (6.55)   (3.34)   (2.62)

RSQ = 0.68, t-statistics in brackets.

In table 5 the percentage deviation from the W&M-calculated values
are shown for both estimations. The conclusion seems to be that generally
the last approach gives a somewhat better fit. But we also notice that
Gullfaks is even more underestimated, 69.5 per cent against 42.9, when data
for interrelated fields are aggregated.

Reserves to peak ratios and production profiles of oil fields

The implied hypothesis behind the intertemporal production profile
function outlined in figure 4 is the following: The volume of capital
category 2 determines recoverable reserves from a reservoir. Distribution
of production in time, on the other hand, is largely determined by the
geo-physical configurations describing the reservoir (the depth of the
reservoir, permeability, etc). It seem likely that within the same
province (the North Sea), the geology is relatively common. As a first
approximation it is thus justifiable to approximate the production profile
by assuming that the shape is independent of economic optimization.

This hypothesis has been tested in two steps:

First we have tested the hypothesis that there is a propotionale or
a linear relation between peak production and total recoverable oil
reserves. The two (linear and proportionale) relations are plotted in
figure 5. The rule of thumb which appear, and seems to be quite robust, is
that peak production amounts to 8-10 per cent of total recoverable
reserves.

The second approach to map the production structure is to estimate
a production profile function defined by:

$$(10) \quad X(t) = \frac{t^a}{b^t}$$

$X(t)$ = production in year t, measured in 1 000 m^3
t = number of years from production start up
a,b = coefficients

As shown in figure 6, the function traces production profiles quite neatly
even for fields of different size.

Table 5. Deviation between W & M - calculated and estimated costs per barrel

	W&M cost per barrel	Estimated costs per barrel	Percent deviation	Percent deviation aggregated fields
Statfjord	6.3	7.0	-10.8	-10.5
Ekofisk	5.9	4.7	20.4	24.5 1)
Frigg	7.2	7.5	-4.2	18.7
Gullfaks	18.5	10.6	42.9	69.5
Valhall	9.0	10.5	-16.8	-14.8
Heimdal	14.7	12.9	12.4	12.8
Ula	12.0	14.9	-23.8	-23.0
Odin	10.0	10.1	-0.1	--
N-Ø Frigg	17.9	11.0	38.8	-
Brent	8.6	7.7	9.5	7.9
Forties	5.8	7.4	-26.5	-22.0
Beryl	9.9	9.3	6.1	3.8
Ninian	11.6	9.4	18.7	18.6
Brae	14.6	12.5	14.3	10.5
Piper	3.9	6.5	-65.8	-38.2
Cormorant	11.5	12.0	-3.8	- 8.5
Magnus	10.4	10.5	-1.1	- 1.9
Fulmar	6.1	9.8	-59.2	-38.2
Claymore	9.2	11.0	-19.6	-19.8
Thistle	12.4	12.7	-2.6	- 7.4
Alwyn North	11.5	10.8	6.7	4.9
Murchison	8.2	10.7	-30.9	-24.9
Dunlin	12.7	12.3	2.9	- 1.3
N-W Hutton	8.1	12.1	-50.3	-35.8
Hutton	17.7	13.4	24.5	27.7
Maureen	19.7	15.7	20.5	19.8
Clyde	21.1	19.2	8.7	2.3
Beatrice	21.3	17.7	16.9	10.9
Montrose	14.7	17.4	-18.1	-21.1
Buchan	14.5	10.7	26.3	37.3
Heather	24.0	22.3	7.1	2.0 2)
Tartan	24.2	21.9	9.8	63.1
Argyll	12.4	15.5	-25.4	29.2 3)
Balmoral	16.9	18.5	-9.5	-14.3
Auk	14.0	11.2	-20.1	-25.4
Highlander	9.4	18.4	-96.0	--
Duncan	15.9	12.1	24.3	--

1) Frigg, Odin and N-Ø Frigg are aggregated into one field, Frigg.
2) Tartan and Highlander are aggregated into one field, Tartan.
3) Argyll and Duncan are aggregated into one field, Argyll.

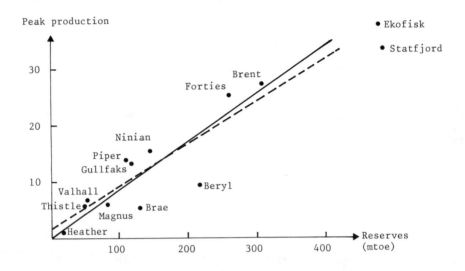

Figure 5. Peak production compared to recoverable reserves[1]

[1] The two plotted relations are:

   i) PEAK = 1.79979 + 0.0758 RESERVE   ii) PEAK = 0.08526 RESERVE

          (3.56)   (18.70)   (23.25)

       RSQ = 0.93   RSQ = 0.89

The procedure necessary to forecast the production profile for a field with known reserves would be as follows: Assume that the amount of economic recoverable reserves is S. From the estimated relation between peak production and the amount of reserves from the previous page we have:

(i) $\quad X^{peak} = \gamma_0 + \gamma_1 S$

where the parameters γ_0 and γ_1 are known. From the first order derivative of function (10) follows:

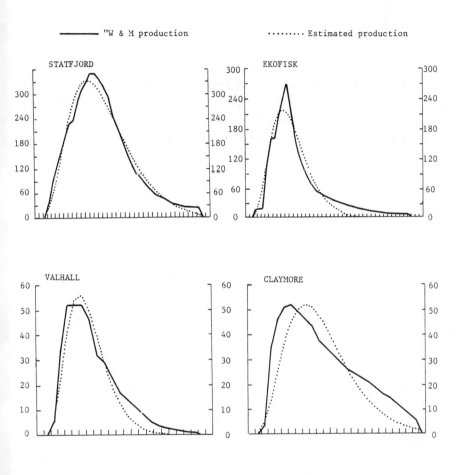

Figure 6. "W & M production" and estimated production profiles on Statfjord, Ekofisk, Valhall and Claymore.

(ii) $X^{peak} = \dfrac{t^{*a}}{b^{t^*}}$,   where $t^* = \dfrac{a}{\ln b}$

Substituting X_{peak} from i) into ii) yields one equation between the two
unknown parameters a and b. The extra equation necessary to determine a

and b follows from:

$$(iii) \quad \int_{0}^{\infty} \frac{t^a}{b^t} \ dt \ = \ S$$

For fields with one-humped production this procedure traces the production profiles quite well. To put it bluntly; the procedure often catches the dromedary but lacks the parameters necessary to cope with the camel. A dismal property of function (10) is that it cuts off the production tails too quickly, especially for large fields. A better approach might therefore be to use (10) to describe the production profile to the left of the inflexion point, and use an exponential "tail function".

5.CONCLUSIONS

Given the key parameters of a field like size of reservoir, water depth, the number of wells, production period etc. our analysis indicate that it is possible - within reasonable ranges of uncertainty - to predict discounted unit cost. Knowing the key parameters, some quite handy and seemingly robust rules of thumb concerning production profiles also appear.

The estimates presented in this paper are of course of marginal value to companies trying to estimate the costs and production performance of one specific new field. Our aim has been to establish some rough fore-casting or check-point routines to be used on a macro-level.

Some prudence in interpreting the results might still be worth-while. Anticipated future cost and production figures are naturally based on historical evidence. Hence what we have detected might to some extent be how the figures were made. From what we know about the construction of W & M figures it is unlikely, though, that we have just mapped the roundabout. Another warning is still worth while: our sample-fields belong to one class of manageable fields; the estimating procedures might not apply as well to another class of fields, for instance challenges like Troll and 34/4.

APPENDIX : THE INVESTMENT PROBLEM IN OFFSHORE CRUDE OIL AND GAS PRODUCTION

BY

KJELL ROLAND

A1. THE OPTIMAL INVESTMENT - AND PRODUCTION PLAN

In section 4 we have introduced the production function (1), operation costs (2), productive capital (3), discounted capital costs (4) and the supply functions for investment goods (5).

Production function:

(1) $X_t = \text{Min} \left[F_{1,t}(K_{1,T}, S, H, Q), F_2 (K_{2,T}, S, H, Q) \right]$

Productive capital:

(2) $K_{i,T} = K_i = \int_0^T I_{i,t} dt,$ $i = 1,2.$

Discounted capital costs:

(3) $\tilde{K}_{i,0} = \tilde{K}_i = \int_0^T \tilde{I}_{i,t} dt,$ $i = 1,2.$

where: $\tilde{I}_{i,t} = q_{i,t} I_{i,t} e^{-rt}$

Supply functions for investment goods:

(4) $q_{i,t} = q_{i,t}(I_{i,t})$, where $\delta q_{i,t}/\delta I_{i,t} > 0,$ $\delta^2 q_{i,t}/\delta I_{i,t}^2 > 0,$

$i = 1,2.$

All variables introduced are defined in section 4. What we need to introduce in addition to (1) - (4), is annual operation costs:

Operation costs:

(5) $\qquad C_t \ = \ \sum\limits_{j=1}^{m} k_{j,t} v_{j,t}$, $\qquad\qquad j = 1,2,\ldots.m.$

where:

C_t = yearly operation costs at time t.

$k_{j,t}$ = price on input no. j at time t.

$v_{j,t}$ = volume of input no. j at time t.

If we assume cost minimization in each period and free competition in the factor markets, then:

$$v_{j,t} \ = \ v_{j,t}(X_t)$$

which again implies:

$$C_t \ = \ \sum\limits_{j=1}^{m} k_{j,t} v_{j,t} = C_t^*(X_t)$$

Given (1), the following per unit operating cost function emerge:

(5) $\qquad C_t \ = \ \text{Min} \left[C_t(K_1,S,H,Q), \ C_t(K_2,S,H,Q) \right]$

We are now able to state the general investment and production problem:

---

(6) $\quad \text{Max}_{T,I_{i,t}} \qquad W(T, K_1, K_2) - \sum\limits_{i=1}^{2} \check{K}_{i,0} \qquad\qquad i=1,2$

$\qquad\qquad\qquad\qquad\qquad\qquad\qquad\qquad\qquad\qquad\qquad\qquad\quad t=1,2\ldots\infty$

(7) s.t. $\qquad\qquad dK_{i,t}/dt = I_{i,t}$

(8) $\qquad\qquad\qquad\quad K_{i,0} = 0$

---

where:

(9) $\quad W \ = \ \int\limits_{t=0}^{\infty} \left[P_t X_t - C_t \right] e^{-rt} dt$

Regarding the discounted capital costs $(\hat{K}_i,\ i=1,2)$, it is important to remember that we assume the supply curves for investment goods (4) to be upwards sloping. Arguments supporting this assumption is limited capacity in supplying industries, crowding on the construction site or it may be that administration and planning costs increases rapidly with the need for more accurate timing of different inputs associated with a reduced construction period.

The investment and production problem consists of finding the profit maximizing investment and production plan. We have to determine the optimal investment period (T), the optimal volumes of fixed capital (K_i), the optimal investment profiles $(I_{i,t})$ and the optimal production program (X_t). Reducing T increases discounted profit (W), but at the cost of increasing investment cost. This is the fundamental trade-off problem determining the optimal investment period. Similarly, increasing capital category 1 increases potential recoverable reserves, i.e. profits, but increases investment costs. In the same way, increasing capital type 2 increases peak production which implies that the production is shifted nearer in time. This of course again increases discounted gross incomes, but also increase investment costs.

The maximization problem (6)-(8) is solvable by the use of control theory as long as the investment problem and the production problem are separable (see Kamien and Schwartz (1981)). This is true with our assumption about the capital equipment: no production prior to T and sunk cost. The only connection between the two optimization problems is through the state variables from the investment period which enters the production period as initial conditions. We solve the total problem by optimizing the investment problem and include the discounted profit from the production phase as a salvage term. The Hamiltonian then looks this way:

$$
(10)\quad H(I_{i,t}, T, \lambda_{i,t}) \;=\; \sum_{i=1}^{2}\left[\,-\hat{I}_{i,t} + \lambda_{i,t} I_{i,t}\,\right] \qquad \begin{array}{l} t=1,2\ldots T \\ i=1,2 \end{array}
$$

Necessary conditions for this problem to be maximized are as follows:

$$
(11)\quad d\lambda_{i,t}/dt \;=\; -\delta H/\delta K_{i,t}
$$

$$
(12)\quad \delta H/\delta I_{i,t} \;=\; 0
$$

$$
\left.\phantom{\begin{array}{c}a\\b\end{array}}\right\} \;\Longrightarrow\;
$$

$$
(13)\quad \lambda_{i,t} \;=\; \text{constant}
$$

$$
=\; d\hat{I}_{i,t}/dI_{i,t}
$$

(14) $H_T + \delta W/\delta T = 0$

(14) is probably easier to interprete in a more explicit form:

(15) $$\sum_{i=1}^{2} [q_{i,T} I_{i,T} e^{-rT} - \lambda_{i,T} I_{i,T}] = [P_T X_T - C_T] e^{-rt}$$

where H_T is the Hamiltonian evaluated at T.

(16) $\lambda_{i,T} = \delta W/\delta K_{i,T}$,   i=1,2, which implies (17) and (18):

(17) $$\lambda_{1,T} = e^{-rT} [\int_{T}^{t(1)} (P_t F'_{1,t} - C'_t) e^{-r(t-T)} dt + \int_{t(2)}^{\infty} (P_t F'_{1,t} - C'_t) e^{-r(t-T)} dt]$$

$$\text{if} \quad F_2(K_2) \leqslant x_p$$

(18) $$\lambda_{2,T} = e^{-rT} [\int_{t(1)}^{t(2)} (P_t F'_2 - C'_t) e^{-r(t-T)} dt] \quad \text{if} \quad F_2(K_2) \leqslant x_p$$

t(1) and t(2) indicates points of intersection of the $F_{1,t}()$ and the $F_2()$ curves (see figure 4). If processing capacity allows for potential peak production to be produced (i.e. max. $F_{1,t}() \leqslant F_2()$), then t(1) = t(2) and the integrals in (17) converges to one integral over the period [T,∞].

Equation (13) gives the necessary condition for the optimal investment program:

OPTIMAL INVESTMENT FLOWS:

The optimal investment flows must satisfy the condition that for all t (t=1,2...T), the marginal discounted cost from investing in capital equipment no. i (i=1,2) is constant and equal to the shadow price of the accumulated capital stock.

The transversality conditions connects the optimal investment path to the production period. From (14) the optimal investment period follows and (17) and (18) are conditions determining the optimal capital stocks:

OPTIMAL INVESTMENT PERIOD:

The optimal investment period (T) must satisfy the condition that the discounted profit from a marginal change in T equals the sum (i=1,2) of the discounted investment costs at T. The investment costs at T are evaluated by the discounted prices of investment at T corrected by the shadow prices of capital stocks.

OPTIMAL VOLUMES OF PHYSICAL CAPITAL:

The optimal volume of capital category no. i (i=1.2) is the point where its shadow price at T equals its marginal contribution to discounted profit over the production period.

The last condition can be stated more explicitly the following way:

-Invest in increasing potential recoverable reserves to the point where the shadow price at T equals discounted marginal income in the two periods where this type of capital limits production (t=T,....t(1) and t=t(2) ...∞).

-Dimension the capacity of the equipment handeling oil and gas offshore so as to make sure that on the margin the shadow price equals the marginal increase in discounted profit in the plateau production period (t=t(1),..t(2)).

A2. A THIRD CATEGORY OF CAPITAL

As mentioned before, in addition to the two categories of capital which enters in the production function (1), a complete description of offshore production of crude oil and gas probably should include at least one other category of capital. In figure 3 this capital is illustrated by the area under the investment curve which is located to the right of production start up (plus possibly a fraction of the investment prior to T.). More precisely, the production process demands input of certain services in addition to those produced by K_1, K_2 and flows of inputs associated with operation costs. These services is produced by a type of capital which, from a technical point, is not required to be permanently installed on the production site to be productive. It is mobile and might for some time or permanently over the lifetime of the field, be hired from outside contractors (dwelling and other types of service plattforms, etc.). This type of capital equipment allows for another kind of flexibility than what is assumed so far: the investment activity is not limited to terminate before production starts up.

Assume, for simplicity, that services (h) from this type of capital is required in fixed proportions to the volume of crude oil and gas produced:

(19) $h_t = \gamma X_t$, $\gamma > 0$

The capital services may be

- produced from K_3 : $h_t = f(K_{3,t})$.

- or hired (h_t') at the fixed price $q_{4,t}$.

$K_{3,t}$ is accumulated investment ($I_{3,t}$) in capital category no. 3. The price of each unit of investment good no. 3 being $q_{3,t}$.

Given a particular production profile ($\bar{X}_t$), $\bar{h}_t$ is needed. The problem whether to rent or to invest in capital type no. 3 can in this situation be separated from the overall investment problem. This investment decision consist in solving the following control problem:

(20)　　Min $\quad \bar{C}_0 \quad = \quad \int\limits_0^\infty e^{-rt} \left[q_{3,t} I_{3,t} + q_{4,t} h_t' \right] dt \quad t=1,2,3\ldots\infty$
　　　　$h_t', I_{3,t}$

S.T.

$$\bar{h}_t \quad = \quad h_t' + f(K_{3,t})$$

(21)　　$K_{3,t} \quad = \quad \int\limits_0^t I_{3,t} dt$

$$K_{3,0} \quad = \quad 0$$

The solution to (20) determines both the investment path and the share of the services that will be rented as functions of the price paths $(q_{3,t}, q_{4,t}, r;\ t=1.2 \ldots\infty)$. The general investment problem outlined in (6)-(8) could be extended to cover the case where capital category no. 3 was included. From (20) and (21) it is possible to derive a relationship showing total discounted costs of supplying the services required in (19) corresponding to a certain production profile (and given all relevant price paths):

(22)　　$\bar{C} \quad = \quad \int\limits_0^\infty e^{-rt} \left[q_{3,t} I_{3,t}^* + q_{4,t} h_t^* \right] dt$

　　　　　$= \quad \bar{C} (X_1, X_2, \ldots, \text{all prices})$

In (22) stars indicate that we look upon optimal values given by the solution of (20) subject to (21). This expression should then be added to the objective function (6). The straightforward use of control theory in section 1 is not applicable any longer, because now the investment period (0,T) and the production period [T,∞] are not separable any more.

A3. Estimating discounted unit costs over fields

Discounted unit costs (CBBL) at t=0 is defined as:

$$(23) \qquad CBBL \quad = \quad \frac{\ddot{K}_1 + \ddot{K}_2 + e^{-rT} \int\limits_{T}^{\infty} C_t e^{-rt} dt}{e^{-rT} \int\limits_{T}^{\infty} X_t e^{-rt} dt}$$

From the first order conditions we know that all endogenous variables depend on the field specific variables S, H, and Q˘ plus all the price paths involved including the discount rate. Taking this into account, it follows that CBBL depends on the same variables. In general, (23) then looks like this:

$$(24) \qquad CBBL \quad = \quad c \ (S, \ H, \ Q, \ \text{all price paths})$$

Based on this information, what we would like to do is to estimate a cost function using the relevant data from different fields. We simplify the problem, first by assuming all expected price paths (including the discount rate) underlying different investors decisions to be equal and constant over time. Furthermore, to arrive at a proper set of right hand side variables we make two assumptions:

PROPOSITION 1: <u>Increasing returns to K_2</u>.

K_2 represents the processing facilities installed off-shore. The crude oil, as it comes out of the well, often contains quantities of natural gas, salt water and sand. These have to be separated from the crude oil. In addition, if the crude is produced under high pressure, flowtanks have to be installed to reduce pressure. In principle, these processes are very similar to what goes on in a refinery and in other chemical industries. Empirical studies of refineries and similar production processes have disclosed increasing returns to capital input (see Moore (1959) and Westphal (1975)). The typical empirical results show elasticity of unit costs of capital with regard to capacity of 0.6 to 0.8.

The most frequently cited reason for the cost of capital to increase less rapidly than its capacity is the following: Capacity is assumed to vary proportional to a volume measure, whereas costs is proportional to the surface area. Examples are cylinders and pipes, for which a doubling of the surface area leads to an approximate tripling of volume.

The first stage of processing the crude and gas off-shore is done by capital equipment dominated by geometrical configurations. This makes it tempting to postulate decreasing unit costs with regard to processing capacity (eg. K_2). An empirical observation supporting this hypothesis is the fact that it seems to be a general rule in the North Sea that investors always dimension the processing capacity on crude oil fields so as to allow peak production (given from the geo-technical conditions and K_1) to be produced. If this is the case, it is necessary to include K_2 (or proxy for K_2) in the list of right hand side variables explaining how unit costs varies over fields. The reason of course being the fact that in this case, unit costs are always reduced as scale is increased independent of price and field specific parametres. Capital type no. 2 is thus a separately operating factor determining unit costs.

Since we lack the information to split total capital costs in K_1 and K_2, we have choosen to use peak production as proxy for K_2.

PROPOSITION 2. <u>Constraints on the feasible investment period (T)</u>

Simple calculations of revenues and costs seem to indicate that the increase in discounted profit by reducing the investment period (T) in most, may be all practical cases, is greater than the increase in costs (in the North Sea). If this is so, then factors different from the marginal optimization of T following (14) determines T. The pure economic arguments in (14) imply that the investment period should be reduced considerably compared to what actually is the case. This is not possible for different reasons. Both technical and organizational factors (capacity, lack of infrastructure, etc.) as well as institutional constraints (distributional effects, constraints on factor mobility etc.) are limiting.

In this case we would like to include T as a variable explaining differences in costs between fields.

A4. CONCLUSION

Based on our model for the off-shore ex-ante investment problem, we arrive at a discounted per unit cost function where the right hand side variables are:

$$(25) \quad CBBL \;=\; C\,(X_p,\; T,\; S,\; H,\; Q)$$

REFERENCES

Campbell, H.F (1980): The effect of capital intensity on the optimal rate of extraction of a mineral deposit. <u>Canadian Journal of Economics Vol 13.</u>

Craft, B.C & al. (1959): <u>Applied petroleum reservoir engineering.</u> Englewood Cliffs, 1959

Kamien M.I., and N.L. Schwartz (1981) : <u>Dynamic Optimization: The Calculus of Variation and Optimal Control in Economics and Management.</u> North Holland.

Lind, R.C. & al. (1982): <u>Discounting for time and risk in energy policy.</u> The John Hopkins University Press.

Lund, Diderik (1984): Estimation of a cost function for offshore oil production. Mimeographed, MIT, March 1984

Moore, F.T (1959) : Economics of scale: Some Statistical Evidence. <u>Quarterly Journal of Economics, no. 73.</u>

Smith, J.L & al. (1983): Regional modeling of oil discovery and production. Working paper, MIT, Energy Laboratory, January 1983.

Westphal, L.W (1975): Planning with economics of scale. In: <u>Economy-wide models and development planning.</u> eds. Blitzer, Clark and Taylor,

Wood & MacKenzie & Co. (1983): North Sea service. Field analysis section, Edinburgh.

PETROLEUM TAXATION: A COMPARISON BETWEEN CANADA AND THE U.S.

BY

ROBERT N. McRAE[1]

ABSTRACT

The first part of the paper outlines the present tax systems in the US and Canada. Then, the relative profitability of a petroleum-based investment in the two countries is explored (for both an onshore and offshore discovery). To add to the scope of the profitability comparison, calculations for the U.K. offshore are included. These calculations are based on the most likely geological risks, and the expected size and cost of the discovery for each of the different regions. This highlights the different levels of profitability to be expected from exploration efforts in the various regions; but it does not permit one to distinguish whether the differences in profitability are caused by the taxation system or due to the geological prospects. To overcome this problem the fiscal system of one country is imposed upon the geological, cost, and price characteristics of another country, allowing a comparison of profitability under a "common pool". This has been done for both the onshore and offshore regions to isolate the differences caused by the taxation system.

1. INTRODUCTION

Petroleum taxation in Canada and the United States was quite similar until the first "oil shock" of 1973. In fact, Canada used the taxation policies of the U.S. in designing some aspects of its tax system-like depletion allowances. There is one major difference in the underlying jurisdiction over petroleum resources between the two countries that has major implications for taxation. In Canada, the provincial governments own the petroleum resources; whereas, in the U.S. private landholders own the mineral rights. This difference becomes blurred when one considers that the

O.Bjerkholt & E.Offerdal, eds., Macroeconomic Prospects for a Small Oil Exporting Country. ISBN 90-247-3183-6.
Copyright 1985, Martinus Nijhoff Publishers, Dordrecht

Canadian government has ownership of all mineral rights in the northern territories and offshore;   and the U.S. government has ownership of mineral rights offshore and for all public lands. Since most of the oil and natural gas production in Canada is from the provinces, and most of the production in the U.S. is from private lands the distinction is important. This may not be so in the future as proportionally more production will likely come from areas under the control of the central government in both Canada and the U.S.

The provincial ownership, more than any other factor, has been responsible for the instigation over the last decade of a very complicated petroleum taxation and pricing system in Canada. It is during this period that both the federal and provincial governments fought over the vast petro-rents suddenly generated by the surge in international oil prices. Both governments had some overlapping claim to the petro-rents.   As each government flexed its muscle, using its power over taxation or pricing, the petroleum industry found itself, unwillingly, in the middle of the dispute. One of the major tools at the disposal of the federal government to control the flow of resource rents to the provincial governments was to exercise its right to set the oil and gas prices for all international and interprovincial sales.   From 1973 to the early 1980's the federal government set these prices at a substantial discount to world - equivalent levels.

In the U.S., the federal government used its power of price-setting to dissipate the petroleum rents (to the consumers).   However, unlike Canada, the main concern was to prevent the petroleum industry from collecting the economic rents. By the late 1970's after the second "oil shock", the U.S. introduced a windfall profits tax and eliminated the price controls for oil. Natural gas is quite another matter, as the Natural Gas Act of 1978 set out a very complicated price decontrol schedule, and left the tax system unfettered. In this paper the discussion of taxation will be limited to those taxes which affect firms engaging in the business of supplying petroleum products. Hence no consideration will be given to any taxes which are aimed directly at petroleum consumption.

For the petroleum investor, the fiscal system is only one of several key variables which will affect the rate of return. The pricing mechanism[2] and the expected size and cost of the discovery will play a key part in the investment decision at the margin.   In theory, the rate of return on investment, adjusted for risk, should be the same across international boundaries (assuming no artificial barriers). Differentials can obviously exist in the short run, especially as countries adjust their tax and

pricing policies after major international shocks. The speed with which
capital flows, especially in light of the important role that multinational
oil companies play, should limit the possibility of differentials in the
rate of return lasting very long.

Although it does not affect the rate of return on investment, many
nations have limitations on the degree of control that is allowed for
foreign investment in the petroleum area. For instance, Canada reserves a
25 % share in "Canada Lands" for its crown corporation, Petro Canada; and
Norway demands that its state oil corporation, Statoil, has at least a 50%
share in the ownership of all licences granted; and in the U.K. the
British National Oil Corporation (BNOC) continues to have an option of
taking up to a 51% share of new licences (whereas before 1980 BNOC took a
mandatory majority equity interest). This state participation is one of
the most effective methods of capturing the economic rents associated with
the exploitation of petroleum resources.

The taxation systems in both the U.S. and Canada have been in a
state of dynamic change in the last decade. Generally, the fiscal changes
have lagged the major oil price shocks of the 1970's. Changes in the
fiscal system will lead to capital gains or losses on existing investment,
and to a revaluation of all new investment. Thus even a significantly more
onerous level of taxation (from the point of view of the investor) will not
likely lead to any change in the level of current production, but will only
affect the future levels of production through the indirect effect of
reduced exploration and development investment.

Petroleum taxation systems should be tailored as much as possible to
the quality ("richness") of the resource; in other words, it should be set
to capture the maximum economic rent. However, this is a difficult task
because of the differences in resource quality. Having stated that
investment flows will adjust to whatever level of taxation is imposed, and
claimed that taxation should be designed to take account of the "richness"
of the resource, it should be clear that a comparison of oil and gas
taxation between countries is going to be difficult. That is not to say
that one cannot learn interesting lessons by examining, on an intercountry
basis, the methods of taxation. It will be in this light that the following
paper will proceed.

Section 2 contains an outline of the taxation system in Canada; and
section 3 contains a similar outline of the taxation system in the U.S. In
section 4 we explore the relative profitability of a petroleumbased
investment in Canada and the U.S. (for both an onshore and offshore
discovery). To add to the scope of the profitability comparison,

calculations for the U.K. offshore are included. These calculations are
based on the most likely geological risks, and the expected size and cost
of the discovery for each of the different regions. This highlights the
different levels of profitability to be expected from exploration efforts
in the various regions; but it does not permit one to distinguish whether
the differences in profitability are caused by the taxation system or due
to the geological prospects. To overcome this problem the fiscal system of
one country is imposed upon the geological, cost, and price characteristics
of another country, allowing a comparison of profitability under a "common
pool". This has been done for both the onshore and offshore regions to
isolate the differences caused by the taxation system.

2. FISCAL SYSTEM FOR CANADA

Background information about recent changes in, and consequences of,
petroleum taxation since the National Energy Program (1980) can be found in
the Memorandum of Agreement (1981), The NEP Update (1982), EMR (1983),
McRae (1982), Helliwell and McRae (1982), and Helliwell, MacGregor and
Plourde (1983).

As mentioned in the introduction, both the provinces and the federal
government have taxation powers that they excercise over the petroleum
industry. Therefore, this section will be subdivided into three: the
first contains the federal tax measures which are universal for both
onshore and offshore production; the second contains the federal fiscal
system specifically designed for the "Canada Lands" (offshore, Yukon, and
the North West Territories); and the third contains the fiscal system of
the province of Alberta.

The first subsection describes federal income tax as it affects the
petroleum industry, the petroleum-specific tax measures such as the
petroleum incentive payments, petroleum and gas revenue tax, and the
incremental oil revenue tax.

The second subsection describes the federal royalty and state
participation scheme for the Canada Lands. A complete description of the
development and production rules are not possible because each lease must
be negotiated with the Canadian Oil and Gas Lands Administration (COGLA).
To date, only a few exploration agreements have been awarded by COGLA.

The third subsection contains the fiscal system for the province of
Alberta. Although there are several other provinces which produce oil and
gas, Alberta produces about 85 % of all Canada's oil and gas. The taxation

system includes a provincial income tax, bidding bonus, gross royalty, and various incentive schemes.

2.1. FEDERAL FISCAL SYSTEM

2.1.1. INCOME TAX

The federal government levies income tax on the taxable profits generated by all firms. The tax rate is 46 %, with a 10 % abatement for income earned in a province. There are various reductions in the basic tax rate allowed for qualifying small businesses. For 1983 only, there is a surcharge of 2.5%.

Taxable income from petroleum activity is determined as follows:

        gross resource income

less   direct operating costs
          general and administrative expenses
          capital cost allowance
          resource allowance
          interest expenses
          Canadian Oil and Gas Property expense
          Canadian development expenses
          Canadian exploration expenses

equals   net resouce profits

less   eligible depJetion allowance

equals   net income subject to tax.

The terms above are qualified as follows:

gross resource income - It is the total proceeds from the sale of oil and gas. With only a few exeptions, no deduction is permissible for royalty payments.

capital cost allowances - All tangible assets are grouped into classes, each with its own depreciation factor. Most classes calculate the capital cost allowances using the declining balance method, although some use the straight line method.

resource allowance - It is equal to 25% of gross resource income minus direct operating costs, general and administrative expenses, capital cost allowances, and Canadian exploration and development overhead expenses. It is meant as a partial offset to the non-deductibility of provincial royalties for federal income tax purposes.

Canadian oil and gas property expense - It covers the cost of acquiring a resource property, including lease or rental payments. These expenses can be written off at a 10% rate using the declining balance method.

Canadian development expense - It includes all delineation and development well costs, except capped exploration wells. These expenses can be written off on a declining balance basis at 30%.

Canadian exploration expense - It includes all seismic, geological, geochemical, and geophysical activity preceeding the completion of a discovery well. Even some wells drilled after a discovery well (dry hole and some capped wells) can be classified as an exploration expense. These expenses are to be written off at 100% in the year incurred.

depletion allowance - It is an additional tax deduction which applies to certain capital costs like oil sands assets, well equipment used in tertiary recovery, and assets used in the processing of heavy oil. These costs earn depletion at the rate of 33 1/3% and can be claimed to a maximum of 25% of resource profits. The general ability to use exploration and development expenses to earn depletion allowance was altered in the National Energy Program (1980). Earned depletion allowance is being phased out (and will disappear by 1984, expect for those items mentioned above) and has been replaced by petroleum incentive payments.

2.1.2 PETROLEUM INCENTIVE PAYMENTS

The National Energy Program (NEP) radically changed the special tax privilege that petroleum firms had enjoyed with respect the depletion allowance. It was to be phased out and replaced with a government grant called the petroleum incentive payment, which varies according to the type of activity (exploration or development), the location of the activity (provincial or Canada Lands), and the degree of foreign ownership. The grant was more generous for exploration than development activity, more generous for activity on Canada Lands than on provincial lands, and more generous for firms with a higher degree of Canadian ownership and control. The aim of the grants was threefold: to shift activity towards exploration on Canada Lands, to provide a strong incentive for Canadianization of the petroleum industry, and to help smaller firms (which might not be in a taxable position) make immidiate use of grants, as opposed to accumulating tax write-offs in the form of depletion allowances.

Where the petroleum incentive payments are used to purchase capital equipment then the capital cost allowance is reduced. The net effect is to tax the grant over the depreciable life of the asset.

Since the NEP provided for a 25% back-in privilege on Canada Lands for the state-owned oil company, Petro Canada, even a completely foreign controlled firm is entitled to a 25% petroleum incentive payment for

Table 1.a. Petroleum Incentive Payments: Provincial lands

	0<=COR<=50	50<COR<=63	63<COR<=71	71<COR
Exploration	0%	15%	25%	35%
Development	0%	10%	15%	20%
Non-conventional	0%	10%	15%	20%

Table 1.b. Petroleum Incentive Payments: Canada Lands

	0<=COR<=50	50<COR<=63	63<COR<=71	71<COR
Exploration	25%	50%	65%	80%
Development	0%	10%	15%	20%
Non-conventional	0%	0%	15%	20%

(COR is the Canadian Ownership Rate, as determined by the Petroleum Monitoring Agency).

exploration activities on Canada Lands. Table 1 gives the details of the petroleum incentive payments.

Since the degree of Canadian ownership can have such an important impact on the level of the grant, the administrative organizations (Alberta has its own organization) are vigilant to ensure that those applying for the grant earn an interest commensurate with its expenditure.

2.1.3 PETROLEUM AND GAS REVENUE TAX

The petroleum and gas revenue tax (PGRT) was introduced in the NEP as part of an attempt by the federal government to increase its share of the petro-rents. It is essentially a federal gross royalty based on production revenue net of operating costs. The basic rate is 16%, but it is subject to a 25% resource allowance, so the effective rate is 12%. However, the PGRT tax payments are not deductible for income tax purposes.

As an offset to the PGRT payments there is a small producer credit of $250,000.00 available to "working" interests held by corporations. There are certain further tax breaks with respect to PGRT for those firms involved in oil sands projects and enhanced oil recovery projects.

2.1.4 INCREMENTAL OIL REVENUE TAX

The incremental oil revenue tax (IORT) was introduced in the federal provincial Memorandum of Agreement (1981) in an attempt to capture the "windfall revenues" of the oil producing firms, which would accrue because of the upward revision in the "made-in-Canada" level of oil prices contained in the federal-provincial agreement compared to the oil prices contained in the NEP. The tax is only to apply to "old" oil discovered before 1981. The tax rate is 50% on the incremental revenue. Royalties are the only deduction allowed. However, the revenue subject to the IORT is not subject to income tax.

Given the high level of provincial royalties many firms prefer to pay the IORT rather than income tax. However, the tax was only in effect from January 1, 1982 to June 1, 1982 and has since been temporarily suspended by each successive federal budget.

2.2 FEDERAL OFFSHORE

The federal government owns the mineral rights to all offshore regions and to the territories (Yukon and NWT). The recently revised system of special taxation for these regions is contained in the Canada Oil and Gas Act. There are two types of royalties levied on the socalled

Canada Lands: a basic royalty of 10% of gross revenue, and a progressive incremental royalty equal to 40% of net profits. The net profits for the progressive incremental royalty are calculated as gross revenue minus operating costs, PGRT, the basic royalty, a notional income tax abatement, an allowed 25% rate of return on invested capital (with the capital base for the return to decrease by 10% annually on a declining balance basis), and a capital cost allowance (16 2/3% annual rate on a straight line basis).

The federal government introduced as part of the NEP the retroactive 25% backin right, reserved for the state-owned oil company, Petro Canada. The Crown may excercise its right any time prior to a development permit being issued, but once the option has been excercised Petro Canada must begin to pay 25% of all costs, appropriate with its "working" interest.

For pre-1981 exploration expenditure on a field declared significant by 1983 and which was first drilled before 1981, an _ex gratia_ payment is made in lieu of a petroleum incentive payment. The payment is to be made out of the Crown share of future production. The payment is equal to 1/4 of 250% of eligible costs incurred before 1981 (grossed up by 15% per annum to the end of 1980 to account for inflation and interest).

The federal government exercises considerable control over all aspects of the exploration and development activities on Canada Lands through the issue of licences through the Canada Oil and Gas Lands Administration (COGLA). Although not strictly a body dealing with taxation matters it does have a very pervasive influence on the activity in the Canada Lands. It is still too early to assess its impact.

2.3 ALBERTA FISCAL SYSTEM

Each producing province has its own petroleum fiscal system. Since Alberta is the most important oil and gas production province its system is described.

Alberta collects its economic rent through three channels: provincial income tax, Crown royalties[3], and bidding bonus payments. Alberta also provides several different types of incentive schemes like royalty reductions, and grants to encourage exploration drilling, geophysical and well-servicing activity.

With respect to provincial income tax collection, Alberta claims a tax of 11% of the federal tax base, adjusted so that royalty payments are allowed as a deduction. A tax reduction, the Alberta Royalty Tax Credit, is provided to individuals and firms that pay provincial royalties. The

tax credit is 50% of Alberta royalties paid up to a maximum of $2 million
per year. For several years in the early 1980's the tax credit was even
more generous.

Alberta's main response to the increase in the world oil price was
to increase its gross royalty rate. The royalty rate is a function of the
date of discovery, the productivity of the well, and the method of
recovery. The marginal royalty rates are 45% for old oil and gas and 35%
for new oil and gas.

Old oil is defined as production from pools discovered prior to
April 1, 1974. All oil discovered after that date, as well as oil produced
by secondary recovery (waterflood) or enhanced recovery methods from "old"
pools, are classified as new oil. Old gas is that which was discovered
prior to January 1, 1974. New gas is that which was discovered after that
date, or gas which was discovered prior to 1974 but was neither consumed
nor sold before 1974.

The actual royalty calculation is complicated and depends upon the
productivity, the method of production, and even the price level for gas.
For gas as the price increases the average royalty rate approaches the
marginal rate. Details of the calculations can be found in EMR (1983). The
average royalty rates are shown in Table 2.

Table 2. Average Royalty Rates for Oil and Gas

	Old oil	New oil	Old gas	New gas
Low productivity well	15%	12%	28%	23%
High productivity well	43%	35%	40%	32%

Source: (EMR (1983), p. 30-38)

3. FISCAL SYSTEM FOR UNITED STATES

Background information about the petroleum taxation system in the
U.S. can be found in Jones (1982) and Verleger (1980,1982).

Both the producing states and the federal government have taxation
powers that they excercise over the petroleum industry. Therefore, this
section will be subdivided into two: the first contains the federal tax
measures which affect both onshore and offshore production; the second

contains the fiscal system for the state of Texas.

The first subsection describes federal income tax as it affects the petroleum industry, and the petroleum-specific windfall profits tax. Unlike Canada, the U.S. federal tax system is the same for petroleum activity offshore as it is onshore.

The second subsection contains the fiscal system for the state of Texas. Although there are other states which produce oil and gas, Texas is the most important. The taxation system only entails a severance tax, as royalties are collected by private landowners, and Texas does not have an income tax.

3.1 FEDERAL FISCAL SYSTEM

3.1.1 INCOME TAX

The federal government levies income tax on the taxable profits generated by all firms. The tax rate is 46%. Petroleum activity is entitled to some tax concessions not available to other firms, such as expensing certain capital costs and depletion allowance; but are subject to a windfall profits tax, unlike other firms.

Taxable income from petroleum activity is determined as follows:

	gross revenue
less	royalty payments
equals	net revenue after royalty
less	operating expenses
	windfall profits tax
	net state and local tax
equals	net operating income
less	expensed capital costs (intangible drilling costs)
	depreciation
	allowable depletion

equals   federal taxable income

times   federal income tax rate of .46

equals   federal income tax

less   investment tax credit

equals   federal income tax payable

The terms above are qualified as follows:

gross revenue - It is calculated from oil and gas sales, valued at the wellhead.

royalty expenses - Most mineral rights in the U.S. are held by private landowners, and as a consequence royalty rates vary considerably. The most common form of royalty is for the owner to take a fixed proportion of the value of the oil or gas produced, usually 12,5%. The most common type of royalty system used for the offshore region is a fixed proportion of 16 2/3%, although in some instances the royalty rate is the bid variable.

operating expenses - These include most expenses incurred after production begins, like direct operating expenses, overhead costs, and employee benefit payments.

expensed capital costs - These include intangible drilling and development costs. The ability to expense such capital costs is supposed to offset some of the unique risks involved in drilling oil and gas. However, if desired it is possible to elect to capitalize rather than expense such items. The general rule to follow in determining if an expenditure can qualify as an intangible drilling and development cost is to ascertain that it has no salvage value. The usual expenses incurred in the preparation of a drill site have no salvage value, and therefore can be expensed.

depreciation - In general all capital assets must be written off on the basis of some sort of depreciation rate. The intangible drilling and development costs mentioned above are an exception. Bonus payments (including legal fees and costs) associated with acquiring a lease must be capitalized, unless it is for an unproductive property which can be

expensed when the lease is surrendered or elapses. Geological and geo-
physical costs are to be capitalized if they result in the acquisition, re-
tention or improvement of a property; but can be considered as intangible
costs if they are used to determine the location for drilling a well. The
Economic Recovery Tax Act of 1981 specified accelerated depreciation rates
for most investment made after 1980. The depreciation rates vary according
to whether the asset is defined as a 3-year, 5-year, 10-year, 15-year
public utility, or 15-year real property. For instance, lease and well
equipment are classified as 5-year property. In addition it is possible to
elect to expense a portion of certain business equipment placed in service
each year. As an alternative to the accelerated depreciation method for
investment after 1981, it is possible to elect to use the
unit-of-production method (the adjusted cost base is multiplied by the
ratio of the annual production to the estimated recoverable reserves).

depletion allowance - After 1974 percentage depletion was almost completely
eliminated for oil and gas production (it is still allowed for some natural
gas producers and some independent oil and gas producers). If applicable,
percentage depletion is calculated as 15% of gross income from oil and gas
production (with the limitation that it cannot exceed 50% of the taxable
income before the depletion allowance deduction). Percentage depletion has
been replaced by cost depletion. Cost depletion can be used to recapture
only those costs associated with acquiring a lease (bonus payments, legal
fees, and geological and geophysical costs that have been capitalized). It
is calculated as the unrecovered depletion costs multiplied by the ratio of
annual production to the estimated recoverable reserves at the beginning of
the year.

Investment tax credit - The Economic Recovery Tax Act of 1981 set forth an
investment tax credit of 6% for 3-year property, and 10% for 5, 10, and
15-year property.

3.1.2 WINDFALL PROFITS TAX

The windfall profits tax was introduced in 1980 as part of the oil
price decontrol program. It was ammended in 1981 as part of the Economic
Recovery Tax Act of 1981: the windfall profits tax was lowered for new
discoveries, and concessions were granted to independent producers and
royalty holders.

The windfall profit is defined as the difference between the revenue received at the wellhead (using the "removal" price) and the revenue that would have occured using an inflation-adjusted base price. The windfall profit is reduced by the state severance tax applicable to this revenue, provided that the severance tax is expressed as of gross revenue (with an upper limit of 15%). The base price uses the tier system which was in effect during the control period. A brief description of the tier structure follows:

tier 1

tax rate for independent producers = 50%

tax rate for other (nonexempt) producers = 70%

adjusted base price = $13.06/b (March 1, 1980) + annual inflation rate

tier 2 - stripper well

tax rate for independent producers = 0%

tax rate for other (nonexempt) producers = 60%

adjusted base price = $15.50/b (March 1, 1980) + annual inflation rate

tier 2 - National Petroleum Reserve

tax rate for independent producers = 30%

tax rate for other (nonexempt) producers = 60%

adjusted base price = $15.50/b (March 1, 1980) + annual inflation rate

tier 3 - new oil

tax rate for independent producers = 25%

tax rate for other (nonexempt) producers = 25%

adjusted base price = $16.96/b (Marc 1, 1980) + annual inflation + 2%

tier 3 - heavy and incremental tertiary oil

tax rate for independent producers = 30%

tax rate for other (nonexempt) producers = 30%

adjusted base price = $16.96/b (March 1, 1980) + annual inflation + 2%

Independent producers are producers who have U.S. retail sales of oil or natural gas less than $5 million per year, and U.S. refinery throughput of less than 50 thousand b/d. The lower rates for independent producers apply only to the first 1.000 b/d of combined tier 1 and tier 2 oil, and any production in excess of this amount is subject to the higher nonexempt rate. The rate for new oil is scheduled to decline from 25% in 1983 to 22,5% in 1984, 20% in 1985 and 15% thereafter. The inflation adjustment is calculated quarterly using the GNP deflator.

Tier 1 oil is defined as oil from an onshore property producing by 1978, or from offshore leases entered into prior to January 1, 1979.

Tier 2 oil can be oil from a stripper well or from a National Petroleum Reserve. A stripper well is one which produces less than 10 b/d averaged over any twelve month period after December 31, 1972.

Tier 3 oil is new oil discovered after December 31, 1978, oil from offshore leases entered into after December 31, 1978, heavy oil, and incremental tertiary oil.

There is a safety net limiting the windfall profits payments: they cannot exceed 90% of the net income.

The windfall profits tax is scheduled to begin a phase-out in 1991 at the latest, with the tax rates being reduced by 3% over a 33 month period.

3.2 FISCAL SYSTEM FOR TEXAS

The fiscal system employed by each state varies considerably. In Texas it is particularly simple because there is no state income tax, unlike most other producing states. The severance taxes in Texas are collected using the following rates:

- oil - $.046 per barrel (but not less than 4,6% of market value)
  plus $.01 per barrel;
- gas - 7,5% of market value (minimum of 121/1500th of $.01 per Mcf).

4. COMPARISON OF THE FISCAL SYSTEMS IN CANADA AND THE U.S.

As mentioned in the introduction it is a difficult task to compare the fiscal systems between countries. This should be evident after wading through the details contained in sections 2 and 3. It would become even more apparent if one had included countries as diverse as the U.K. and Indonesia. Each country has assessed the likely economic rent associated

with its oil and gas resources, and designed a fiscal system to capture
some of that rent.

A quick comparison of the Canadian and U.S. petroleum taxation
systems will demonstrate many similarities. In general, the U.S. system is
less complicated and appears to offer a lower average tax take, especially
when comparing the provincial system in Alberta and the state system in
Texas. The relatively high average provincial royalty rates in combination
with the non-deductible federal royalty rate (which by itself is equal to
the average deductible royalty in Texas) seems by itself to more than tip
the balance in favour of Texas. The Canadian petroleum incentive payments
probably are more generous than the cost depletion allowance in the U.S.
Such a statement, as imprecise as it is, cannot be made with much accuracy
since the petroleum incentive payments are very sensitive to the degree of
Canadian control - and are only promised to exist until the end of 1986.
As well we must take account of the windfall profits tax in the U.S., which
does not have a operational parallel in Canada. As a crude comparison it
would seem that the U.S. system relies somewhat more on "profit" oriented
taxes, whereas the Canadian system relies more on the gross royalty to
collect the economic rent.

The Canadian offshore fiscal system is much simpler than the
provincial system. With the basic royalty, the progressive incremental
royalty, and PGRT (and the forced state participation) the Canadian system
shares some similarities with the systems in the U.K. and Norway. The
system in Canada seems to be more "profit" oriented than the provincial
system, hence more flexible. However, as pointed out previously, there is
still a considerable amount of uncertainty surrounding the continuation of
the petroleum incentive payments (which are very generous for Canadian
owned firms undertaking exploration activity), and until very recently
uncertainty as to the actual ownership of the mineral rights off the
province of Newfoundland (the Supreme Court has said they belong to Canada,
not the province). As well, the petroleum industry is generally nervous
with a government which has changed the rules so drastically over the last
decade. Even without this long list of qualifiers it would be hard to
compare the existing offshore systems in Canada and the U.S. - again
because of the differences in design.

However crude, the above attempts at comparison really miss the
point that the tax systems must be assessed in conjunction with the
expected geological prospects. To see how an investor would compare the
tax systems we need to have much more information at hand: the cost, price,
and output, as well as tax data associated with a "typical investment".

Then we could compare the profitability between jurisdictions. Fortunately, I can finish this paper by providing such a comparison, thanks to study done by the Canadian Energy Research Institute (CERI) of Calgary.

The information contained in Table 3 provides a means to compare the taxation systems in Canada, the U.S. and the U.K. It is based on onshore activity through a comparison of the fiscal systems in Texas (West Texas) and Alberta (Fenn West); and on offshore activity through a comparison of the fiscal systems in Canada (the Hibernia area of the east coast offshore), the U.K. (Brent area), and the U.S.(offshore Lousiana in 80 to 120 metres of water).

There are obviously numerous assumptions which must be made in order to generate the numbers in Table 3. Without going into too much detail, the numbers are generated by a commercially available software program called Profitability of Oil and Gas Opportunities (POGO for short). The software includes the necessary taxation systems and parameters, and the user must provide details of the geological characterists of the pool, the costs associated with exploration, development and production, and certain parameters like the real discount rate, and the expected future oil prices. The most likely geological prospects (and their associated costs) for the areas under consideration are contained in the CERI report.

The tax systems for Canada and the U.S. have been discussed in the previous sections. The U.K. system is briefly described in Michell (1982), except that since he wrote the paper the special petroleum duty has been eliminated and the rate for the petroleum revenue tax has increased. The chief components of the tax system are a royalty of 12,5%, a petroleum revenue tax at 75%, and a corporation income tax at 52%.

The analysis behind the numbers in Table 3 all involve a discovery of a new pool (although in a known field). The oil price is virtually identical in each region. The concentration is on oil production, so any gas discoveries are assumed to be sold in the ground, unexploited. In the introduction it was argued that it was too hard to disentangle the taxation aspects from the complicated pricing and marketing problems surrounding gas, hence the focus on oil.

One of the more important assumptions about the nature of the firm is that it is in a position to fully utilize the tax write-offs in the year in which they incur. In other words, the analysis is done on a "flow-through" basis.

One must decide which measure to use in comparing the relative

Table 3. Profitability of Petroleum Investment
          Source: CERI (1983)

	Alberta	Texas	U.K. offshore	U.S. offshore	Canada offshore
Typical pool - no risk					
Investment (million 1982 $C) .	2,0	6,9	1176,5	113,7	2062,7
AIT internal rate of return (%)	98,9	91,9	16,4	22,9	20,5
AIT net income/investment	3,5	3,3	1,3	1,6	1,4
Revenue shares (%)					
Federal government	36,2	32,4	51,6	40,1	38,8
State/provincial government	(31,5	4,0)			
Industry (gross)	32,3	51,1	48,4	59,9	61,2
Industry (net of operating)	29,1	46,1	28,4	43,3	48,2
Typical pool - risk					
Investment (million 1982 $C) .	1,0	1,4	247,3	9,2	720,9
AIT internal rate of return (%)	84,6	70,7	n/a	94,6	20,0
AIT net income/investment	2,7	ʼ2,7	1,2	1,6	1,4
Probability for risk case					
Oil	0,33	0,16	0,20	0,05	0,33
Gas	0,33	0,09	0,00	0,20	0,00
Dry hole	0,34	0,75	0,80	0,75	0,67

	Texas tax system imposed on Alberta Canada	U.K. tax system imposed on offshore Canada	Offshore U.S. tax system imposed on offshore
Common pool - no risk			
Investment (million 1982 $C)	2,0	2 062,7	2 062,7
AIT internal rate of return (%)	98,7	15,0	18,5
AIT net income/investment ...	5,0	1,2	1,4
Revenue shares (%)			
Federal government	35,7	49,0	39,6
State/provincial government	3,9		
Industry (gross)	47,8	51,0	60,4
Industry (net of operating)	44,6	38,0	47,4
Common pool - risk			
Investment (million 1982 $C)	1,0	720,9	720,9
AIT internal rate of return (%)	78,2	n/a	17,2
AIT net income/investment ...	3,6	1,2	1,3

Notes to accompany Table 3.
AIT - after income tax, $C - Canadian dollars, n/a - not available

net income = gross production revenue - royalties - operating expenses -
special taxes (PGRT in Canada, windfall profits tax and severence taxes in
the U.S., and petroleum revenue tax in the U.K.) - federal and
state/provincial taxes.
The investment data for Canada does not have the petroleum incentive
payments netted out. Since they can be large for the offshore exploration
investment, the results for offshore Canada will be biased.

profitability. Two measures are provided: the after income tax internal rate of return, and the ratio of after income tax net income to the initial investment (see Van Meurs (1971)). The latter measure gives a sort of benefit-cost ratio. A real rate of 10% is used in all discounting. For simplicity it is assumed that all costs and prices remain constant in real terms (sensitivity analysis shows some, but very little inflation bias in the tax systems).

Each case was analysed twice: once assuming a 100% probability of success, and again using assumptions about the probability of discovering oil, gas, or a dry hole to assess the expected costs and returns.

To remove the differences in geological prospects (and costs) from the comparison excercise, and focus more directly on the fiscal systems, there are some results reported which superimpose the fiscal system of another country on the physical and cost characteristics associated with the Alberta discovery and with the east coast offshore discovery. In this way, one can see the results of "what if" Canada adopted the U.S. offshore fiscal system in place of the existing system, and so on.

Many interesting facts come to light by examining the contents of Table 3. If we concentrate on the certain discovery case (abstracting from the various probabilities of success) then we see that the onshore pools (Alberta and Texas) have roughly the same level of profitability, and that the offshore pools all have roughly the same, but lower, level of profitability. The same ranking holds true under the expected case (using various probabilities for the discovery of oil, gas, or a dry hole). One is struck by the much larger investment required in offshore activity – especially in Canada. However, under the risk-adjusted case the investment required is substantially lower (but still higher than onshore investment) because the cost of the dry holes are far less than the total investment necessary to fully develop a pool. The internal rate of return for the U.S. offshore is greatly increased because of the high probability of striking gas.

The numbers for the Alberta case are strongly influenced by the royalty holiday incentive (allows for certain select successful exploration wells to receive a five year royalty holiday – for the exploration well only, not for the subsequent development wells). Without the royalty holiday the after income tax rate of return falls from 99% to 56% and the after income tax net income to investment ratio falls from 3.5 to 2.6.

The Canadian ownership rate (COR) is the key variable in determining the size of the petroleum incentive payment in Canada. The base case assumption is that the exploratory firm is 100 % Canadian owned. However, if the COR is less than 50 %, hence qualifying for the lowest level of petroleum incentive payments, it does not have much of an influence on the Alberta profitability. Surprisingly, it does not even have too large an effect on the offshore Canada pool: a COR less than 50 % causes a reduction in the after income tax rate of return from 20.5 % to 17.5 %, and a decline in the after income tax net income to investment ratio from 1.4 to 1.3.

The revenue shares provide the basis for a very interesting story. The government take is highest for the onshore Canada (Alberta) pool, primarily because of the large provincial share. But the government revenue share for offshore Canada is only slightly higher than the lowest government share (Texas), leaving the net industry revenue share slightly larger for offshore Canada than Texas. The lowest net industry share is for Alberta and the offshore U.K.

To abstract from the interaction of different geological, cost and taxation systems, the second part of Table 3 contains some profitability numbers for some hypothetical experiments involving the imposition of the Texas fiscal system on the Alberta pool, and the imposition of the U.K. and the U.S. offshore fiscal systems on the offshore Canada pool. The imposition of the Texas fiscal system on an Alberta pool would result in a substantially better profitability rating, mainly because of the lower state/provincial government taxes (royalty and income taxes). The imposition of the U.K. fiscal system on the offshore Canada pool would lead to a lower level of profitability, mainly due to the higher U.K. federal tax bite. Since the U.S. and Canadian offshore profitability was very similar in the first part of the table it is not too surprising that the imposition of the U.S. offshore fiscal system on the offshore Canada pool does not make much difference to the profitability.

Some general observations will conclude this section. A comparison of the onshore pools, accounting for the risk of gas and dry holes, gives an identical level of profitability. This is so despite the fact that the net industry share is substantially higher in Texas. Since Alberta still has relatively good geological prospects (ie. relatively "rich" resource) it can increase its tax take to extract the economic rent without affecting the exploration activity too much. The last statement must be qualified because of the well-known problems with high "front-end" gross royalty taxes, which dominate the Alberta fiscal system. A comparison of the offshore Canada with offshore U.S. pools indicates roughly equal levels of profitability. Therefore, despite the different components used in the fiscal systems in Canada and the U.S., it seems that when the different geological prospects are considered, there is little reason to prefer one jurisdiction over the other (except to note that onshore activity is more rewarding than offshore activity). The U.K. offshore fiscal system is less favourable to the investor than the other systems, but its tax burden is not much heavier than the other two offshore systems.

The above analysis reveals an acceptable degree of profitability for new investment in Canada, but the tax system is such that much higher taxes exist for production of old oil. This has resulted in some difficulty in raising new investment from internally-generated funds to pursue exploration, assuming an imperfection in the capital markets.

The analysis of the tax system indicates that most of the risk is borne by the private petroleum firms, but with the government bearing a substantial share depending upon the degree of state particiation. Despite the level of taxation it seems that firms are earning some supernormal profits. With respect to risk, the firms operating in the U.K. sector of the North Sea have some constraints, in that they cannot spread the oil-specific tax write-offs outside the "ring fence".

There are some distortions evident in the tax system, especially in Canada. The petroleum incentive payments encourage exploration effort in the "Canada Lands" (with its lower profitability), and it discourages effort from the foreign-controlled firms. As well, the high level of combined provincial and federal royalty rates discourages effort at exploiting marginal deposits.

NOTES

1) I wish to acknowledge my deepest appreciation to the Canadian Energy Research Institute of Calgary for making available to me a recently completed (and still confidential) consulting study, of which I made extensive use of two reports: one describes fiscal systems in six countries, and the other compares oil and gas investment returns in Canada, the U.S. and the U.K.

2) When examining profitability it is possible to ignore the differences caused by pricing for oil. Since 1981 the Canadian government has allowed producers to sell new oil at the world price. Since 1980 the United States has allowed all oil ("new" and "old") to be sold by producers at the world price. In Canada "old" oil is still priced at a discount to the world oil price. The complexities and uncertainty sur-

rownding future pricing and marketing of natural gas in both Canada and the U.S. really precludes trying to disentangle the relative taxation systems from the pricing rules as well as the geological prospects.

3) (Income from freehold mineral rights and Indian Lands are the main sources of non-Crown royalty payments). Special royalty arrangements exist for enchanged oil recovery, synthetic oil, and experimental projects. None of the above special features will be discussed.

REFERENCES

Canada, Department of Energy, Mines and Resources, The National Energy Program 1980, October 1980.

Canada, Memorandum of Agreement Between the Government of Canada and the Government of Alberta Relating to Energy Pricing and Taxation, September 1981.

Canada, Department of Energy, Mines and Resources, The National Energy Program Update 1982, May 1982.

Canadian Energy Research Institute, "A Comparison of Oil and Gas Investment Returns in Canada, the United States and the United Kingdom", May 1983, confidential.

Canada, Department of Energy, Mines and Resources, (Financial and Fiscal Analysis Branch), Petroleum Fiscal Systems in Canada: A Summary, October 1983.

Helliwell, J.F. and R. N. McRae, "Resolving the Energy Conflict: from The National Energy Program to the Energy Agreements", Canadian Public Policy, Winter 1982, pp. 14-23.

Helliwell, J. F., M. E. MacGregor and A. Plourde, "The National Energy Program Meets Falling World Oil Prices", Canadian Public Policy, September 1983.

Jacoby, H. D. and J. L. Smith, "The Effects of Taxes and Price Regulation on the Supply of Offshore Gas", MIT Energy Laboratory Working Paper, November 1983.

Jones, J. R. (ed.), Oil and Gas Federal Income Tax Manual, 11th Edition, Chicago: Arthur Anderson & Co., 1982.

McRae, R. N., "A Major Shift in Canada's Energy Policy: Impact of the National Energy Program", The Journal of Energy and Development, Spring 1982, pp. 173-198.

Mitchell, J., "Taxation of Oil and Gas Revenues: The United Kingdom", The Energy Journal, Vol. 3, No. 2, 1982, pp. 39-50.

Moose,J. S., "British and American Tax Treatment of U.K. North Sea Oil Fields", The Energy Journal, Vol. 3, No. 2, 1982, pp. 55-63

Van Meurs, A. P. H., Petroleum Economics and Offshore Mining Legislation, Elsevier Publishing Co., Amsterdam, 1971.

Verleger, P. K. Jr., "Assessment of the Effects of the Windfall Profits Tax on Crude Oil Supply", The Energy Journal, Vol. 1, no. 4, 1980, pp. 41-58.

Verleger, P. K. Jr., "Taxation of Oil and Gas Revenues: The United States", The Energy Journal, Vol. 3, No. 2, 1982, pp. 33-38.

PART FOUR:

OIL REVENUES AND LONG-TERM MACROECONOMIC PLANNING

REGIONAL IMPACTS OF PETROLEUM ACTIVITIES IN NORWAY

BY

ALETTE SCHREINER AND TOR SKOGLUND

ABSTRACT

The regional distribution of total employment is affected directly by the regional distribution of the petroleum activities, and indirectly by the domestic use of oil and gas revenues. The first part of this paper gives a survey of the regional economic aspects of the petroleum activities, and possible impacts on recent regional developments in Norway are briefly discussed. In the second part of the paper future regional consequences of the petroleum activities are analysed. Particular attention is paid to the regional impacts of more extensive petroleum activities off the coast of Northern Norway. The analysis is based on calculations on a multiregional input-output model constructed by the Central Bureau of Statistics.

1. INTRODUCTION

The petroleum industry has in the course of few years become an important industry in Norway. Value added in the petroleum sector constituted in 1983 about 18 per cent of GDP, while the share of crude oil and natural gas in total exports was about 35 per cent. At the same time, the petroleum sector's share of total employment was less than 1 per cent. The strong geographical concentration of most of the petroleum activities entails, however, that the employment effects are considerable in the regions mostly affected by petroleum activities.

The regional distribution of employment can be said to be affected by petroleum activities in two ways: directly by the regional distribution of employment in the petroleum industry and indirectly by the domestic use of oil and gas revenues which now amount to about 20 per cent of total government revenues. In the first part of the paper we give a survey of the regional economic aspects of the petroleum activities, including a

O.Bjerkholt & E.Offerdal, eds., Macroeconomic Prospects for a Small Oil Exporting Country. ISBN 90-247-3183-6.
Copyright 1985, Martinus Nijhoff Publishers, Dordrecht.

review of the regional development in the petroleum activities in Norway up to now. Possible impacts on the recent regional development in population, migration and employment are briefly discussed. No attempts are made, however, to solve the difficult methodological problem of separating the effects of the petroleum activities from other effects influencing regional employment.

In the second part of the paper we will analyse possible future regional consequences of petroleum activity. Although a relatively moderate growth in total oil and gas production is foreseen, some important changes in the regional distribution are likely to take place. Of particular interest are the impacts of establishing petroleum activities off the coast of Northern Norway. This region is now facing serious employment problems and it has been suggested that petroleum activities may provide a powerful stimulus to the regional economy. No decision concerning future oil or gas production in Northern Norway is, however, yet taken.

We define the petroleum sector for our purposes as including drilling, extraction and pipeline transportation of oil and gas. The statistical units constituting the sector are mainly oil and rig companies. Work carried out by subcontractors and deliveries of investment and intermediate goods by other enterprises are interpreted as production in the respective sectors. In the following the latter is referred to as petroleum related activities.

Our analysis is based on a regional breakdown of projections of the development in the national economy, under different assumptions about the distribution of the petroleum activities between Southern and Northern Norway. By comparing calculated regional labour demand with regional projections of labour supply, we hope to get an indication of the prospects of attaining a balanced development in the labour market in the various regions.

2. THE REGIONAL IMPACT OF THE PETROLEUM ACTIVITIES

In 1966 drilling started on the Norwegian continental shelf. In 1971 the first field came on stream in the Ekofisk area and in 1975, with a production of 8.7 mtoe, Norway became a net exporter of petroleum. Since then production has increased rapidly, with a production of 55.0 mtoe in 1983 which is maximum so far. There has been a gradual shift northward of the activity on the continental shelf. In 1981 the exploration activity was extended to include the area north of the 62nd parallel.

There seems to be broad political agreement in Norway that

increased Norwegian participation in the petroleum activities should be encouraged. Statoil, the Norwegian State Oil Company, was established in 1973. Since then the share in the exploration and production activities by Norwegian companies has increased steadily. This holds true also for the number of employed on offshore installations and in deliveries to the petroleum sector.

2.1. REGIONAL DEVELOPMENT IN POPULATION, MIGRATION AND EMPLOYMENT

The overall trend in the regional population pattern displayed in table 1, is the migration from Northern and Western Norway, and to some extent Trøndelag, to the southern and eastern parts of the country. Agder and Rogaland in the south has a faster growth in population than in any other region. This is the combined result of high fertility and large net immigration. Eastern Norway has had a considerable net immigration, but a low fertility rate, while the opposite has been the case for Northern Norway. The development of the petroleum activity may explain the increase in net migration to Rogaland after 1970.

It appears from table 2 that there was a decline in total employment in Northern Norway in the 1960s, particularly due to a decline in fishing and agriculture. The decline in these industries continued in the 1970s, but was then more than offset by an increase in employment in the service industries. With the severe employment problems now facing this part of the country the migration from Northern Norway has increased during the last years.

2.2. REGIONAL ASPECTS OF THE PETROLEUM ACTIVITIES

The production of oil and gas in the North Sea can be said to affect the regional economic structure in two different ways. First, there is the income earned by the owners of the Norwegian factors of production employed in the petroleum sector and by Norwegian enterprises producing goods and services for delivery to the petroleum sector. The income flow from the petroleum sector benefit the owners of the factors of production in a large number of enterprises throughout the economy as well as the government through the payment of income taxes. However, if we assume that in the case of no petroleum activity there would have been alternative uses for these factors of production with a corresponding yield, the income

Table 1   Population growth and net migration by region. 1961-82.   Annual
average in per cent of total population

	1961-70		1971-80		1981-82	
Region	Popul. growth	Of which net migration	Popul. growth	Of which net migration	Popul. growth	Of which net migration
Oslo/Akershus	1.4	0.6	0.2	-0.1	0.2	0.1
Rest of Eastern Norway	0.6	0.1	0.6	0.4	0.4	0.4
Agder	1.0	0.3	1.1	0.6	0.9	0.5
Rogaland	1.2	0.1	1.4	0.5	1.2	0.5
Western Norway	0.7	-0.3	0.5	-0.1	0.3	-0.1
Trøndelag	0.7	-0.2	0.5	0.1	0.3	0.0
Northern Norway	0.4	-0.8	0.3	-0.3	0.1	-0.5
Total	0.8	0.0	0.5	0.1	0.4	0.1

(Source: Population and migration statistics from the Central Bureau of
Statistics).

Table 2 Employment by region 1962-80. 1000 employed persons

Region	1962	1970	1980	Per cent annual growth	
				1962-70	1970-80
Oslo/Akershus	366	408	464	1.4	1.3
Rest of Eastern Norway	431	437	510	0.2	1.6
Agder	76	80	95	0.6	1.7
Rogaland	99	104	143	0.6	3.2
Western Norway	277	282	329	0.2	1.6
Trøndelag	137	140	173	0.3	2.1
Northern Norway	180	167	200	-0.9	1.8
Total	1 566	1 618	1 914	0.4	1.7

(Source: Unpublished employment statistics from the Central Bureau of statistics)

level (excluding government revenues from the special petroleum taxes)
would not have been affected except to the extent that the remuneration to
capital and labour in the petroleum sector is higher than in alternative
uses. However, the industrial structure is affected, and thereby the
regional distribution of employment. The employees on the continental shelf
are recruited from all over the country, although a majority lives in
Rogaland. This is also the case with other petroleum related activities,
especially those with temporary employment. The dispersion of the employees
by place of residence and the commuting over long distances resulting from
this, is made possible by the practice of prolonged shifts, for example

three weeks of work followed by three weeks of leisure. This means that it is mainly the distribution of the employees by place of residence that determine the dispersion of income through employment in the petroleum activities.

Second, there is the government income from taxes on the production of oil and gas. These revenues are often interpreted as a scarcity rent, which is the compensation to the owner for depletion of an exhaustible resource. Part of the scarcity rent or "oil rent" is retained, however, by the oil companies, i.e. excess return to capital over and above capital return in alternative use. A wellknown implication of domestic use of these revenues is a reduction in the production of tradeables (other than petroleum) and an increase in the production of nontradeables. Due to regional differences in the industrial structure, a transfer of employment from tradeables to nontradeables will have different impacts on total employment in different regions.

2.3. THE REGIONAL DISTRIBUTION OF EMPLOYMENT IN THE PETROLEUM ACTIVITIES

Roughly two thirds of the employees in the petroleum sector have their work offshore. The remaining third is employed in auxiliary units onshore and in the offices of the oil companies. Table 3 shows the regional distribution of employment in the petroleum sector and petroleum related activities. The employees are distributed according to place of work or, for those working offshore, according to the company's place of registration. The category "Exploration, drilling and production etc." corresponds roughly to the petroleum sector according to our definition. The employment is strongly concentrated to Rogaland, though the share has been declining. A possible explanation of the employment growth in Oslo/Akershus is that part of the growth in the administrative and engineering units of the oil companies has taken place in this region.

The shift northwards in the offshore activities seem to have had only small impacts on the geographical distribution of employment in these activities. Originally, Stavanger in Rogaland was chosen as the "petroleum capital" because of its favourable position in relation to the Ekofisk area. Gradually a comprehensive "petroleum environment" has developed in Stavanger as a result of the concentration of petroleum activities in the area. Thus, staying in Stavanger represents an "environmental advantage" which may compensate for the disadvantages of gradually longer distances to the petroleum fields. What actually seems to happen, is that subdivisions

are established on places closer to the new fields (for example in Harstad
in Northern Norway) while the main offices remain in Stavanger (and to some
extent in Oslo).

Mainly due to the mobility of the drilling rigs, the employed in
drilling companies are living more dispersed than the employed in the oil
companies. While 65 per cent of the latter live in Rogaland, only 25 per
cent of the employees in drilling live in this region. Another 25 per cent
live in Eastern Norway and yet another quarter live in Western
Norway.[1]

Table 3. Regional distribution and total employment in petroleum
related activities. 1974, 1979 and 1983. Percentages and number
of employees

Region	Exploration, drilling and production, etc.			Bases, transp- portation, catering, administra- tion, etc			Construction and maintenanc of platforms and supply vessels, etc.		
	1974	1979	1983	1974	1979	1983	1974	1979	1983
Oslo/Akershus	1.4	7.2	18.3	5.0	10.1	11.7	17.1	15.6	15.2
Rest of Eastern Norway	-	0.1	2.1	-	0.5	2.3	13.6	7.0	13.6
Agder	0.3	2.6	0.7	0.1	2.9	8.3	7.2	5.9	10.1
Rogaland	83.5	79.5	64.4	73.5	70.3	48.0	15.0	36.2	28.7
Western Norway	6.4	5.3	9.1	19.6	16.1	27.4	35.6	24.7	24.3
Trøndelag	6.4	4.0	4.1	-	-	0.3	10.7	9.9	6.3
Northern Norway	2.0	1.2	1.3	1.8	0.2	2.0	0.8	0.7	1.8
Total	100.0	100.0	100.0	100.0	100.0	100.0	100.0	100.0	100.0
Total employment ...	2.594	9.098	17.593	2.002	7.491	7.557	9.630	17.601	23.089

Source: The Directorate of Labour.

The second category mentioned in table 3, "Bases, transportation,
catering, administration etc." includes various services related to the
production and drilling activities. These activities provide so to speak
the physical connection between the offshore installations and the
mainland. Due to the costs of transportation the localization of the
supply activities is to a large extent determined by the localization of
the offshore installations which they are meant to serve. This may explain
the increasing number of employees in the supply activities in Western
Norway, and the large dispersion of employment in these activities in
general.

The last category "Construction and maintenance of platforms and supply vessels, etc.", include the production and maintenance of investment goods for the petroleum sector. The regional distribution of these activities is mainly determined by the distribution of the production capacity in shipbuilding and related industries. These enterprises are situated all along the coast. The geographical distribution of production and employment has not been stable over the years due to fluctuating offshore investment activity and competition between domestic and foreign enterprises. The small scale of the production units in Northern Norway may, in addition to the disadvantage of long distances to the offshore activities, explain their low share of production and employment in these activities.

The figures in table 3 give an illustration of the regional impacts of the petroleum activities, where only the direct deliveries of investment and intermediate goods are included. In the discussion in section 4 the full input-output effects are taken into consideration.

2.4. IMPACTS OF THE PETROLEUM ACTIVITIES IN ROGALAND

The high concentration of petroleum activities in Rogaland has brought about great changes in the industrial structure, and has contributed to a general increase in the economic activity in the region. Regional input-output analysis has indicated that in 1980 25.000-30.000 persons were directly and indirectly related to petroleum activities in Rogaland (Thorsen (1982)). This amount to almost 18 per cent of total employment in the county, according to table 2. In addition, the high profitability in the petroleum sector has lead to income inequality between those who are involved in the petroleum activities and those who are not.

The increase in local demand as a result of the petroleum activities has led to a considerable growth in industries producing for the local market. For example, the annual growth in employment in the service industries in Rogaland was 6.7 per cent from 1970 to 1980, while the corresponding figure was 4.6 per cent for the whole economy. In the construction industry the annual growth in employment in Rogaland and the whole country was 2.0 and -0.1 per cent, respectively.[2]

The increase in employment in petroleum related activities has been made possible partly by a significant immigration (see table 1) and partly by increased labour market participation. As a result of scarcity of labour in the expanding industries the wage level has increased more than in other regions. This has lead to reduced profitability and reduction in employment in enterprises where increased costs of production cannot easily be compensated for by corresponding increase in product prices. The extent of the transfer of labour between industries within Rogaland as compared to the rest of the country, is analysed in Hervik et.al. (1983).

3. NATIONAL SCENARIOS UNDERLYING THE REGIONAL ANALYSIS

Our analysis of future regional impacts of the petroleum activities rest heavily on assumptions concerning the long-term economic development at the national level. As a point of departure we have chosen two scenarios for the Norwegian economy over the period 1980-2000. These scenarios have been elaborated by a commission appointed by the government to analyse the various impacts of future petroleum activities, NOU (1983). The two scenarios are the reference scenario and a scenario that implies extensive domestic use of oil and gas revenues. The scenarios are based on calculations on the MSG model. The MSG model has for more than fifteen years been used as a tool in analysing the long-term economic development in Norway. It is characterized as a multisector growth model. The model calculates the development in the distribution of labour, capital and production over industries. In recent years the model has been used to analyse the impacts of petroleum activities and domestic use of oil and gas revenues, see Bjerkholt, Lorentsen and Strøm (1981). A brief description of the MSG model is given in the appendix.

Table 4 shows the development in employment as calculated in the two scenarios: the reference scenario and a scenario implying increased domestic use of petroleum revenues.

The reference scenario outlines an economic development towards the turn of the century that implies a lower rate of growth than in the past 20 years. This is due to the assumed reduction both in the rate of growth of employment and in productivity. The average annual growth in real GDP is estimated to less than 2 per cent for the period 1980-2000, while the average annual growth rate was close to 5 per cent in the period 1970-80.

Total labour supply is exogenously determined. The estimates are based on projections by the national labour supply model MATAUK. Full utilization of the projected labour supply is assumed.

From our point of view, the calculated development in employment in the various industries is of special interest. The projection results are summarized in the following:

- Continued decline in employment in agriculture, forestry and fishing is projected, but slower than in the period 1970-1980. The least decline is expected in fisheries.

- Continued decline is also projected in the manufacturing industries and particularly in those exposed to competition from abroad.

- A decline in employment is expected in the construction industry, in which there were a significant growth in employment in the 1970s.

- The growth in employment in transportation, electricity supply and private services is expected to continue.

- In wholesale and retail trade growth in employment is expected to slow down compared to the 1970s.

- A significant slow-down of growth in employment in government administration, compared to the period 1970-1980 is expected.

The production of oil and gas is assumed to be 65 mtoe in 1990 and 80 mtoe in the year 2000 . The oil price is estimated to USD 34 per barrel in the period 1982 to 1985. From then on a real price increase of 2 per cent per year is assumed. This imply relatively optimistic estimates of the future revenues from the petroleum activity. The domestic use of these revenues will affect the future industrial structure. The reference scenario implies an increasing surplus on the current account. Thus there is room for a more extensive domestic use of the oil revenues.

The scenario with increased domestic use of the oil revenues is based on the same assumptions about oil and gas production and prices, and thus the same development in the petroleum revenues as the reference scenario, but a lower rate of growth in the surplus on the current account is assumed. The increase in domestic income utilization is assumed to be evenly distributed between consumption and investment, and the private and public sector. About one third of the extra income to be used is assumed to be met by reduced traditional exports, and two thirds by increased imports.

An annual average increase in real GDP of 2.5 per cent from 1980 to year 2000 is calculated in this scenario. As a result of increased

domestic demand, an increase in labour participation rates, and thereby a
higher rate of growth in employment is assumed. Total domestic use of

Table 4. Employment by industry in Norway 1970-1980 and projected
employment for the period 1980-2000 by means of the MSG model.
Per cent annual average growth in man-years

| Industry | 1970-1980 | Per cent of total employ-ment in 1980 | 1980 - 2000 | |
			Reference scenario	Increased domestic use of petroleum revenues
Agriculture, forestry fishing	-3.4	8.1	-1.6	-2.2
Oil and gas production etc	-	0.5	5.4	5.4
Manufacture of machinery and equipment, incl. oil platform building	0.9	7.5	0.1	0.3
Other manufacturing industries	-0.6	14.9	-0.9	-0.5
Construction	0.9	8.5	-0.8	0.7
Ocean transport	-5.0	1.7	-1.3	-1.4
Public administration and defence	2.2	7.1	0.8	0.9
Other private and govern-ment services	2.6	51.7	1.5	1.8
Total	1.0	100.0	0.7	1.0

Source: National Accounts and NOU (1983).

goods and services is calculated to be about 17 per cent higher in the year
2000 than in the reference scenario.

As expected, this scenario shows a stronger decline in employment
in the export industries than the reference scenario. For the industries
exposed to foreign competition in the domstic market the situation is
different because part of the increased domestic demand is directed towards
their products. The result is that the estimated reduction in employment in
these industries is smaller than in the reference scenario.

For agriculture, forestry and fishing the decline in employment is
stronger than in the referece scenario, while there is little change in
employment in the sheltered manufacturing industries. In the construction
industry the decline in employment is turned to a moderate growth and in
the service sector there is a significantly faster growth in employment in
this scenario. Part of the growth in employment in the service industries
is assumed to be met by increased labour market participation, especially

for women. Withouth this, the changes in the future industrial structure compared to the reference scenario would have been larger.

4. ANALYSIS OF REGIONAL IMPACTS OF FUTURE PETROLEUM ACTIVITIES IN NORWAY

4.1. MODELS AND ASSUMPTIONS USED IN THE REGIONAL ANALYSIS

Our main model tool in the regional analysis is the REGION model, see Skoglund (1980). The REGION model is the first attempt to build a quantified multiregional model in the Central Bureau of Statistics. The model has been operational since 1979. The model is essentially a top-down model constructed to be used for regional breakdown analysis of national scenarios calculated by the MSG model. The overall objective in constructing this model has been to improve the coordination between national and regional economic planning. A survey of the structure of the regional calculations is given in figure 1.

REGION comprises about 30 industries and 20 regions. In addition there is a number of sectors for final categories of delivery. The industrial sector classification is the same as in the MSG model. The regional unit is the county. The basic theoretical approach used in the REGION model is regional input-output analysis within a commodity-by-industry framework. The sectors are linked by a subdivision of the commodity flows into intraregional flows (commodities which are used and produced in the same region), interregional flows (commodities produced in one region and used in another) and international flows (exports and imports). Constant input coefficients are assumed for each type of commodity flow. The production of each interregional commodity is delivered to a "pool of commodities", where each region has a fixed share of the total delivery of each commodity. Thus it is assumed that demand for interregional commodities from one region is met by the same regional pattern of supply as equivalant demand from another region. Diffusion of increased activity in one region to the neighbouring regions is as a result of this probably underestimated. The production of intraregional commodities is determined by regional demand. Private consumption in each region is determined by total value added in the region. It is further assumed that labour demand by industry and region is determined by the growth in production in the respective industry and region.

The regional development projected by REGION is to a large extent determined by the estimated regional pattern of production and commodity

214

flows in the base year and of the development in the national economy. Due to the assumption of fixed shares in the regional distribution of interregional commodities, the model calculations tend to generate only moderate changes in the regional industry pattern for those industries

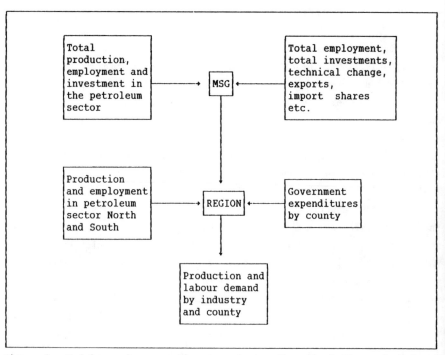

Figure 1. Models and assumptions used in the calculations of regional production and labour demand.

where the greatest part of the production is delivered out of the county. The regional forecasts for these industries will basically be a reflection of the same structural changes at the national level. Changes in these industries will, however, through the assumptions of the model, affect the development in the service industries and other industries who are primarily oriented towards the regional market. The same effects will follow from exogenous changes in the regional distribution of government expenditures and changes in the distribution of petroleum activities.

In the model calculations discussed in section 4.2 we have assumed that the regional distribution of parts of the government expenditures and employment is determined by regional population forecasts. The regional population growth and particularly the projected changes in age composition

is assumed to influence the regional development of health services and
education.

More attention has, however, been paid to the modelling of the
petroleum activities in REGION. In section 2 we discussed how the localization of the petroleum activities on the continental shelf would influence
the regional distribution of production of deliveries to the petroleum
sector. In the present analysis we have taken account of this in a very
simple way by dividing the petroleum activities on the Norwegian
continental shelf into a Southern and a Northern area. The line of
division corresponds roughly to the border between Southern and Northern
Norway. According to this division, the petroleum sector, as defined in
section 1, is divided into two production sectors, petroleum sector North
and South respectively. The two sectors are assumed to have the same input
structure, but the distribution of the production of supplies by region is
assumed to be different. It is also assumed that the distribution of the
employees by place of residence is different in the two sectors. Employment
and production are exogenously determined for the two sectors separately
and this enables us to study regional effects of changes in the
geographical pattern of petroleum activities on the continental shelf.

As to the production of intermediate goods and services, we have
assumed that 50 per cent of the total domestic deliveries to petroleum
sector North is produced in Northern Norway. Correspondingly, we assume
that 50 per cent of the employed in petroleum sector North live in Northern
Norway. We have very little empirical basis for estimating these shares.
If we allow for a time of transition for the adaption of enterprises in
Northern Norway to production for the petroleum sector, we nevertheless
believe that our estimates are within the range of possibility. As for
investments, we have made no particular assumptions about the share of
deliveries to petroleum sector North from North Norwegian enterprises.

No restrictions on the supply side (i.e. labour, capital, land) are
explicitly taken care of in the REGION model. Scarcity of land and labour
may for example put a limit to the growth in production in rapidly
expanding areas. As an attempt to compensate for this deficiency, we have
compared the estimated development in regional labour demand with
projections of the regional supply of labour. Our projections of labour
supply by region is a break-down of projections by the Norwegian national
labour supply model MATAUK. By using the latest Norwegian regional
population projections as the main framework and exogenous forecasts of
labour force participation rates and working hours, the growth in potential
labour supply by county is derived. Two sets of migration assumptions are

used, one alternative that disregard migration between counties and one
alternative based on a constant pattern of migration (estimated in the
period 1977-1980). The system of models used in the labour supply
projections are further described in the appendix.[3)]

4.2. MAIN RESULTS OF THE REGIONAL CALCULATIONS

Altogether three REGION scenarios for the period 1980-2000 are
considered. We label them A,B and C. They are based on the two projections for the national economy over the period 1980-2000 discussed in
section 3 and on our own assumptions about the distribution of production
and employment between the two petroleum sectors as briefly described in
table 5. Our scenarios A and B are based on the MSG reference scenario,
while our scenario C is based on the MSG scenario that implies extensive
domestic use of the oil and gas revenues. Scenario A and B differ only with
regard to the assumptions made about the regional development of the
petroleum activities. In scenario A we assume only moderate growth in
production and employment in the petroleum sector in the north. In scenario
B we assume that there will be a considerable expansion of the activity in
the north, and correspondingly reduced growth in production and employment
in the south. In scenario C the development in the petroleum sector is
assumed to be as in scenario A.

The structural changes in production and labour demand by industry
at the national level, as it is calculated by the MSG model, have decisive
influence on the regional projections of labour demand. Regions with a
considerable share of the employment in industries that are expanding in
the national (interregional) or international market, will get an increase
in the demand directed towards the local industries (intraregional
production), and thus an increase in the demand for labour from these
industries. There are, however, also differences in the development within
the same industry in different regions due to differences in the input
structure and composition of production.

The most striking results in scenario A as they appear from table
6, are probably the relatively high rate of growth in labour demand in
Oslo/Akershus and Rogaland, and the low rate of growth in the remaining
part of Eastern Norway. Oslo/Akershus is expected to maintain an
approximately constant number of employed in the manufacturing industries.
This region also has a considerable share of employment in the expanding
private and government services. In the last decade, however, the

Table 5. The main assumptions of the three scenarios

Scenario	Petroleum activity in Northern Norway	Development of the current account	Development in total employment
A (Reference)	Moderate growth in exploration, no production before year 2000	Increasing surplus, that is, moderate domestic use of the petroleum revenues	Moderate growth
B (Increased petroleum activities in Northern Norway,	Intensification of exploration activities, production starts be-fore year 2000. Northern Norway has 50 per cent share in em-ployment and deliveries of intermediate goods	As A	As A
C (Increased domestic use of petroleum revenues)	As A	Slower growth of surplus	Faster growth due to increased labour market participation rates

Table 6. Projections of labour demand and labour supply by region 1980-2000. Per cent annual average growth in man-years

Region	Labour demand			Labour supply		
	Reference scenario Scenario A	Increased petro-leum activi-ties in Northern Norway Scenario B	Increased domestic use of petro-leum revenues Scenario C	No mig-ration	Migra-tion rates as in 1977-80	Increased labour market partici-pation rates, no migration
Oslo/ Akershus	1.0	1.0	1.4	0.3	0.5	0.6
Rest of Eastern Norway	0.3	0.3	0.7	0.5	0.7	0.8
Agder	0.8	0.8	1.0	0.9	1.1	1.3
Rogaland	0.9	0.9	1.1	1.1	1.3	1.4
Western Norway	0.8	0.8	1.0	0.9	0.6	1.2
Trøndelag	0.5	0.5	0.8	0.8	0.7	1.1
Northern Norway	0.5	0.6	0.7	1.0	0.6	1.3
Total	0.7	0.7	1.0	0.7	0.7	1.0

Oslo/Akershus region has had a lower rate of growth in employment than should be expected from the industrial structure. If this trend prevails in the future, the model calculations will probably tend to overestimate the rate of growth in labour demand in this region.

The main cause of the high rate of growth in labour demand in Rogaland is the petroleum activities. In addition to the assumed growth in labour demand in the petroleum sector, Rogaland has got a large share of the deliveries of goods and services to the petroleum sector, such as building of ships and oil platforms, and various kinds of services. The growth in production in these activities leads, through the intraregional input-output relationships and a regional multiplier process, to a further growth in the regional demand for labour.

The low rate of growth in labour demand in Eastern Norway except Oslo/Akershus, may at least to some extent, be explained by a combination of the extensive decline in labour demand in agriculture and a disadvantegous composition of the manufacturing industries. This negative development in the basic industries further leads to a low rate of growth in labour demand from the service industries.

Agder and Western Norway also benefit from the petroleum activities, although to a less extent than Rogaland. Besides, the rather moderate decline in labour demand in fishing compared to agriculture underlying the national scenarios, implies a relative advantage for these coastal regions compared to the inland regions in Eastern Norway.

In Trøndelag, as well as in Northern Norway only a moderate rate of growth in total labour demand is projected. In Trøndelag, there is a considerable decline in the labour demand from agriculture. The main positive factors are the rather constant labour demand from manufacturing of machinery and equipment and the growth in labour demand from building of ships and oil platforms. The projected development in Northern Norway is discussed in the next section.

The northward shift in the petroleum activities that is assumed to take place in scenario B, leads, as expected to increased growth in the total demand for labour in Northern Norway. The projected regional pattern of development is, however, not much changed. As in scenario A, a relatively high rate of growth is projected in Rogaland while the growth in Northern Norway still is lower than the national average. These rather minor reallocation effects are mainly related to the fact that Rogaland and the rest of Southern Norway will be important suppliers of goods and services to the petroleum activities in Northern Norway.

Scenario C is based on the MSG scenario where domestic use of the

petroleum revenues is assumed to increase. At the national level, a higher
rate of growth in the manufacturing industries is calculated. At the same
time, there is an increase in labour demand from the manufacturing
industries producing for the home market at the expence of those producing
for exports (except the petroleum sector). All regions seem to benefit
from this development. The largest increase in the rate of growth in
labour demand compared to the reference scenario is calculated to be found
in Eastern Norway. It seems like this region benefit from the higher rate
of growth in import-competing industries. Besides, Eastern Norway, and
particularly Oslo/Akershus, has considerable employment in construction and
other service industries, and are consequently influenced by the prospects
of increased national growth in these sectors. According to our calculations, Western and Northern Norway are the regions that comparatively will
have the least advantage of the increased use of petroleum revenues.

If we compare the estimated labour demand in scenario A and B with
the labour supply projections, it appears that in the case of no migration,
there will be excess supply of labour in all regions except in
Oslo/Akershus. If we assume that a migration pattern as estimated in the
period 1977-1980 is maintained, this leads to a positive net migration from
Northern and Western to Southern and Eastern Norway. The excess supply of
labour is by this reduced in Western Norway, Trøndelag and Northern Norway
and increased in Eastern Norway except Oslo/Akershus, and in Agder and
Rogaland. Still, there is a lack of balance between Oslo/Akershus and the
rest of Eastern Norway. This is at present, and will probably also in the
future, be compensated for by extensive commuting to Oslo/Akershus from the
surrounding regions.

The labour supply projections based on increased labour market
participation rates, imply only small changes in the regional distribution
of labour supply. Comparing with the projected labour demand in scenario C
we can see from table 6 that the most significant imbalances arise in
Oslo/Akershus and Northern Norway. It seems that the growth in total
employment underlying this scenario can only by achieved by migration from
Northern Norway to Oslo/Akershus or by a strengthening of the economic
development in Northern Norway at the expence of Oslo/Akershus.

4.3. PROJECTED LABOUR DEMAND IN NORTHERN NORWAY

From table 7 it appears that all three scenarios imply a considerable reduction in labour demand in the manufacturing industries in

Northern Norway. There is also a reduction in labour demand from agriculture, forestry and fishing. The decline in the construction industry projected in the MSG reference scenario has extensive impacts for Northern Norway, where it is a rather important industry[4].

The impacts for Northern Norway of a northward shift in the petroleum activities can be seen by a comparison of projected labour demand in scenario A and B. For the manufacturing industries, scenario B implies a reduced decline in labour demand compared to scenario A, of altogether 600 man-years over the projection period 1980-2000. In addition an increase of 1 100 man-years carried out in the petroleum sector by persons who have their place of residence in Northern Norway is assumed. However, the total increase in labour demand is higher, due to the increased rate of growth in the service industries. A possible explanation of the relatively small increase in labour demand from the manufacturing industries due to the northward shift in the petroleum activities, is that the internal deliveries within the region are limited, so that the cumulative effects within the region of deliveries to the petroleum sector are small. Besides, we have assumed that no production of investment goods will take place in Northern Norway. In the case of such production, the increase in labour demand may amount to several thousand man-years. Existing production capacity and technology to undertake such assignments is limited. This kind of employment would moreover mainly be of a temporary character, resulting in fluctuations in the regional demand for labour.

For Northern Norway, scenario C imply the same development in total labour demand from the manufacturing industries as scenario A. There is, however, a redistribution of the labour demand from "Other manufacturing industries" to the manufacturing of machinery and equipment. In the construction and service industries there is a considerable increase in the rate of growth in demand for labour.

Compared to scenario A and B this scenario imply the highest rate of growth of labour demand in Northern Norway. At the same time, however, Northern Norway's share in the growth in labour demand at the national level is smaller than in the two other scenarios. The main reason for this is that the share of employment in the manufacturing industries that are expanding at the national level is small, at the same time as a further decline in labour demand from agriculture and fishing takes place.

It seems that with maintenance of the present pattern of migration, petroleum activity off the coast of Northern Norway may, according to our calculations, contribute to a more balanced development in the labour market in this part of the country. However, the impact of the petroleum

activity is limited, and the rate of growth in labour supply still exceeds
the rate of growth in labour demand. If out-migration is not allowed for,
the calculated excess supply of labour in Northern Norway is considerable.
It seems that the ability and opportunity of North Norwegian enterprises to

Table 7.   Employment by industry in Northern Norway in 1970 - 1980 and
           projected change in labour demand 1980 - 2000. Man-years

Industry	1970-1980	1980-2000		
		Reference scenario	Increased petroleum activities in Northern Norway	Increased domestic use of petroleum revenues
		Scenario A	Scenario B	Scenario C
Agriculture, fishing and forestry	-16 100	-5 400	-5 200	-7 700
Oil and gas pro- duction etc.	300	400	1 500	400
Manufacture of machinery and equip- ment, incl. oil platform building, etc.	2 300	-600	-200	-300
Other manufacturing industries	3 500	-5 300	-5 100	-5 600
Construction	2 200	-2 500	-2 500	2 300
Ocean transport	-2 900	-600	-600	-800
Public administration and defence	5 900	2 700	2 700	2 900
Other private and government services	28 700	29 900	31 200	32 900
Total	23 900	18 600	21 800	24 100
Per cent share of national growth	14.3	7.6	8.9	6.6

Source: Unpublished employment statistics from the Central Bureau of
        Statistics.

undertake assignments from the petroleum sector will be decisive for the
possibility that the petroleum activities will contribute to a balanced
development in the labour market in Northern Norway. In the production
phase, which we, in scenario B assume has just started at the end of the
projection period, the possibilities of increased participation from North
Norwegian enterprises should be better. First of all, this phase lasts
longer (up to 20-30 years), and the offshore installations require regular
deliveries of various goods and services, and thereby offer permanent

employment to a number of people.

The calculated increase in labour demand in scenario C is far from sufficient to balance the increase in labour supply in Northern Norway. The result of this imbalance will probably be increased out- migration and/or increased unemployment in Northern Norway, if not a significant economic growth in this part of the country takes place. Regional unemployment, hidden or open, may imply that the assumptions made at the national level about labour market participation rates and employment, may not be realized.

5. CONCLUSIONS

Two main conclusions may be drawn from our analysis:

- Extension of the petroleum activities to the coast off Northern Norway will diminish the projected imbalance in the labour market in this part of the country. However, in order to attain a reduced out-migration compared to the present figures, it is necessary that the participation of North Norwegian enterprises and labour in the petroleum activities is considerably higher than we have assumed in our calculations.

- Our analysis also indicates that rural regions will benefit comparatively less from increased domestic use of oil and gas revenues that the central regions. This is mainly due to the concentration of the service industries in more central, densely populated regions.

In our discussion of the prospects for regional economic development, we have paid little attention to the possible effects of regional policies. A balanced growth in different parts of the country is considered to be highly desirable and several policy instruments are available in order to influence the regional distribution of production and employment.

The models used in the regional analysis are not very sophisticated from a theoretical point of view. The lack of relationships describing the adaptions of persons and companies within a regional framework is evident. The main advantage is that national consistency is taken care of.

Our analysis is based on independent regional projections of what we have called "demand" and "supply" of labour. The regional demand projections are derived from industry forecasts and the regional supply projections are derived from populations forecasts. This approach raises some important problems of interpretations. On the supply side this problem is closely linked to the problem of defining labour force and labour force participation rates. The definition underlying our model calculations is based on the common statistical definition which excludes socalled "hidden employment" etc. It is obvious, however, that the defintion of labour force is not independent of the demand side of the labour market. The projection of labour market participation rates should be considered in the light of the projected economic development. This is to some extent done in the national scenarios, but not in the regional calculations.

On the demand side it may be argued that the regional distribution of production and employment also depends on the labour supply pattern. A region with excess supply of labour will tend to attract new firms while scarcity of labour may put a limit on the economic growth in other regions. An appropriate treatment of these effects is only possible within a model where regional labour demand and supply are determined simultaneously.

APPENDIX: THE MAIN FEATURES OF THE MODELS USED IN THE ANALYSIS

THE MSG MODEL

The MSG model traces out the long-term growth paths of the economy, especially the distribution of labour, capital and production over about 30 industries, the changes in household consumption patterns, and the development in the corresponding equilibrium prices.

For each industry the input coefficients of labour, capital, energy and other materials are determined by cost minimization. The mix of oil products and electricity as energy inputs is also determined endogenously from relative prices. For each industry there is assumed to be a trend of technical change. The equilibrium commodity prices are then determined by unit costs taking into account the repercussions through input-output relationships.

On the quantity side the allocation of production by industry is determined by the final demand where exports and government expenditures are exogenous and household consumption and private gross investment endogenous. Imports are calculated from import shares differentiated by commodity and purchasing industry.

Industry demand for capital and labour services per unit of output is derived through cost minimization. Private gross investment is determined in a closed loop with the scale of production by industry. The scale of production determines capital services and capital stock by industry. Fixed capital composition within each sector then determines private gross investment by commodity.

For given prices the commodity composition of household consumption depends only on its total which is determined so that total capacity use is ensured.

The model thus depicts an economy at full (or specified) capacity utilisation. The main variables given exogenously are the total labour force, the rate of return on capital, the parameters of technical change, and the exogenous components of final demand.

THE REGION MODEL

The REGION model comprises basically the same industries and consumption sectors as the MSG model. The regional unit used in the model is county. With 20 regions (19 counties and a dummy region for non-regionalized activities) and about 30 industries the model gives a rather disaggregate description of the Norwegian economy. The counties are comparatively small regional units, the population varies between 80.000 and 450.000. The main reason for choosing counties as regional units in the model is that the counties as administrative units have become of increasing importance in regional planning in Norway. This approach creates, however, serious problems in the modelling of interregional linkages.

The basic theoretical approach used in the REGION model is regional input-output within a commodity-by-industry framework. The model contains no price relationships. For each industry in all regions we assume fixed proportions between input and output of commodities. The industries and regions are linked by a subdivision of the commodity flows in intraregional flows (commodities produced and used in the same region), interregional flows (commodities produced in one region and used in another region), and international flows (exports and imports). Constant input coefficients

are assumed for each type of commodity flow. The input coefficients are
differentiated by commodity, industry and region. The production of intraregional commodities is determined by the regional demand. The production
of interregional commodities is determined by the assumption of constant
regional shares for each commodity. The model does not specify interregional commodity flows between pairs of regions, but it is assumed that
demand in all regions is met by the same regional pattern of supply.
Exports are exogenously given on the national level and distributed to
regions according to estimated market shares. The import figures
calculated by constant import shares are adjusted by given national import
figures.

Private consumption and investment are also specified by region and
in different ways linked to the regional production activities. Private
consumption is assumed to be determined by the total value added in the
regions. In the case of private gross investment, national figures are
exogenously given in each industry and subdivided to regions according to
production shares calculated in the model. The consumption and investment
in central and local government are exogenously given in each region. It is
furthermore assumed that the labour demand in each regional industry is
determined by the calculated growth in production and exogenously given
growth in labour productivity. Some industries (among them ocean transport
and petroleum activities on the continental shelf) are not entirely regio-
nalized but intermediate demand, investment and labour demand are exogenously given and allocated to regions according to estimated shares.

The national accounts by county, which have been constructed by the
Central Bureau of Statistics for the years 1973, 1976 and 1980, are the
main empirical bases for estimating the coefficients of the model. The
regional accounts are constructed by breakdown of national figures and give
complete input-output tables by county on a very disaggregate industrial
level (about 180 industries and 300 commodities). In order to estimate the
interregional and international trade relations in the model, we have
applied an indirect method. Our approach has been to utilize national
coefficients on the disaggregate industrial level of the accounts and by
aggregation to the industrial level of the model, we obtain structural
differences between regions.

As a consequence of the top-down approach most of the exogenous
variables in the REGION model are either exogenous or endogenous in the MSG
model. Exogenous variables are only specified on a regional level for
central and local government expenditures and for petroleum activities
concerning the distribution between south and north. For some variables

national consistency are obtained by an adjustment technique.   The main endogenous variables in the model are production and labour demand diffe-rentiated by industry and county.

THE MODELS AND ASSUMPTIONS USED IN THE REGIONAL LABOUR SUPPLY PROJECTIONS

The projections of regional labour supply used in this paper are the first results from a submodel in an integrated system of models for regional economic and demographic projections called DRØM. This model system, not yet fully operational, will project migration on basis of relative labour market tightness of the counties. The REGION model will later on be more closely linked to this model system. The now operational submodel of regional labour supply is here used to calculate independent labour supply projections for the counties, based on given regional pro-jection of population by age and sex. The regional labour supply projec-tions are furthermore based on a top-down approach using national projec-tions from the MATAUK model as exogenous variables. MATAUK is the labour supply model of the Central Bureau of Statistics and this model is also used in the process of determining the exogenous assumptions of labour force and labour supply in the MSG model.

The structure of the models and assumptions used in the labour supply projections is outlined in figure 2. The regional population model is of standard cohort survival type. Demographic transition rates are estimated on data from the current population register of Norway.   The latest available projections are based on two alternatives concerning migration. One alternative disregard migration, in the other alternative the pattern of migration is assumed to remain the same as observed in the base period 1977 - 1980. Both the national labour supply projection and its regional breakdown are consistent with the latest regional population projections made by the Central Bureau of Statistics.

The MATAUK model projects labour force and hours supplied by one-year age groups, sex, education (129 groups) and marital status (for women). Exogenous variables and parameters are:

- Population by age and sex
- The distribution of the women by marital status
- Rates of transition between educational groups
- Labour force participation rates and hours worked per member

of the labour force

In MATAUK, the distribution of women by marital status is taken from a model assuming fixed transition rates on the 1979 level. Fixed transition rates between educational statuses are also assumed. The MATAUK projections used by us are based on trends in the labour force participation rates and hours worked. These trends are calculated for the 1976-81 period, but are assumed to level out through the projection period.

The regional projections of the DRØM submodel gives labour force and hours supplied by county, one-year age groups, sex, education (4 groups) and marital status (2 groups of women). Exogenous variables and parameters are:

- Population by county, age and sex
- Proportions of the population by age and sex on the national level belonging to each group of educational and marital status
- National labour force participation rates and hours worked
- Regional marriage rates
- Parameters giving regional relative differences in proportions of the population belonging to each educational group
- Parameters giving regional relative differences in labour participation rates and hours worked

Most of these variables are supposed to be supplied from the other models mentioned. The sets of regional differences are taken from analysis of the 1980 population census.

Figure 2. Models and assumptions used in the regional labour supply
           projections

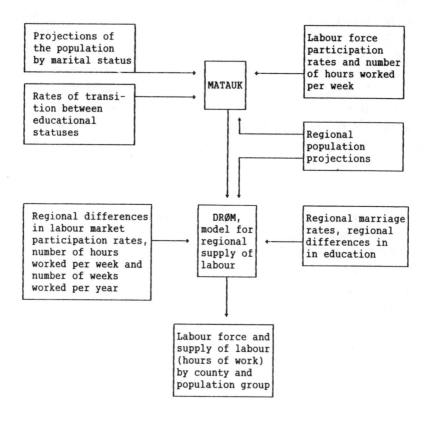

NOTES

1) All figures from The Directorate of Labour.

2) Source: Unpublished employment statistics from the Central Bureau of
    Statistics.

3) The projections of regional labour supply have been prepared by
    Knut Ø. Sørensen in the Central Bureau of Statistics.

4) More details on the calculated development in Northern Norway are
    reported in Schreiner and Skoglund (1984).

REFERENCES

Bjerkholt, O., L. Lorentsen and S. Strøm (1981): "Using the Oil and Gas Revenues: The Norwegian Case." In T. Barker and V. Brailovsky: <u>Oil or Industry?</u> Academic Press, London 1981. Also as Artikler from the Central Bureau of Statistics, No. 133.

Hervik, A.,A. Sæther and O. Hauge (1983): <u>"Regional-økonomiske perspektiv på valg av utvinningstempo i Nordsjøen."</u> Report No. 8301 from Møreforskning.

NOU (1983):Det framtidige omfanget av petroleumsvirksomheten pa norsk sokkel. Norges offentlige utredninger, NOU 1983: 27.

Schreiner, A. and T. Skoglund (1984): <u>"Virkninger av oljevirksomhet i Nord-Norge."</u> Reports from the Central Bureau of Statistics, No. 84/17.

Skoglund, T. (1980): <u>"REGION. En modell for regional kryssløpsanalyse."</u> Artikler from the Central Bureau of Statistics, No. 122.

Thorsen, I.(1982): "En regional kryssløpsmodell for Rogaland." Unpublished thesis at the University of Oslo.

7210
4313 ?
1132 ?
1322
7230   U.K.

231 - 47

THE WEALTH EFFECT OF NORTH SEA OIL

BY

HOMA MOTAMEN

ABSTRACT

This paper puts forward a methodology for analysing the impact of alternative oil depletion policies at national level. This is done by developing a long run macroeconomic model and combining it with the method of optimal control. The model presented here is formulated with special reference to North Sea oil in the UK, but it can be applied, with the necessary modifications, to determine depletion strategies to any oil-rich economy with a flexible exchange rate.

1. INTRODUCTION

There seems to be a tendency to determine the rate of oil extraction independently of the decisions to invest the proceeds of the resource. In this paper a general framework is set out, whereby these two important policy variables can be analysed jointly. The methodology proposed is one of optimal control theory combined with a long-run macroeconomic model of an industrial oil-producing country. The model developed here is structured with special reference to the UK economy but it can be applied, with the necessary modifications, to any industrialized economy having a flexible exchange rate.

The analytical solutions to this planning model are shown in this paper. They are determined through a simultaneous solution of the problem.

O.Bjerkholt & E. Offerdal, eds., Macroeconomic Prospects for a Small Oil Exporting Country. ISBN 90-247-3183-6.
Copyright 1985, Martinus Nijhoff Publishers, Dordrecht.

The model is an open economy one and the objective is global maximization of non-oil wealth, which in turn implies that the economy has a choice between investing at home and overseas. Since the problem is a dynamic one, the proper allocation of the resource involves determing when and where to invest, that is, when to invest overseas and when to invest at home. Here the problem of absorption capacity of the economy for a newly-acquired revenue, namely oil, becomes relevant. This can be achieved through the method of optimal control where the allocation of the resource between the home and overseas sectors is checked against the final target.

2. STRUCTURE OF THE MACROECONOMIC MODEL OF THE UK

The macroeconomic model formulated here is a fairly aggregate one, comprising seventeen equations, which explain the overall structure of the British economy. It is an open-economy model designed to bring out the role of the newly-developed petroleum sector and to highlight its potential in influencing directly and indirectly the rest of the economy. The model is essentially a long-run model, given the specific nature of the problem posed in this study. The time period under consideration is roughly two-and-a-half decades, which is assumed to span the life of North Sea oil. There are altogether seven identities and ten behavioural equations in the macroeconomic model as shown below and we shall explain each equation individually.

The economy is broken down into three main sectors: oil, non-oil domestic and non-oil overseas. Although the size of the oil sector is substantially smaller than that of the non-oil, it was necessary to draw the distinction in order to carry out a planning exercise for the proceeds of the resource. Equation (1) which is the first of the identities, gives the national income as the sum of output from these sectores. More specifically, gross national income at market prices, N_t, comprises:

(i)   gross domestic non-oil value-added at factor cost, D_t, plus expenditure taxes on non-oil output, 1_t^{11}, to give gross domestic product at market prices;

(ii) value-added in the oil sector at market prices, P_t; and

(iii) net income from overseas, F_t.

The reasons for expressing P_t at market prices will become more clear after equation (4) has been explained.

Equation (2) depicts an aggregate production function of the economy outside the petroleum sector. The non-oil domestic output, D_t, is shown as a non-linear function of the lagged values of capital, K_t, and labour, L_t. It is assumed that in the long run the production function exhibits decreasing returns to scale with respect to the capital stock variable. This is portrayed by restricting the value of the exponent of the capital stock to less than one. This restriction on the exponent of the capital variable is imposed here, for it is believed to characterize the UK economy best, in the light of the many obstacles it faces in the way of production, such as work stoppages at different production levels and various industrial and labour problems. As a result, ceteris paribus, the proportional increases in output decline as more of the capital input is added. Technical progress is also built into the production function and is formulated as an increasing function of time.

Raw materials used in the domestic production are postulated to be proportional to the level of current non-oil domestic output. This is shown in equation (3) whereby as output rises the demand for raw material increases. The value of output generated in the oil sector, P_t, is given by equation (4) as the product of the oil price, π_t, and the quantity of oil produced, q_t. The price of oil is taken as an exogenous variable.

Since the UK is not a member of the price-setting cartel, OPEC, it is thought best to regard the economy as a "pricetaker".[1] Equation (4) also has an added identity attached to it which splits total oil revenue into two parts:[2] the public sector share of oil, l_t^1, and the private sector, namely the companies' share of oil P_t^c.

While q_t, is a flow variable determining the rate of extraction of crude oil, Q_t is the stock variable which measures the volume of oil reserves beneath the North Sea floor. Equation (5) is a first order difference equation which gives the volume of production in each time period as the change in reserves over two consecutive time periods. So the volume of reserves in the last time period, Q_{t-1}, less the level of oil extracted this period, together determine the current volume of reserves remaining in the sea bed, Q_t. With a fixed level of reserves, Q_0, this would imply that if there is any production in a given time period, say t, by definition Q_t would be larger than Q_{t+1}. We shall explain later how q_t is used as a control variable and Q as a state variable in our Optimal Control model.

The public sector share of oil revenue comprises royalties, corporation tax, and petroleum revenue tax (PRT) and advanced petroleum revenue tax.[3] This makes the government revenue from this sector a function of oil output, oil prices and the exchange rate.[4] The relationship is presented in equation (6).

Gross domestic fixed capital formation, I_t, is expressed as changes in capital stock from one period to the next - equation (7). This is shown by means of a first order difference eqation. Capital stock, K_t, and investment are both measured as "gross" to avoid complications over calculations of the appropriate depreciation rates. Not only has estimation of depreciation been a controversial and unresolved question, it is also of no direct relevance to the problem we are studying. It should be noted that the variable I_t, embraces investment in the non-oil sector only and excludes any capital expenditure in the petroleum sector. Moreover, I_t applies essentially to productive investment. This implies that the flow of investment in our model comprises two specific categories:

(a)   direct investment to establish productive capacity and raise total domestic output, such as investment in manufacturing plants or agricultural machinery;

(b)   investment on productive infrastructure to facilitate the expansion of direct investment. This serves indirectly to raise productive capacity, for example through construction of more roads, electricity plants, renovating port facilities and warehouses.

Investment on social infrastructure is not, however, included in I_t. Expenditure to meet social needs, such as hospitals and schools, are included in the item public sector expenditure, G_t. This classification is used here on the argument that although social infrastructure may be a prerequisite of productive investment, its existence does not necessarily imply that productive investment will be induced. Therefore, the incremental output-capital ratio in this model is applicable only to items (a) and (b) above and not to social infrastructure. [5]

Investment in the oil sector is treated separately. It is assumed as exogenous to the model, for the firms investing in the North Sea are mainly multinational companies. Their capital accordingly, is not necessarily UK owned, and is supplied from their profits made in different parts of the world. Such capital would be regarded as part of their international assets. Thus capital expenditure in the petroleum sector enters the model as an exogenous variable through equation (6) where government receipts from oil is computed. Here the companies' investment expenditure is offset against their revenue in calculating their tax liabilities to the government.

Equation (8) gives net income from abroad, F_t, as a function of the portfolio of assets overseas during the previous period, E_{t-1}. Overseas income rises in constant proportion, θ, to overseas assets in the previous period. E_t in this context includes debts which would be negative assets. F_t, accordingly, can take positive or negative values.

The net change in foreign assets from one period to the next is shown in equation (9) as the balance of payments on the current account, B_t. Although this assumption may not necessarily hold in the short run, it is perfectly valid in the context of our model, as we are considering the relationship over a long period.

Equation (11) depicts a simple long-run consumption function which gives aggregate private consumption as dependent on disposable income. The latter is defined as the sum of domestic non-oil income, less income-related taxes, l_t^{111}, and net income from abroad. This formulation is based on the classic permanent income hypothesis which conforms with the long-run nature of the model. It could be argued that the consumption function should include the revenue from the oil sector, P_t, as one of its explanatory variables. However, although the oil sector may affect the size of its peculiar characteristics it has little direct influence. The components of P_t are shown in equation (4) to consist of the public sector share, l_t^1, and the oil companies' share, P_t^c. Due to the multinational nature of the oil companies, most of their revenue tends to flow abroad and to become distributed among their various bases overseas. The only accountable part of this revenue that would remain in the UK would be payments to British labour employed and payments to the non-oil UK industries providing inputs to the North Sea oil industry. The former category of payments, though small, is likely to have more of an indirect effect and its inclusion in the consumption function is likely to cause greater inaccuracy than its omission.

The volume of income-related taxes l_t^{111}, and that of the expenditure tax, l_t^{11}, are determined through equations (12) and (13) respectively. The former is directly proportional to the sum of the values of non-oil domestic income and non-oil overseas income. [6] This fixed proportion is shown by means of coefficient ε.

Equation (14) is simply a rearrangement of the national income accounting identity. It defines the balance of payments on the current account, B_t, as the residual of net national income minus aggregate expenditure. Suffice it to say that the components of expenditure constitute aggregate domestic demand. It should also be noted that B_t is a composite term of visible and invisible exports and imports.

Equation (15) is another identity, which defines total imports M_t, as the difference between total exports, X_t, and the balance of payments on the current account. Total exports are then further subdivided into non-oil exports, V_t, and the share of oil which is exported. The value of oil

Table 1. Notations used in the macroeconomic model   (i) Variables

N_t	=	Gross national income
D_t	=	Value added in the non-oil sector at factor cost
P_t	=	Value added in the oil sector, market prices
F_t	=	Income from abroad
K_t	=	Fixed capital stock gross
I_t	=	Gross non-oil fixed capital formation
L_t	=	Labour input
R_t	=	Raw materials used in domestic production
π_t	=	International price of crude oil
Q_t	=	Stock of oil reserves
q_t	=	Quantity of crude oil extracted annually from North Sea
1_t^1	=	Total government take from North Sea oil
1_t^{11}	=	Expenditure tax
1_t^{111}	=	Income-related tax
P_t^c	=	Company share of value added of oil
E_t	=	Stock of assets abroad
C_t	=	Personal consumption
B_t	=	Current account balance (changes in reserves)
G_t	=	Government expenditure
X_t	=	Total exports
V_t	=	Non-oil exports
S_t	=	Effective exchange rate
h_t	=	Rate of change of effective exchange rate

exported is a "net" concept, and it is net of the foreign oil imported in the UK. ω is taken to be a constant parameter over the time horizon under consideration. This may not be a true situation and the value of net exports may change during the life of the North Sea oil. Therefore, although in the first instance we will consider a constant parameter, fluctuations in this parameter can be examined in the context of this model.

Equation (16) is a behavioural equation expressing non-oil exports as a non-linear function of the last period's effective exchange rate, S_{t-1}. The underlying assumption behind this relationship is that non-oil exports move inversely with the exchange rate, so that as the latter rises in any period, the quantity of the former falls in the next period and vice versa. It is thus postulated that the first derivative of this equation is negative.

(ii)   Parameters

g	=	Scale variable in the production function
β	=	Rate of technical progress
α	=	Elasticity of response for capital
γ	=	Elasticity of response for labour
ξ	=	Raw materials used as a proportion of current output
θ	=	Yield on investment overseas
η	=	Average propensity to consume
ε	=	Coefficient of income-related tax
ω	=	Proportion of oil exported
σ	=	Coefficient of expenditure tax
m_0, m_1	=	Parameters of the export equation
ℓ_0, ℓ_1, ℓ_2	=	Parameters of the foreign exchange equation
♦	=	Essential imported share of raw materials used in non-oil production
μ	=	Essential imported share of aggregate consumption
v_0	=	a combination of parameters σ, η and ε defined as $(v_0 \equiv 1 + \sigma\eta - \varepsilon\sigma\eta - \eta + \varepsilon\eta)$ to facilitate exposition of argument
v_1	=	a combination of parameters σ, η, ε and μ defined as $(1 + \sigma\eta(1+\varepsilon) - \eta(1-\varepsilon) + \mu\eta(1-\varepsilon)]$ to facilitate exposition of a argument
v_2	=	$v_1 + \phi\xi$ (by definition)

(iii) The macroeconomic model

(1) $N_t = D_t + 1_t^{11} + P_t + F_t$

(2) $D_t = g(1+\beta)^t K_{t-1}^\alpha L_{t-1}^\gamma$ $\quad\quad \beta \geqslant 0 \quad 0 < \alpha < 1 \quad 0 < \gamma < 1$

(3) $R_t = \varepsilon D_t$

(4) $P_t = \pi_t q_t \equiv 1_t^1 + P_t^c$

(5) $q_t = Q_{t-1} - Q_t$

(6) $1_t^1 = f(q_t, P_t, S_t)^*$

(7) $I_t = K_t - K_{t-1}$

(8) $F_t = \theta E_{t-1}$ $\quad\quad \theta > 0$

(9) $E_t = B_t + [E_{t-1}/(1 + h_t)]$

(10) $h_t = \dfrac{S_t - S_{t-1}}{S_{t-1}}$

(11) $C_t = \eta(D_t - 1_t^{111} + F_t) \equiv \eta(1-\varepsilon)(D_t + F_t)$

(12) $1_t^{111} = \varepsilon(D_t + F_t)$

(13) $1_t^{11} = \sigma C_t$

(14) $B_t = N_t - C_t - I_t - G_t$

(15) $M_t = X_t - B_t \equiv V_t + \omega P_t - B_t$

(16) $V_t = m_0 S_{t-1}^{m_1}$ $\quad\quad \dfrac{dV_t}{dS_{t-1}} < 0$

(17) $S_t = \Omega_0 + \Omega_1 (\pi_t q_t)^{\Omega_2}$ $\quad\quad \dfrac{dS_t}{dq_t} > 0$

* The formula for total government take from the oil sector is applied.

Movements in the effective exchange rate have in turn been related to the volume of oil revenue. Equation (17) determines this relationship through a non-linear function with a positive first derivative and a negative second derivative. It is assumed to have a fairly substantial positive intercept on the basis that clearly the exchange rate will be positive even when total oil revenue is zero.

In constructing this dynamic model it is assumed that investment is correctly allocated to match the economy's pattern of demand. It was pointed out before that, to study the planning strategy for North Sea oil revenue, we used the method of Optimal Control. The procedure for applying this method involved two stages. First a macroeconomic model of the UK economy had to be built, which we already explained. Second the problem had to be formulated in such a way that it could be applied to the technique of Optimal Control. In other words an explicit economic target and certain intertemporal constraints had to be expressed.

The optimization problem can be formally stated as:

$$\text{Max} \sum_{t=1}^{T} I_t + \sum_{t=1}^{T} B_t$$

Subject to

(18) $\quad B_t \leqslant X_t - \phi R_t - \mu C_t$

$Q_T \geqslant 0$

$I_t \geqslant 0 \quad q_t \geqslant 0$

The state variables are K_t, E_t and Q_t. The control variables are I_t, and q_t; and the exogenous variables are π_t, L_t and G_t. The remaining variables are endogenous.

3. REDUCED FORM OF THE MODEL

The reduced form of the model is obtained by expressing the entire model, the equations of motion and the constraints, in terms of the state, control and exogenous variables (Motamen (1983)).

The optimal control problem can be restated as:

$$\text{Max} \sum_{t=1}^{T} I_t + \sum_{t=1}^{T} [- I_t + v_0(D_t + F_t) + \pi_t q_t - G_t]$$

subject to

$$v_2 D_t + v_1 F_t - I_t - m_0 \left[\Omega_0 + \Omega_1 (\pi_t q_t)^{\Omega_2}\right]^{m_1} + (1 - \omega)\pi_t q_t - G \leqslant 0$$

and

(18a) $\left(-\sum_{t=1}^{T} q_t + Q_0\right) \geqslant 0$

where

$$I_t \geqslant 0 \qquad q_t \geqslant 0 \qquad \text{for } t = 1, \ldots, T$$

Setting the Lagrangian, W, we introduce λ_{1t} as the Lagrange multiplier associated with the first constraint in time period t and λ_2 as the Lagrange multiplier associated with the second constraint. Note that the second Lagrange multiplier does not have time as its subscript because λ_2 is related to only one time period, which is the terminal period.

4. THE ANALYTICAL SOLUTIONS

The Kuhn-Tucker (Arrow and Kurz (1971),(Intriligator (1971)) conditions show interdependencies between the Lagrangian multipliers λ_{1T-j} and λ_{1T-j+1}. We use this relationship to analyse the solutions. these are summarized below under five alternative conditions.

Condition 1:

When both

$$\lambda_{1T-j} = \lambda_{1T-j+1} = 0, \quad \text{then} \quad v_0(D'_{T-j+1} - F'_{T-j+1}) = 0$$

which means:

(19) $D'_{T-j+1} = F'_{T-j+1}$

In other words when the balance of payments constraint is non-binding in both periods t and t-1, the optimal policy would be to equalize rates of return on domestic and foreign investment at the margin, that is, to invest in the sector with the highest rate of return.

Condition 2:

When

$$\lambda_{1T-j} = 0 \qquad \text{and} \qquad \lambda_{1T-j+1} > 0$$

then:

(20) $\quad F'_{T-j+1} < D'_{T-j+1}$

Condition 3:

When both

$$\lambda_{1T-j} > 0 \qquad \text{and} \qquad \lambda_{1T-j+1} > 0$$

The relationship is indeterminate i.e.

(21) $\qquad\qquad D'_{T-j+1} \gtrless F'_{T-j+1}$

Condition 4:

when

$$\lambda_{1T-j} > 0 \qquad \text{and} \qquad \lambda_{1T-j+1} = 0$$

then

(22) $\quad F'_{T-j+1} > D'_{T-j+1}$

i.e. when the balance of payments constraint becomes non-binding a higher rate of return on overseas than home investment is required.

Condition 5:

When we return to

$$\lambda_{1T-j} = 0 \qquad \text{and} \qquad \lambda_{1T-j+1} = 0$$

again

$$F'_{T-j+1} = D'_{T-j+1}$$

meaning equalizing rates of return at the margin on home and overseas investment is optimal (Motamen (1983)).

To complete our solutions, we also have to analyse the Kuhn-Tucker conditions with respect to q_{T-j}.

These are summarized below:

Condition 1:

Consider the case when the balance of payments constraints are non-binding in all the K periods, i.e. when $\lambda_{1K} = 0$ for $K = T - j + 1, \ldots, T$.

We can conclude that

$$(23) \quad \frac{\Delta\pi_{T-j+1}}{\pi_{T-j}} > \theta$$

This solution has important implications as far as the optimal depletion of the oil stock is concerned. It implies that when the balance of payments constraint is non-binding the rate of change of the resource prices has to be greater than the rate of return on investment. It is important to note that the solution reached here is a modified version of Hotelling's (1931) solution. For Hotelling's rule to hold, the proportional rate of change in prices must equal the going rate of interest. The solution is reached where the miner operates in a competitive market and acts primarily as the seller of the resource. In our solution where the state is the owner of the resource, (i.e. both producer and consumer of the resource), the optimal depletion calls for the rate of return to be less than the percentage rate of price change, which in turn calls for a slower depletion rate for oil. We shall further elaborate on this solution later in section 5.

Condition 2:

This is when

$$\lambda_{1T-j} = 0, \quad \lambda_{1T-j+1} > 0 \quad \text{and} \quad \lambda_{1k} = 0$$

$$k = T - j + 2, \ldots, T$$

then:

$$(24) \quad \pi_{T-j} + \sum_{K=T-j+1}^{T} v_0 \frac{\partial F_K}{\partial q_{T-j}} > \lambda_2$$

Condition 3:

When

$$\lambda_{1T-j} > 0, \quad \lambda_{1T-j+1} > 0 \text{ and } \lambda_{1K} = 0$$

for $K = T - j + 2, \ldots, T,$

we obtain

$$(25) \quad \pi_{T-j} + \sum_{K=T-j+1}^{T} v_0 \frac{\partial F_K}{\partial q_{T-j}} > \lambda_{1T-j+1} \, v_1 \frac{\partial F_{T-j+1}}{\partial q_{T-j}}$$

Therefore, without specific values of the parameters, it would be difficult to obtain any more specific solution.

Condition 4:

Alternatively when

$$\lambda_{1T-j} > 0, \quad \lambda_{1T-j+1} = 0 \quad \text{and} \quad \lambda_{1K} = 0$$

for $K = T - j + 2, \ldots, T$

then

$$(26) \quad \pi_{T-j} + \sum_{K=T-j+1}^{T} v_0 \frac{\partial F_K}{\partial q_{T-j}} > \lambda_2$$

This is the same as the solution reached under condition 2 above.

Condition 5:

This last stage is when the constraints are non-binding over all the remaining periods.

$$\lambda_{1K} = 0 \qquad K = T - j, \ldots, T$$

This is the same as Condition I outlined earlier and the same solution hold.

The economic implication of conditions 2 and 4 when the constraint is binding in periods T-j and T-j+1 is the following: when the balance of payments constraint becomes binding, the optimal policy would be to cut down on oil production. The rationale for this solution is that if the constraints were not binding, the inequality (26) would become an equality such that

$$(27) \quad \pi_{T-j} + \sum_{K=T-j+1}^{T} v_0 \frac{\partial F_K}{\partial q_{T-j}} = \lambda_2$$

One has to investigate what causes the balance of payments constraint to become binding and to turn the equality (27) into an inequality. Clearly one of the terms on the left hand side of equation (27) has to rise to change it into the inequality (26). Of the two variables, either the price of oil π_{T-j} has to increase or the term $\partial F_K/\partial q_{T-j}$ has to rise. Bearing in mind that $\partial F_K/\partial q_{T-j}$ is itself a function of the prices of oil over time it implies that petroleum prices π_{T-j}'s are higher in inequality (26) compared with equality (27). This, in turn, suggests that higher petroleum prices can make the balance of payments constraint binding. The reason for this is the strengthening effect on sterling that higher oil revenue can cause (as shown in equation (17) of the macro model). The high exchange rate in turn forces the non-oil exports V_t to decline and deteriorate the trade balance. Under these circumstances, since the oil price is exogenous the only variable we can control is the value of q_t, the production of oil, and a reduction of q_t would make the constraint nonbinding. Thus, as far as policy is concerned, this implies that when the balance of payments constraint becomes binding, the optimal policy would be to cut back on oil production.

5. CONCLUSIONS

The implications of the solutions stated in section 4 are considered briefly here. The interrelationship of the Lagrange multipliers were analysed separately for the variable K_t, (domestic non-oil capital formation) and q_t (the production of oil) under five different conditions, or stages. However, since the different stages related to the two variables coincide with one another - for instance, stage I, related to the variable K , is the same as stage I related to variable q - their implications can

t   t
be explained simultaneously. As far as policy is concerned these concurrent
stages can be portrayed as described next.

During stage I when the balance of payments constraint is non-
binding over a certain period of time, equalizing rates of return at the
margin between home and overseas investment is the optimal policy. At the
same time, under these conditions the rule for the production of oil should
be according to a modified version of Hotelling's rule. The optimal
depletion rate calls for the rate of change of oil prices over time to be
less than the rate of interest. It is less by the value of a fraction
consisting of v_0, a combination of some parameters, and the yield on
overseas investment (Motamen (1983)). v_0, which is defined in Table 1,
comprises the parameters average propensity to consume, income-related tax
coefficient and expenditure tax coefficient. Effectively, v_0 is some form
of savings propensity which takes into account tax leakages. So depending
on the magnitude of these parameters, the rate of return on overseas
investment and the rate of change of the price of oil, the depletion of
petroleum is determined.

When the constraint first becomes binding, i.e. when $\lambda_{1T-j} = 0$
and $\lambda_{1T-j+1} > 0$ (stage II), this implies that imports have to be kept at
their minimum level. The optimal solution says invest overseas and cut back
on oil production. This is because, given the structure of the economy, if
under these circumstances investment at home takes place, more imports will
be required. The higher volume of imports would not be offset by the
non-oil exports alone, due to the high exchange rate, and most of the oil
earnings of foreign exchange would have to be used up to pay for imports.
Moreover, the economy would be put on an expansion path such that when the
oil runs out and the foreign exchange dwindles, a gap would emerge between
the receipts and the payments.

When the balance of payments constraint is binding over consecutive
periods, i.e. when $\lambda_{1T-j} > 0$ and $\lambda_{1T-j+1} > 0$, we have labelled this as
stage III. As far as the allocation of investment between home and overseas
is concerned, the solution is indeterminate and one has to resort to stage
IV which gives a clear-cut direction for policy. However, as far as the
depletion rule is concerned, we obtain a conclusive solution: namely, cut
back on oil extraction. In other words when the balance of payments is
binding over a period, the optimal policy is to reduce petroleum
production, and this will, in turn, reduce the exchange rate and help
improve non-oil exports.

Stage IV is when the constraint is binding in period T-j and non-binding in T-j+1. Then, the optimal policy calls for more investment at home, albeit at a lower rate of return than that achieved overseas, accompanied by a reduction in petroleum extraction. The rationale for domestic investment is to boost non-oil exports and to gain other sources of foreign exchange besides oil. In other words, at this stage the economy has to plan to reduce its dependence on petroleum. Although import requirements will increase as a result of the high domestic investment, as was pointed out in stage II, by this time the income from overseas assets would have sufficiently grown (having accumulated during stages II and III) to offset for the dwindling oil revenue. Investment in non-oil exports at home during stage IV will ensure a smooth transition into a state with non-replenishable source of income.

NOTES

1) Some would argue that a better term to describe the behaviour of the UK is price-follower in line with OPEC pricing decisions for a comparable crude to that of the UK. Either term would nevertheless confirm the assumption of exogeneity about the price of oil in the British economy.

2) This is the reason for expressing P_t at market prices in equation (1) above, for it includes l_t^1 , the tax on petroleum output.

3) Supplementary petroleum duty was a category of oil taxation which was operative until the end of 1982 and was phased out subsequently. Advanced Petroleum Revenue Tax replaced it from 1983.

4) This is a rather crucial variable in the model, for it is the spending of oil proceeds that is the concern of this study.

5) The first partial derivatives of non-oil output, D_t, in equation (2) in the text with respect to the lagged value of capital stock, K_{t-1}, determines the incremental output-capital ratio outside the petroleum sector.

6) Our definition of income related-taxes includes direct income tax, corporation tax and national insurance.

247

REFERENCES

Arrow,K. J. and M. Kurz, (1971): <u>Public Investment, the Rate of Return and Optimal Fiscal Policy</u>, (Baltimore: Johns Hopkins University Press) pp. 26-55,

Hotelling, H. (9131): "The Economics of Exhaustible Resources", <u>Journal of Political Economy</u>, Vol. 39 (1931), pp. 137-75.

Intriligator, M. D. (1971): <u>Mathematical Optimization and Economic Theory</u>, (Englewood Cliffs, N.J. : Prentice Hall), pp. 292-3.

Motamen, H. (1980): <u>Expenditure of Oil Revenue</u>, St. Martins press, New York 1980.

Motamen, H. (1983): <u>Macroeconomies of North Sea Oil in the United Kingdom</u>, Heinemann Educational Books, London.

2⁴⁹⁻⁸ʳ

USING THE OIL REVENUES: A LONG RUN PERSPECTIVE

BY

ROAR BERGAN AND ERIK OFFERDAL

ABSTRACT

This paper discusses the long run macroeconomic planning problems of a
small, open economy earning an resource rent. A two-sector optimal growth
model for Norway is introduced, in which the planning objective is to maximize the sum of discounted utility of consumption. The model is solved using standard dynamic optimization techniques, and the properties of the optimal growth paths are discussed. A special emphasis is placed on optimal
consumption and balance of payments policies in a small open economy, and
the role of the real exchange rate.
     A numerical version of the model, with coefficients estimated on Nor-
wegian data, has been implemented. This version is solved for a base run,
using official projections of oil and gas revenues as input. Impact calculations are performed on the numerical model to analyze two questions: How
should optimal policies be adjusted to an exogenous increase in oil revenues appearing in the distant future? Secondly, how should optimal policies
be adjusted if there somehow are institutional constraints on the development of the balance of payments?

1. INTRODUCTION

During the last ten years revenues from oil and gas extraction have
become a major element in the Norwegian economy. In 1975 the oil sector
contributed approximately 3% to GDP and 7% to total export revenues,
whereas in 1984 these figures had increased to almost 20% and 40%,
respectively. Furthermore, given a reasonable oil price development, the
reserves on the Norwegian continental shelf are of such magnitude that the

oil revenues will continue to be of great importance well into the next century. The policy issue of how and when Norway should spend these revenues is therefore of vital importance.

The Norwegian discussion on the macroeconomic impacts of petroleum revenues has primarily focused on the so-called Dutch Disease problems, i.e. the impacts on industry structure of domestic spending of the revenues (e.g. Eide (1974), Bjerkholt, Lorentsen and Strøm (1981)). If Norway is to reap the benefits of oil revenues, this necessarily implies transfer of productive resources from sectors producing tradeables to sectors producing nontradeables, thus entailing some deindustrialization. In a market economy with full utilization of resources, the price of nontradeables will then have to increase relative to tradeables to satisfy increased domestic demand. (See Corden (1982) for a survey of the Dutch Disease literature).

There is a long-standing tradition in Norwegian macroeconomic planning of extensive use of econometric models, both for short term stabilization purposes and long term studies of industrial development. Naturally, such model tools come in handy for more detailed analysis of the impacts of oil revenues. Recently, two expert committees appointed by the Government have published their reports, one on perspectives for the Norwegian economy in general up to year 2000 (NOU 1983:37), and the second on the future extent of petroleum activities in Norway (NOU 1983:27). Both committees applied the same multisectoral growth model of the Johansen type, called the MSG model (Johansen (1960), Bjerkholt et.al. (1983)) for their analysis. This model has been used by the Ministry of Finance over the last decade for long term projections of the Norwegian economy. The MSG model is an approximation to a perfect-competition market economy with full mobility of production factors, and traces out growth paths of the economy, especially the distribution of labour, capital and production over about 30 industries, the changes in consumption patterns and the development of equilibrium prices.

The use of the model falls mainly within an instrument-target approach: it is discussed how macroeconomic growth rates and industry structure will vary under different assumptions regarding the use of oil revenues and current account policies. Several impact calculations have been made to see how different profiles of spending the oil revenues will affect the future growth of the sectors producing tradeables, and thus obtain numerical estimates of the deindustrialization process and the trade-off between oil and industry (Barker and Brailovsky (1981)).

It is our view that a more satisfactory way of analyzing the crucial planning problems raised by the oil wealth is a more explicit dynamic optimizing approach. The revenues are by their very nature a temporary phenomenon; some time in the future the oil wells will inevitably run dry. A vital element in long term planning for an open economy is always the conflict between present consumption and a long run current account equili- brium, but the fact that oil revenues sometime will vanish, makes this con- flict even more prevalent. Therefore, the relevant question ought to be: which implications will the oil revenues have for consumption growth, capi- tal accumulation and current account policies, given that one in some sense want the <u>maximum</u> benefit of these revenues over a long term planning hori- zon? A natural approach in answering this question might be to employ one of the established macroeconomic models, such as for example MSG. We have, however, chosen to formulate a new model as we feel that the MSG model is not very well suited for discussions of dynamic optimality. This is partly due to its static nature, and partly to the treatment of foreign trade.

From economic growth theory it is well known that an optimal growth path is characterized by several sets of conditions. One set is the static optimality conditions that ensures the efficient allocation of resources at each point in time. Another set of conditions concerns the dynamic optima- lity in the development of consumption and investment over time. In our opinion the MSG model is reasonably well suited to deal with the former of these efficiency conditions, but not the latter.

This may be illustrated by means of the familiar one-sector, two-period framework, depicted in figure 1. Assume that an economy has a given fund OR available in period 1 that may either be consumed directly, invested in some production/transformation process at a falling rate of return, or invested in internationally at an exogenously given rate of return. In figure 1 the return on domestic investment is illustrated by the slope of the concave production possibility frontier, while the return on foreign assets is illustrated by the slope of the line AA. An economy maximizing the utility of the consumption stream over the two periods, will be in equilibrium when the slope of the intertemporal indifference and transformation curves both equal the slope of the curve AA. Or equivalently, when the marginal rate of intertemporal substitution in consumption minus one, the consumer rate of interest by definition, equals the rates of return on the two investment opportunities. In figure 1 this means that one should aim at B and C for investment and consumption respectively. The economy then consumes OC_1 and invests RX_1 domestically. This will give a discrepancy between first period income and spending, in figure 1 equal to the distance X_1C_1, which is financed by borrowing abroad and thus yielding a current account deficit. The crucial point is of

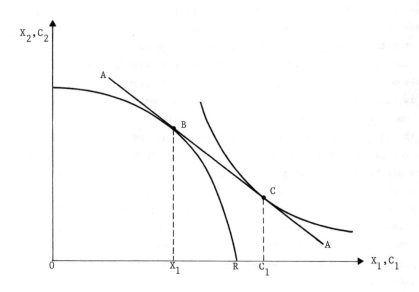

Figure 1. Optimal consumption and saving in the two period case

course that for an open economy with a possibility of unlimited
lending/borrowing at a given interest rate, the investment and consumption
decisions are completely separable.

An extension of the above conditions to a multiperiod framework is
quite straightforward and yields similar conclusions; the rate of growth in
consumption along an optimal growth path is determined by the marginal
valuation of increased consumption today versus increased investment now
which gives a return in the form of increased consumption possibilities in
the future. In MSG, however, there are no forward markets tying together
the different time periods, and thus no feedback mechanisms between the
domestic rate of return on capital and consumption growth. The rate of return on foreign assets does not enter the model at all, and the rate of
return on domestic investment is given exogenously. Total consumption is
determined residually to ensure full utilization of resources. Thus, although the MSG model may give projections of a sequence of static optimal
resource allocations, there is no market mechanism that will ensure dynamic
optimality.

Equally important, the model portrays a picture of general equilibrium
in a closed economy, and only introduces international trade via exogenous
exports and imports. This means that the distinction between sectors as to

how they behave in international markets become trivial, and the usual small-country assumptions of given world market prices and supply-side determined exports are missing. However, most of the literature on the domestic spending of oil revenues specifically focuses on the changes in relative prices between tradeables and nontradeables, the so-called real exchange rate, and on structural changes between sectors producing the two kinds of commodities. As shown by Bruno (1976) and Dornbusch (1983) the introduction of nontraded goods is not trivial in an optimal growth context. The price of nontradeables relative to the price of tradeables will have a major influence on the real interest rates relevant to consumption and investment decisions.

The present paper is devoted to present a dynamic optimization model for the Norwegian economy. We have chosen to keep the model rather simple, but we still feel that the model can be used to illustrate some of the problems recently discussed in Norway concerning current account strategies and the size of the traded goods sector.

2. THE MODEL

The model presented below, is a simple extension of the dependent economy model (see Dornbusch (1980)), incorporating the distinction between tradeables and nontradeables. Since the model is intended to be used for a planning horizon of 70 years, we have followed Dervis et.al. (1984) in confining the model to technical and definitional relationships, and avoiding behavioural equations. (See Bruno and Sachs (1982) for a similar model of a more market-oriented type). A schematic presentation of the model is given in table 1. The parametric specification of the functions, notation, and parameter values, are found in the appendix.

The basic features of the model are the following:

i)   There are three domestic sectors of production, each producing one of the following goods: A traded (T), a nontraded (N), and a composite oil and gas good (O). A fourth, non-competitive import good (I) is used for all domestic purposes. Since Norway is a small open economy, we have assumed that the three tradeables in the model are traded at world market prices that are exogenous to Norway.

ii) The traded and nontraded sectors are producing according to linearly homogeneous CES production functions with Hicks-neutral technical progress,

Table 1. A schematic description of the model.

$$\text{Max } W \;=\; \sum_{t=1}^{T} NC_t(1+\beta)^{-t}U(C_t)$$ Objective function

$$U(C_t) \;=\; \frac{1}{1-\theta}\, C_t^{1-\theta}$$ Instantaneous utility

$$CC_t \;=\; C_t NC_t \;=\; f(CN_t, CT_t, CI_t)$$ Consumption aggregation

$$\left.\begin{array}{l} XN_t \;=\; F_N(KN_{t-1}, LN_t; t) \\[2ex] XT_t \;=\; F_T(KT_{t-1}, LT_t; t) \end{array}\right\}$$ Production functions

$$\left.\begin{array}{l} XN_t \;=\; \sum_i a_{Ni}Xi_t + j_N J_t + CN_t \\[1.5ex] XT_t \;=\; \sum_i a_{Ti}Xi_t + j_T J_t + CT_t + AT_t \\[1.5ex] XO_t \;=\; \sum_i a_{Oi}Xi_t + j_O J_t + AO_t \\[1.5ex] I_t \;=\; \sum_i a_{Ii}Xi_t + j_I J_t + CI_t \end{array}\right\}$$ Input-output structure

$$J_t \;=\; JN_t + JT_t + JO_t$$ Total investment

$$\left.\begin{array}{l} KN_t \;=\; KN_{t-1} + JN_t - d_N KN_t \\[2ex] KT_t \;=\; KT_{t-1} + JT_t - d_T KT_t \end{array}\right\}$$ Capital accumulation

$$BAL_t \;=\; PT_t AT_t + PO_t AO_t - PI_t I_t + rf_t V_{t-1} + S_t$$ Current account

$$V_t \;=\; V_{t-1} + BAL_t$$ Foreign Asset Accumulation

$$\left.\begin{array}{l} L_t \;=\; LT_t + LN_t \\[2ex] K_t \;=\; KT_t + KN_t \end{array}\right\}$$ Primary factors

$$JN_t \geqslant 0 \qquad\qquad JT_t \geqslant 0$$ Non-negativity constraints

$$V_T \geqslant V_T^{*} \qquad K_T \geqslant K_T^{*}$$ Terminal constraints

using capital and labour as inputs. Capital is sector specific in the sense that non-negative gross investment in each sector of production is assumed. Total labour supply is given exogenously. Capital is "produced" by a fixed coefficient technology from the four goods of the model. Intermediate input of the four goods to the three domestic sectors of production is determined by fixed input-output coefficients.

iii) There is no explicit production function for the petroleum sector. Instead, production and investment profiles are given exogenously while no labour is required in the production of petroleum. In making these assumptions, we avoid the very important question of how Norway should deplete her petroleum reserves in an optimal way. Our interest lies, however, primarily in the optimal spending of oil revenues. To ensure that the development of the current account did not deviate from those obtained by the two expert committees because of different assumptions as regards the petroleum sector, we preferred to have a time profile of the oil revenues that, at least for the first two decades, was in accordance with the two committees. Further, to illustrate that the petroleum incomes are of a temporary nature, we wanted oil and gas production to fade out before the end of the planning period.

iv) We have imposed a terminal constraint on the stock of net foreign assets, but there are no restrictions on the current account surplus/deficit during the planning period. The rate of return on foreign assets is for the present assumed exogenous, independent of the size of net claims.

v) Nontraded goods, traded goods and non-competitive imports are used for consumption purposes. A Cobb-Douglas function is used to obtain a measure of per capita real consumption to enter the instantaneous utility function. (See Dornbusch (1983)). Our choice of instantaneous utility function implies that the flexibility of the marginal utility of income, or income flexibility for short, is constant.

vi) The intertemporal optimization problem is to find a growth path of the economy that maximizes the discounted value of instantaneous per capita consumption weighted by the number of consumers, given the terminal constraints on net foreign assets and domestic non-oil capital.

Although the model itself is rather simple, it proves to be difficult to find the full analytical solution to the optimization problem. In the appendix it is shown how the model can be solved using a variant of the Kuhn-Tucker theorem (see Arrow and Kurz (1970)). In the following we shall confine ourselves to look at some aspects of the solution that deals with the relationship between different interest concepts. In doing this, we shall make use of the shadow prices attached to each of the equations of the model. It is therefore useful to recall the interpretation of these prices: The shadow price of a good measures the increase in the objective function of an increased delivery of one unit of the good at time t. The value of the shadow price is what the representative consumer is willing to pay at t=0 for one unit of the good delivered at time t. The structure of shadow prices gives the structure of relative market prices necessary to obtain the optimal solution in a perfect forsight economy.

It is known from economic theory that along an optimal growth path, the rate of decline of marginal utility ,or the consumer rate of interest, must equal the return on capital equipment and the return on investment in foreign assets. This was illustrated for a one-good economy in section 1. In a multi-sector economy where the relative prices are changing, the picture is somewhat more complicated. The equality above will then only hold if and only if the different rates of return are defined in a common unit of measurement. If the return on different assets are, for example, measured in the assets themselves, these "own rates of interest" should not be equal. In our model, this means that if the growth path is to be optimal, then the interest rate on foreign assets in terms of "dollars" is not necessarily equal to the net return on investment in domestic fixed capital in terms of the capital good. Below, we shall first find the expressions for some of the own rates of return in our model. Next, we shall show that the relationship between these different interest concepts in a crucial way depends on the relative price between nontraded and traded goods, known as the real exchange rate. The basis for this discussion is the first order conditions for an optimal solution as spelled out in the appendix. For expositonary reasons, we shall suppress most of the algebra and only comment upon a few salient results.

For simplicity, we shall assume that the world market prices of non-competitive imports (PI_t) and the traded good (PT_t) are equal and constant throughout the planning period. Units of measurement are chosen so that $PI_t=PT_t=1$. (Non-competitive imports and the traded good could then have been aggregated to one good in the following). It may then be shown that:

(1) $$P_{It} = P_{Tt} = \lambda_{Ft} = \lambda_{Vt}$$

λ_{Ft} and λ_{Vt} are the shadow prices attached to respectively the current account and net foreign assets at time t and p_{it} is the shadow price of good i. The real exchange rate at time t can then be defined as:

(2) $$pr_t = P_{Nt}/P_{Tt}$$

We are now ready to take a closer look at some of the interest rates of the model.

The period-to-period return on foreign assets, rf_t, is assumed to be exogenous. One "dollar" invested abroad at time (t-1) will be repaid by $(1+rf_t)$ dollars at time t. rf_t is therefore the own rate of interest on foreign assets from time (t-1) to time t. This is also seen from:

(3) $$rf_t = (\lambda_{V(t-1)} - \lambda_{Vt})/\lambda_{Vt}$$

The shadow prices of (1) are thus all falling at a rate equal to the "dollar" interest rate on foreign assets.

When the non-negativity constraints on gross investments are not binding, the shadow prices attached to the stock of fixed capital in the non-traded and traded sectors of production should be equal and equal to the shadow price of new capital equipment. The own rate of interest on fixed capital is then:

(4) $$r_t = (P_{J(t-1)} - P_{Jt})/P_{Jt}$$

i.e the rate of change in the shadow price attached to new capital equipment.

Let us now turn to the consumer rate of interest. Our choice of consumption aggregation function makes it possible to interpret $CC_t = NC_t C_t$ as an exact index of total real consumption at time t. The consumer rate of interest, or the rate of decline of marginal utility along the growth path is then:

$$(5) \qquad RCC_t = (\frac{\partial W}{\partial CC_{t-1}} - \frac{\partial W}{\partial CC_t}) / \frac{\partial W}{\partial CC_t} = (1+\beta)(C_t/C_{t-1})^\theta - 1$$

where $W = \sum_{t=1}^{T}(1+\beta)^{-t}(1-\theta)^{-1}NC_t^\theta CC_t^{1-\theta}$

In (5), β is the rate of time preference and θ the negative of the income flexibility.

We shall now see how the development of the real exchange rate in our model affects the relationship between the interest concepts above. By assuming a constant oil price ($PO_t=PO$), the following expression for the net rate of return on domestic capital can be found:

$$(6) \qquad r_t = \frac{(j_N pr_{t-1} + k)rf_t + j_N(pr_{t-1} - pr_t)}{j_N pr_t + k}$$

where $k = j_T + j_I + j_O PO$

It appears from (6) that:

$$(7) \qquad \begin{array}{lll} r_t < rf_t & \text{iff} & pr_{t-1} < pr_t \\ r_t = rf_t & \text{iff} & pr_{t-1} = pr_t \\ r_t > rf_t & \text{iff} & pr_{t-1} > pr_t \end{array}$$

Only if the real exchange rate is constant from t-1 to t should the net rate of return on domestic capital be equal to the return on foreign assets. If, however, the real exchange rate is appreciating, one should aim at lower demand for capital return in terms of the capital good. The reason for this is, of course, that the relative price between the capital good and "dollars" is then increasing from (t-1) to t; one unit of the capital good will buy more dollars at time t than it did at time (t-1). If one expects the real exchange rate to increase, it is therefore wrong to invest in domestic capital up to the point where the rate of return in terms of the capital good equals the the exogenous return on foreign assets in terms of dollars.

The relationship between the consumer rate of interest and the return on foreign assets, is found to be:

(8) $$RCC_t = (1 + rf_t)(pr_{t-1}/pr_t)^{\alpha N} - 1$$

Here, αN is the share of nontraded goods in total consumption. It then follows that:

(9)
$$
\begin{aligned}
RCC_t < rf_t \quad &\text{iff} \quad pr_{t-1} < pr_t \\
RCC_t = rf_t \quad &\text{iff} \quad pr_{t-1} = pr_t \\
RCC_t > rf_t \quad &\text{iff} \quad pr_{t-1} > pr_t
\end{aligned}
$$

If the real exchange rate is constant, the consumer rate of interest will equal the rate of interest on foreign assets. But, if the relative price of nontraded to traded goods is rising, then the real interest rate relevant to consumption decisions, will be lower than the exogenous rf_t. The reason is again that when a real appreciation is taking place, the consumption basket is getting more valuable over time relative to foreign assets. If the relative prices are changing, it is thus not correct to demand equality between the consumer rate of interest computed by a formula like (5) and the world market interest rate on "dollars".

As stated earlier, when they are measured in a common unit of measurement, the net rate of return on domestic capital must equal the return on foreign assets which again must equal the consumer rate of interest, if the growth path is to be optimal. To see that this is so in our model, we shall compute the rate of return on foreign assets at time t, measured in units of the consumption basket. Assume that at time $(t-1)$, m units of the aggregate consumption good is exchanged for dollars and invested abroad. One unit of the consumption basket will at $(t-1)$ buy an amount of $(p^*_{1(t-1)}/\lambda_{v(t-1)})$ dollars, where $p^*_{1(t-1)} = P_{1(t-1)}/NC_{t-1}$ is the shadow price of the aggregate consumption good. The amount of dollars invested abroad at (t-1) is therefore $m(p^*_{1(t-1)}/\lambda_{V(t-1)})$. One period later one will receive $m(p^*_{1(t-1)}/\lambda_{V(t-1)})(1 + rf_t)$ dollars which then can be exchanged for units of the consumption basket at a relative price of (λ_{Vt}/p^*_{1t}). One will thus receive:

$$ m\,\frac{p^*_1(t-1)}{\lambda_{V(t-1)}}(1 + rf_t)\frac{\lambda_{Vt}}{p^*_{1t}} \;=\; m\,\frac{p^*_1(t-1)}{p^*_{1t}}(1 + rf_t)\frac{\lambda_{Vt}}{\lambda_{V(t-1)}} \;=\; m(1 + RCC_t) $$

units of the consumption basket. The return on foreign assets in terms of the consumption basket is therefore:

$$ \frac{m\,(1 + RCC_t) - m}{m} \;=\; RCC_t $$

that is, the consumption rate of interest. A similar line of reasoning can be used to show that the net rate of return on domestic capital in terms of the aggregate consumption good, is also equal to the consumption rate of interest.

Let us now turn to two problems related to our specification of the welfare index. The Cobb-Douglas function used to obtain an index of total consumption, is easily seen to imply unitary price and income elasticities. Along a growth path it is therefore only changes in relative prices that will change the composition of consumption. This may be considered unrealistic since one normally would expect the income elasticity of nontraded goods to be significantly higher than that of traded ones.

Another aspect of our model is that the rate of optimal consumption growth becomes highly dependent on some of the exogenous assumptions. The growth in consumption can be written as:

$$ (10) \qquad C_t/C_{t-1} \;=\; \left[\left[(1+rf_t)/(1+\beta)\right](pr_{t-1}/\,pr_t)^{\alpha N} \right]^{1/\theta} $$

It follows from (10) that if we use the parameter values of the reference scenario, to be presented in section 3.2, (rf=0.04, β=0.01 and θ=1.6) and assume a constant real exchange rate, consumption growth is 1.85 per cent along the optimal trajectory. Table 2 shows the effect on optimal consumption growth of changes in the parameter values.

Table 2: Optimal consumption growth under different assumptions (real exchange rate kept constant)

Assumptions			Optimal growth in per capita consumption (%)
β	rf_t	θ	
0.01	0.04	1.6	1.85
0.00	0.04	1.6	2.18
0.01	0.03	1.6	1.23
0.01	0.04	1.1	2.70

(10) also points to the fact that even with a fixed foreign rate of interest, fluctuations in the real exchange rate will lead to fluctuations in optimal consumption growth - especially if the nontraded good carries a substantial weight in total consumption.

3. THE NUMERICAL RESULTS

This chapter discusses three scenarios:

- A reference scenario, where Norway will experience rapidly increasing oil revenues up to 2010, whereafter they decline sharply to an insignificant level by the year 2050.

- Scenario 2 where Norway, other things equal, get an extra dose of oil revenues due to sustained peak production, thirty years hence.

- Scenario 3 with the reference scenario oil revenues, but with a constraint on the current account keeping the surplus/deficit within a 10 billion NOK limit.

The reference scenario will provide the first insights into the nature of dynamically efficient accumulation policies, and work as a reference case for the two latter simulations.

The second scenario is included to illustrate the effects of increased oil revenues. This corresponds to well known simulation experiments on the MSG model, here conducted within a dynamic optimization framework to see how optimal policies should be adjusted.

It might be claimed that the above simulations give optimal policy rules that cannot be followed in a real world economy with institutional constraints. In the third scenario the effects of imposing constraints on the current account is studied. This of course restricts the possibilities for intertemporal consumption smoothing - the incomes will have to be used domestically on a spend-as-you-earn basis. Our aim in the third scenario is to study the structural shifts and accumulation policies necessary to support this restriction.

The numerical results below, were obtained by using the CONOPT algorithm. (Drud and Meeraus (1980)).

3.1. EXOGENOUS ASSUMPTIONS

When using the model we have strived towards using the same exogenous assumptions as those used by the two expert committees (NOU 1983:27 and NOU 1983:37).

Population growth: There are two variables pertaining to population growth in the model; the number of consuming households, and the size of the labour force. The number of households grows at a rate of 0.3 per cent up to 1985, at a rate of 0.2 per cent from 1985 to 2010 and is thereafter held constant. Total labour force grows at a rate of 0.7 per cent from 1980 to 1985, 0.3 per cent to 1990 and is thereafter constant.

Technical progress: In each of the domestic production sectors there is an index for Hicks-neutral technical progress, growing by 1.5 per cent annually from 1985 onwards.

Prices: There are four exogenous prices in the model, all assumed to be determined in world markets. The interest rate on foreign assets is constant at a level of 4 per cent in real terms. The import good is chosen as numeraire, and for our present purposes we have also chosen to rule out terms of trade changes between imports and the traded good over the planning horizon. Considering the composition of Norwegian non-oil exports, this may not be a particularly realistic assumption. It does however make it possible to treat non-competitive imports and the traded good as one good, called tradeables, which will be convenient when discussing the simulation results. The present model specification has been chosen to allow terms of trade changes in later simulations.

For all three scenarios, the price of crude oil is assumed to grow at a 2 per cent annual rate in real terms up to 2010 and thereafter remain constant at the 2010 level. This assumption is, by and large, in accordance with both expert committees mentioned above.

Oil production: For the reference scenario and for scenario 3 with current account restrictions, we have assumed oil and gas production to grow from its 1980-level of 50 mtoe to 80 mtoe in 2000 and 90 mtoe in 2010. Thereafter it declines sharply in both these scenarios to an insignificant level of 2 mtoe in 2050. In scenario 2 with higher oil revenues, we assume that the production level will remain at the peak of 90 mtoe from 2010 to 2020, and thereafter falls off to a level approximately equal to the reference scenario level in 2050. The assumptions regarding the oil production are summarized in fig. 2.

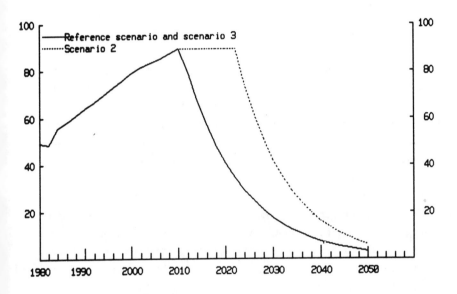

Figure 2. Oil production profiles.
         Million tonnes oil equivalents (mtoe).

Investments: Exogenous gross capital formation consists of fixed capital formation in the petroleum sector and increases in stocks. Investment in the petroleum sector is assumed to reach 20 billion NOK by 1985, a level which is sustained onto 1995. Thereafter oil investment falls to zero by 2005. Inventory build-up is assumed to grow at a rate of 2 per cent annually.

Objective function parameters. The income flexibility is kept at -1.6
in the simulations reported below (see (Biørn and Jansen (1982)). The rate
of time preference is held at 1 per cent annually.

Terminal constraints: We have imposed terminal constraints on the
stocks of non-oil productive capital and foreign reserves. The stock of
capital bequeathed to generations beyond the 2050-horizon is required to be
no less than 2,500 billion NOK, as opposed to its 1980 level of 882 billion
NOK. Total foreign reserves is required to be no less than 300 billion NOK,
as opposed to the 1980 situation with foreign debts amounting to 93 billion
NOK.

3.2. THE REFERENCE SCENARIO

In all the simulations below, the 1980-values are fixed at their historical levels. There are thus no possibilities of an instant reallocation
of productive resources to jump onto a smooth long run growth path.

It appears from figure 3 that the reference scenario may be divided
into three periods: The first 2-4 years, the next decade and the rest of
the planning period. During the first of these periods, the imbalances of
the base year economy is corrected to obtain the equality between interest
rates as shown in section 2 and the level of consumption is adjusted to its
optimal path. It is important to note that while the growth of consumption
is heavily dependent on some of the exogenous parameters of the model (see
section 2), the level is determined by the overall income possibilities of
the Norwegian economy over the planning horizon. In the reference scenario
this leads to an initial boost in consumption from its historical
1980-value. For the next eight years, per capita consumption is growing at
an average annual rate of 1.58 per cent. The remaining years are
characterized by a smooth, and higher, consumption growth of 1.81 percent
annually on average.

Growth in total domestic investment in the first two decades, is
strongly influenced by the variations in the exogenous investment in the
petroleum sector . Figure 3 therefore also shows the development in endogenous investment only. It appears that after an initial slowdown, these
investments have the fastest growth in the years up to the beginning of the
1990's. In contrast to consumption growth, the growth in investment thereafter slows down.

The development of total consumption and investment is of course

265

F i g u r e s :   R e f e r e n c e   S c e n a r i o

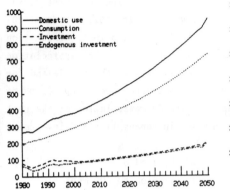

Figure 3. Use of goods and services
Billion NOK

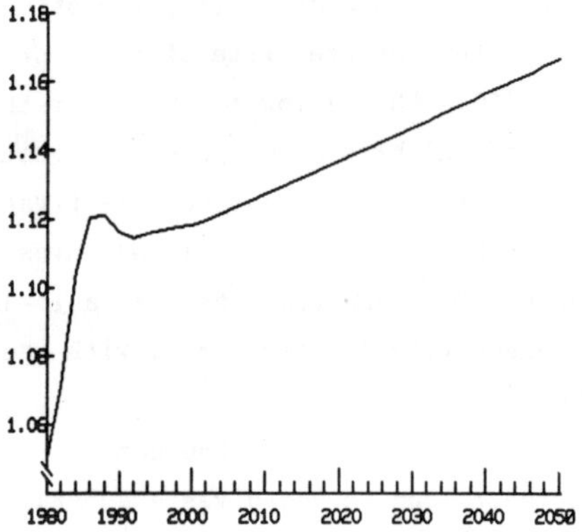

Figure 4. Real exchange rate

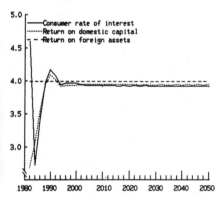

Figure 5. Real interest rates

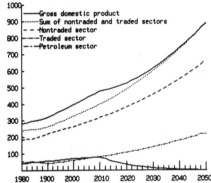

Figure 6. GDP by sector
Billion NOK

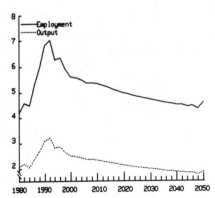

Figure 7. Size of nontraded to
traded sector

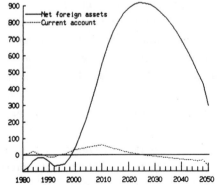

Figure 9. Current account and foreign
assets. Billion NOK

closely related to the development of the real exchange rate shown in figure 4. According to (8), the strong appreciation during the first decade lowers the consumer rate of interest (see figure 5). It follows from (8) and (10) that a lower consumer rate of interest implies lower consumption growth, which is also the case. Equation (6) shows that the appreciation that takes place during the first decade also lowers the the demand for return on domestic capital and investment is therefore speeded up. From the early 1990's onwards, there is a lower, but steady appreciation of the real exchange rate, in accordance with the changes in consumption and investment growth.

Figure 6 shows the composition of GDP by kind of economic activity. The petroleum sector gives a substantial contribution to GDP up to 2010, whereafter production is gradually fading out. As regards the traded and nontraded sectors, there are substantial structural shifts in production and employment as can also be seen from figure 7. Up to the early 1990's, there is a marked reallocation of of labour towards the nontraded sector in accordance with the strong real exchange rate appreciation during these years. Output in the traded good sector is in fact 21 per cent lower in 1990 than it were in the base year. From 1992 onwards, the reallocation of labour is, however, reversed. To enable Norway to pay for her imports in the years of falling oil revenues, the gross product of the traded good sector will thereafter have the highest growth rate throughout the planning period. It should be stressed that this build-up of the traded good sector starts almost twenty years before Norway faces declining petroleum revenues, and in a period where these revenues are growing fast! This points to the importance of taking a long run view when discussing the optimal size of the traded good sector in Norway.

The change in the structure of production after 1990 may at first glance seem to be at variance with the development of the real exchange rate. The real exchange rate then steadily appreciates while at the same time the traded good sector grows at a significantly higher rate than the nontraded sector. The explanation to this lies in a simple application of the Rybczynski theorem. We have assumed a constant labour force after 1990, while the economy's stock of capital grows steadily. It follows from this theorem that, if the relative prices are constant, the sector which is most capital intensive, in our case the traded good sector, will grow fastest. This is illustrated in figure 8.

The Rybczynski-effect will shift the transformation frontier between traded and nontraded goods in an asymmetrical fashion. At a given real exchange rate, production of non tradeables will therefore decrease along the

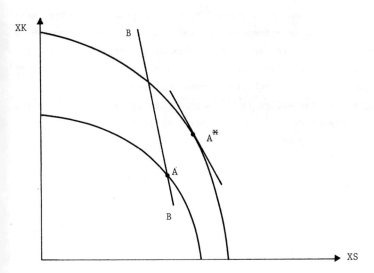

Figure 8. The Rybczynski-effect and real exchange rate appreciation

line BB. The demand for non tradeables is, however, steadily increasing, and this will put an upward pressure on the real exchange rate, changing the equilibrium from A to A*.

The possibility of running current account surpluses or deficits separates current incomes and spendings and makes it possible to smooth the consumption path. Foreign assets will be accumulated according to their rate of return, considerations taken to their terminal value. Figure 9 shows the development of the current account and net foreign assets in the reference scenario. Up to 1995 there is a high level of investment in the petroleum sector, a growth in oil and gas revenues and a declining export of tradeables. This leads the current account to fluctuate, with subsequent surpluses and deficits. As the oil investment is fading out and the export of tradeables is recovering, the current account is showing substantial surpluses for 30 years yielding a stock of foreign reserves of 900 billion NOK by 2025. During the remaining years of the planning period, Norway is decumulating this stock, approaching the terminal foreign reserves of 300 billion NOK.

268

3.3. SCENARIO 2: INCREASED OIL REVENUES

Scenario 2 is included to illustrate the "Dutch Disease effects" mentioned in section 1 in an intertemporal context: In an open economy with a nontraded sector, an extra income flow, in this case a resource rent, will lead to a change in the structure of relative prices in favour of nontradeables and thus in the domestic structure of production.

The effects on consumption is shown in figure 10. Although the extra incomes appear thirty years hence, the consumption <u>level</u> increases by 2.5 % already the first year, and thereafter grows at the same rate as in the

F i g u r e s : S c e n a r i o 2 : Increased oil revenues

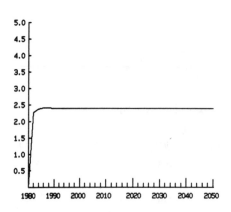

Figure 10. Consumption. Percentage deviation from the reference scenario

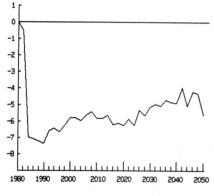

Figure 11. Traded sector production. Percentage deviation from the reference scenario

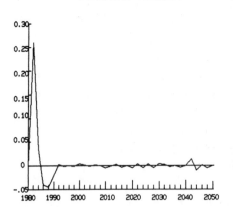

Figure 12. Real exchange rate. Percentage deviation from the reference scenario

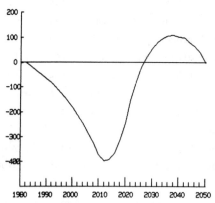

Figure 13. Net foreign assets. Absolute deviation from the ref.scen. Billion NOK

reference scenario. This illustrates nicely the how dependent the optimal level of consumption today is on the oil revenue forcasts.

The initial rise in consumption requires a transfer of productive resources towards the nontraded sector. As shown in figure 11, over the first five years production in the traded good sector declines to a level approximately 8 % below the level of the reference scenario, and thereafter grows at the same rate but from a permanently lower level. A real exchange rate appreciation follows to make the necessary reallocations come about (see figure 12).

The shifts in consumption and production structure implies that the economy starts the domestic spending of the extra incomes immediately by increasing imports and running a lower current account surplus than other-wise before the extra incomes appear. This may be seen from figure 13. The net stock of foreign reserves is significantly lower than in the reference scenario up to about 2015. After this point, however, an increased share of the revenues are accumulated abroad.

3.4 SCENARIO 3: THE CONSEQUENCES OF AN ANNUAL CURRENT ACCOUNT CONSTRAINT

We showed in section 3.2 that the optimal policy in the reference scenario was characterized by large surpluses and deficits on the current account. If there are institutional limitations on the possibility of following a policy of sustained current account imbalances, this optimal policy is not viable. Assume that the interest rate on foreign reserves were 3 per cent instead of 4 per cent. In the absence of uncertainty, our model then implies that the optimal current account policy is a debt accumulation of the same magnitude as the reference scenario reserve accu-mulation. Looking back to the intense discussion over Norway's debt accu-mulation in the mid-seventies, it is clearly out of the question that such a policy proposal would be implemented, however optimal. In this section the consequences of imposing annual current account constraints on the op-timization problem is analyzed.

Current account constraints could be imposed in several ways. We have chosen to allow annual balances of up to 10 billion NOK in either direc-tion. When the current account is confined within this tunnel, it is pos-sible to maintain the reference scenario terminal condition of a stock of net foreign asset of 300 billion NOK in 2050.

The existence of a current account constraint, means that the accumulation of foreign assets is no longer allowed to take place according to their marginal return. Still, the relationship between the consumer rate of interest and the return on domestic investment must hold. If either the upper or lower constraint on the current account is binding, a gap between the domestic rates of return and the foreign interest rate will appear as a result of the non-negative shadow price attached to this extra constraint.

Figure 14 shows the development of the current account in scenario 3 and the reference scenario. Due to the terminal condition, the economy is now forced to stay at the upper limit of the allowed tunnel for most of the planning period. The large surpluses in the reference scenario from 2000 to 2025 is no longer possible and the deficits during the last 20 years are correspondingly smaller.

A crude characterization of the effects on the Norwegian economy, is that domestic use of goods and services are now speeded up during the years of smaller current account surpluses and slowed down during the years of smaller deficits. The most striking feature compared to the reference scenario, is the larger volatility of the growth rates. Consumption is now speeded up considerably during the years from 1995 to 2005 (see figure 15). In 2005 consumption is approximately 15 billion NOK higher than in the reference scenario. From 2005 to 2035 the growth rate of consumption is lower and thereafter almost the same as in the reference scenario. In 2050 the level of total consumption is almost 5 per cent lower than in the reference scenario.

The real exchange rate development necessary to support this growth path is shown in figure 16. In most of the years up to 2000, the current account surplus is larger in the present case compared to the reference scenario. This calls for a slowdown in domestic spending and a reallocation of resources from the nontraded to the traded sector. To achieve this, the relative price between nontraded and traded goods must fall, which is illustrated by the figure. For the next 20 years, however, there is a substantial increase in domestic spending which leads the real exchange rate to appreciate relative to the reference scenario. This appreciation then turns into a relative depreciation by 2020, as the need for export of tradeables is growing.

The relative distribution of production between the nontraded and traded sectors is easily understood from the above discussion. As apparent in figure 17, the nontraded sector is relatively larger during the years of higher domestic spending while the opposite is true for the rest of the period. It is especially interesting to note the development of the traded

271

Figures: Scenario 3:   Annual current account constraint

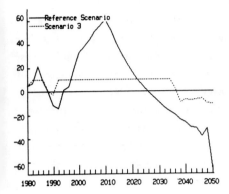

Figure 14. Current account
           Billion NOK

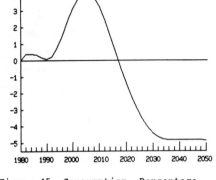

Figure 15. Consumption. Percentage
           deviation from Ref. Scen.

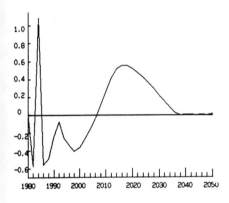

Figure 16. Real exchange rate
           Percentage deviation
           from Reference Scenario

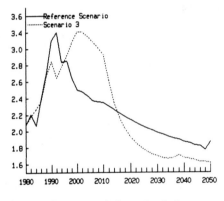

Figure 17. Nontraded to traded sec-
           tor production

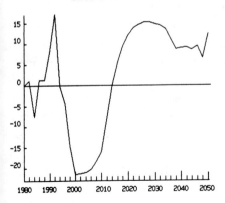

Figure 18. Production in the traded
           sector. Percentage deviation
           from Reference Scenario

good sector. Due to the slowdown in domestic spending in the 1990-2000 period, the maximum relative squeeze of the traded sector is now delayed by
10 years. The gross output is 50 billion NOK, or 20 per cent, lower in the
traded sector in 2004 in this alternative scenario (see figure 18). During
the decade from 2010 to 2020, however, a major restructuring of the economy
takes place. The need to compensate the declining oil revenues by export of
tradeables makes for a fast output growth of the traded goods sector in
those years. This reshuffling of resources is also found in the reference
scenario, but in the present case it is larger and takes place within a
shorter time period. This illustrates the inherent conflict between the
wish to minimize the reallocation of labour between sectors and a policy of
restricting the surplus/deficit on the current account.

4. CONCLUSIONS

The modelling work presented in this paper is still at an experimental
level and it would be unwarranted to draw any policy conclusions from the
results obtained. We do, however, feel that the present work justifies
some conclusions as regards modelling efforts.

We have argued that the existing models of economic planning in Norway
are not very well suited for long run analysis of optimal accumulation
policies. Instead, some kind of dynamic optimization model is needed to
deal with some of the urgent planning problems of today. Even in a simple
model such as the one presented here, changes in exogenous input may
generate effects that are not immediately transparent. This should be amply
illustrated above by the way the interest rates vary with changes in the
real exchange rate. There can therefore be no doubt that the use of
numerical optimization models as a supplement to larger, traditional
simulation models, may provide policy makers with useful insights. An
especially interesting idea is to run an optimization model in tandem with
the MSG model: First the aggregated optimization model is used to generate
time-paths for investment, the current account and important relative
prices. Second, these results are used as input to simulations on the MSG
model. To follow this procedure would surely weaken our criticism of the
present use of the MSG model.

We have found that even small changes in parameters and exogenous
assuptions may generate growth trajectories with highly different
properties and implications for policy. One implication of this, is that
the present formulation of the model should be exposed to a careful

scrutiny. Some obvious candidates for future work on our model are:

- a more general specification of the consumption system, permitting different income and price elasticities.

- more general production functions allowing for substitution between labour, capital and material input.

- better representation of uncertainty related to oil and gas revenues. At present we have assumed this uncertainty away, and thereby obtained results based on perfect forsight, a rare case in a planning context. Considering the magnitude of future petroleum revenues in the Norwegian economy, a better representation of this uncertainty is of vital importance.

APPENDIX: A PRECISE DESCRIPTION OF THE MODEL

A.1.   VARIABLES AND EQUATIONS

Variables

Ai_t :   Net exports of good i. i=T,O
BAL_t :   Current account surplus
C_t :   Per capita consumption
CC_t :   Index of total consumption
Ci_t :   Consumption of good i. i=N,T,I
I_t :   Imports of the non-competitive import good
J_t :   Total gross capital formation
Ji_t :   Gross capital formation in sector i. i=N,T,O
K_t :   Total non-oil real capital stock at the end of period t
Ki_t :   Stock of fixed capital in sector i at the end of period t. i=N,T
L_t :   Total labour supply
Li_t :   Employment in sector i. i=N,T
NC_t :   Number of consumers (index)
Pi_t :   World market price of good i. i=T,O,I
rf_t :   Rate of return on foreign assets
S_t :   Net transfers from abroad
V_t :   Stock of net foreign assets at the end of period t
Xi_t :   Gross output of sector i. i=N,T,O
εi_t :   Rate of Hicks-neutral technical progress in sector i. i=N,T

Exogenous: JO_t, L_t, NC_t, Pi_t, rf_t, S_t, XO_t, εi_t

Coefficients

a_{ij} :   Input-output coefficients. Unit requirement of good i in sector j
a_{NE} :   The exported share of gross output in the nontraded sector
d_i :   Rate of depreciation in sector i. i=N,T
j_i :   Share of good i in the composite capital good. i=N,T,O,I
αi :   Good i's budget share in consumption. i=N,T,I
β :   Rate of time preference
γi :   Scale parameter of the production functions. i=N,T
δi :   Share parameter of the production functions. i=N,T
θ :   Negative of the flexibility of marginal utility of income
ϱi :   Substitution parameter of the production functions. i=N,T

Goods

N   :   Nontraded
T   :   Traded
O   :   Oil and gas
I   :   Non-competitive imports

Equations

Objective function:

$$(A1) \qquad \text{Max } W(C_{1980}, \ldots, C_{2050}) = \sum_t NC_t (1+\beta)^{-t} \frac{1}{(1-\theta)} C_t^{1-\theta}$$

Per capita consumption:

$$(A2) \qquad C_t = NC_t^{-1} A \; CN_t^{\alpha N} \; CT_t^{\alpha T} \; CI_t^{\alpha I}$$

Production functions:

$$(A3) \qquad XN_t = \left[\prod_{\tau=1}^{t} (1+\epsilon N_\tau) \right] \gamma N \left[\delta N \; KN_{t-1}^{-\varrho N} + (1-\delta N) LN_t^{-\varrho N} \right]^{-\frac{1}{\varrho N}}$$

$$(A4) \qquad XT_t = \left[\prod_{\tau=1}^{t} (1+\epsilon T_\tau) \right] \gamma T \left[\delta T \; KT_{t-1}^{-\varrho T} + (1-\delta T) LT_t^{-\varrho T} \right]^{-\frac{1}{\varrho T}}$$

Material balances:

$$(A5) \qquad XN_t = a_{NN} XN_t + a_{NT} XT_t + a_{NO} XO_t + j_N J_t + a_{NE} XN_t + CN_t$$

$$(A6) \qquad XT_t = a_{TN} XN_t + a_{TT} XT_t + a_{TO} XO_t + j_T J_t + AT_t + CT_t$$

$$(A7) \qquad XO_t = a_{ON} XN_t + a_{OT} XT_t + a_{OO} XO_t + j_O J_t + AO_t$$

$$(A8) \qquad I_t = a_{IN} XN_t + a_{IT} XT_t + a_{IO} XO_t + j_I J_t + CI_t$$

Total investments:

$$(A9) \qquad J_t = JN_t + JT_t + JO_t$$

Capital accumulation:

(A10) $KN_t = KN_{t-1} + JN_t - d_N KN_t$

(A11) $KT_t = KT_{t-1} + JT_t - d_T KT_t$

Current account surplus:

(A12) $BAL_t = PT_t AT_t + PT_t a_{NE} XN_t + PO_t AO_t - PI_t I_t + rf_t V_{t-1} + S_t$

Accumulation of net foreign assets:

(A13) $V_t = V_{t-1} + BAL_t$

Total labour input:

(A14) $L_t = LN_t + LT_t$

Stock of non-oil fixed capital

(A15) $K_t = KN_t + KT_t$

Non-negativity of gross investments:

(A16) $JN_t \geqslant 0$

(A17) $JT_t \geqslant 0$

Terminal conditions:

(A18) $V_T \geqslant V_T^{\star}$

(A19) $K_T \geqslant K_T^{\star}$

A.2. SOLUTION OF THE MODEL

The model can be solved using a variant of the Kuhn-Tucker theorem (see Arrow and Kurz (1970)).

The Lagrangian of the problem is:

$$
\begin{aligned}
L =\ & \sum_t NC_t(1+\beta)^{-t}\frac{1}{(1-\theta)}\,C_t^{1-\theta} \\[4pt]
& -\sum_t p_{1t}\left(C_t - NC_t^{-1}A\,CN_t^{\alpha N}CT_t^{\alpha T}CI_t^{\alpha I}\right) \\[4pt]
& -\sum_t v_{Nt}\left[XN_t - \left[\prod_{\tau=1}^{t}(1+\varepsilon N_\tau)\right]\gamma N\left[\delta N\,KN_{t-1}^{-\varrho N}+(1-\delta N)LN_t^{-\varrho N}\right]^{-\frac{1}{\varrho N}}\right] \\[4pt]
& -\sum_t v_{Tt}\left[XT_t - \left[\prod_{\tau=1}^{t}(1+\varepsilon T_\tau)\right]\gamma T\left[\delta T\,KT_{t-1}^{-\varrho T}+(1-\delta T)LT_t^{-\varrho T}\right]^{-\frac{1}{\varrho T}}\right] \\[4pt]
& -\sum_t p_{Nt}\left(a_{NN}XN_t + a_{NT}XT_t + a_{NO}XO_t + j_N J_t + CN_t + a_{NE}XN_t - XN_t\right) \\[4pt]
& -\sum_t p_{Tt}\left(a_{TN}XN_t + a_{TT}XI_t + a_{TO}XO_t + j_T J_t + CT_t + AT_t - XT_t\right) \\[4pt]
& -\sum_t p_{Ot}\left(a_{ON}XN_t + a_{OT}XT_t + a_{OO}XO_t + j_O J_t + AO_t - XO_t\right) \\[4pt]
& -\sum_t p_{It}\left(a_{IN}XN_t + a_{IT}XT_t + a_{IT}XO_t + j_I J_t + CI_t - I_t\right) \\[4pt]
& -\sum_t p_{Jt}\left(JN_t + JT_t + JO_t - J_t\right) \\[4pt]
& -\sum_t q_{Nt}\left((1+d_N)KN_t - KN_{t-1} - JN_t\right) \\[4pt]
& -\sum_t q_{Tt}\left((1+d_T)KT_t - KT_{t-1} - JT_t\right) \\[4pt]
& -\sum_t \lambda_{Ft}\left(BAL_t - PT_t AT_t - PT_t a_{NE}XN_t - PO_t AO_t + PI_t I_t - rf_t V_{t-1} - S_t\right) \\[4pt]
& -\sum_t \lambda_{Vt}\left(V_t - V_{t-1} - BAL_t\right)
\end{aligned}
$$

$$- \Sigma\ w_t(LN_t + LT_t - L_t)$$
$$_t$$

$$- \Sigma\ q_t(KN_t + KT_t - K_t)$$
$$_t$$

$$+ \Sigma\ qk_{Nt}JN_t$$
$$_t$$

$$- \Sigma\ qk_{Tt}JT_t$$
$$_t$$

$$- qe_K(K_T^* - K_T)$$

$$- qe_V(V_T^* - V_T)$$

Note that in the above problem the objective function is concave while all the constraints are convex functions. The necessary conditions for a solution to the optimization problem are then:

$$\frac{\partial L}{\partial C_t} \rightarrow (S1) \qquad P_{1t} = NC_t\ (1+\beta)^{-t}\ C_t^{-\theta}$$

$$\frac{\partial L}{\partial CN_t} \rightarrow (S2) \qquad P_{1t}\alpha N\ \frac{C_t}{CN_t} = P_{Nt}$$

$$\frac{\partial L}{\partial CT_t} \rightarrow (S3) \qquad P_{1t}\alpha T\ \frac{C_t}{CT_t} = P_{Tt}$$

$$\frac{\partial L}{\partial CI_t} \rightarrow (S4) \qquad P_{1t}\alpha I\ \frac{C_t}{CI_t} = P_{It}$$

$$\frac{\partial L}{\partial XN_t} \rightarrow (S5) \qquad v_{Nt} = (1 - a_{NN} - a_{NE})P_{Nt} - (a_{TN} - a_{NE})P_{Tt} - a_{ON}P_{Ot} - a_{IN}P_{It}$$

$$\frac{\partial L}{\partial XT_t} \rightarrow (S6) \qquad v_{Tt} = (1 - a_{TT})P_{Tt} - a_{NT}P_{Nt} - a_{OT}P_{Ot} - a_{IT}P_{It}$$

$$\frac{\partial L}{\partial AO_t} \rightarrow (S7) \qquad P_{Ot} = \lambda_{Ft}PO_t$$

$$\frac{\partial L}{\partial AK_t} \rightarrow \text{(S8)} \qquad p_{Tt} = \lambda_{Ft} PT_t$$

$$\frac{\partial L}{\partial I_t} \rightarrow \text{(S9)} \qquad p_{It} = \lambda_{Ft} PI_t$$

$$\frac{\partial L}{\partial BAL_t} \rightarrow \text{(S10)} \qquad \lambda_{Ft} = \lambda_{Vt}$$

$$\frac{\partial L}{\partial V_{t-1}} \rightarrow \text{(S11)} \qquad \lambda_{Ft} rf_t + \lambda_{Vt} = \lambda_{V(t-1)} \qquad \text{for } t < T$$

$$\lambda_{FT} rf_T + \lambda_{VT} + q e_V = \lambda_{V(T-1)} \qquad \text{for } t = T$$

$$\frac{\partial L}{\partial J_t} \rightarrow \text{(S12)} \qquad p_{Jt} = j_N p_{Nt} + j_T p_{Tt} + j_O p_{Ot} + j_I p_{It}$$

$$\frac{\partial L}{\partial KN_{t-1}} \rightarrow \text{(S13)} \qquad v_{Nt} \left[\delta N / (\gamma N \prod_{\tau=1}^{t} (1+\epsilon N_\tau))^{\varrho N} \right] \left[\frac{XN_t}{KN_{t-1}} \right]^{(1+\varrho N)}$$

$$= (1+d_N) q_{N(t-1)} - q_{Nt}$$

$$\frac{\partial L}{\partial KT_{t-1}} \rightarrow \text{(S14)} \qquad v_{Tt} \left[\delta T / (\gamma T \prod_{\tau=1}^{t} (1+\epsilon T_\tau))^{\varrho T} \right] \left[\frac{XT_t}{KT_{t-1}} \right]^{(1+\varrho T)}$$

$$= (1+d_T) q_{T(t-1)} - q_{Tt}$$

$$\frac{\partial L}{\partial JN_t} \rightarrow \text{(S15)} \qquad - p_{Jt} + q_{Nt} + qk_{Nt} = 0$$

$$qk_{Nt} JN_t = 0$$

$$\frac{\partial L}{\partial JT_t} \rightarrow \text{(S16)} \qquad - p_{Jt} + q_{Tt} + qk_{Tt} = 0$$

$$qk_{Tt} JT_t = 0$$

$$\frac{\partial L}{\partial LN_t} \rightarrow \text{(S17)} \qquad v_{Nt} \left[(1-\delta N) / (\gamma N \prod_{\tau=1}^{t} (1+\epsilon N_\tau))^{\varrho N} \right] \left[\frac{XN_t}{LN_t} \right]^{(1+\varrho N)} = w_t$$

$$\frac{\partial L}{\partial LT_t} \rightarrow \text{(S18)} \qquad v_{Tt} \left[(1-\delta T)/(\gamma T \prod_{\tau=1}^{t} (1+\varepsilon T_\tau))^{\varrho T} \right] \left[\frac{XT_t}{LT_t} \right]^{(1+\varrho T)} = w_t$$

$$\frac{\partial L}{\partial K_t} \rightarrow \text{(S19)} \qquad q_t = 0 \qquad \text{for } t < T$$

$$q_T = qe_K$$

A.3. THE PARAMETERS

The model is calibrated to national accounts data for the Norwegian economy of 1980.

The input-output coefficients a_{ij} is computed as the ratio of intermediate use of good i in sector j to gross output in sector j. The numerical values for the a_{ij}'s and j_j's are found in table A1.

TABLE A1: Input-output coefficients.

Delivering sector	Receiving sector Nontraded	Traded	Petroleum	Investments
Nontraded	0.3202425	0.1739225	0.032824	0.565474
Traded	0.1037555	0.1996519	0.0243144	0.18966567
Petroleum	0.0004502	0.008779	0.00640828	0.0195557
Imports	0.0574218	0.3001504	0.0159074	0.2253048
Total	0.4818700	0.6825038	0.07945408	1.0000

The production functions are estimated on national accounts data for the 1962-1980 period. However, the share parameters δi have been adjusted to obtain the actual factor shares of 1980 from the equation:

$$\delta i/(1-\delta i) = (LS_i/PS_i)(Ki/Li)^{\varrho i} \qquad i=N,T$$

where LS_i and PS_i are respectively the share of labour income and profits

281

in factor income.   The equation is derived straightforward from (A3) and
(S15) above.

TABLE A2:   Parameters of the production functions and
            consumption aggregation function

$\gamma N = 1.84255$	$\delta N = 0.393298$	$\varrho N = 0.333$
$\gamma T = 3.8006439$	$\delta T = 0.441015$	$\varrho T = 0.191$
$\alpha N = 0.806$	$\alpha T = 0.059$	$\alpha I = 0.135$

REFERENCES

Arrow, K.J. and M. Kurz (1970): "Public Investment, the Rate of Return and
Optimal Fiscal Policy". John Hopkins University Press, Baltimore.

Barker, T. and V. Brailovsky (Eds.) (1981): "Oil or Industry?" Academic
Press, London.

Biørn, E. and E.S. Jansen (1982): "Econometrics of Incomplete Cross-
Section/Time-Series Data: Consumer Demand in Norwegian Households
1975-1977. Central Bureau of Statistics, Oslo

Bjerkholt, O., L. Lorentsen and S. Strøm (1981): "Using the oil and gas
revenues: The Norwegian case". In Barker and Brailovsky.

Bjerkholt, O., S. Longva, Ø. Olsen and S. Strøm (Eds.) (1983): "Analysis
of Supply and Demand of Electricity in the Norwegian Economy".
Central Bureau of Statistics, Oslo.

Bruno, M. (1976): "The Two-Sector Open Economy and the Real Exchange
Rate". American Economic Review, Vol. 66, no. 4.

Bruno, M. and J. Sachs (1982): "Energy and Resource Allocation: A Dynamic
Model of the "Dutch Disease"". Review of Economic Studies, XLIX, pp.
845-859.

Corden, W.M. (1982): "Booming Sector and Dutch Disease Economics: A survey". Working Paper 079. The Australian National University, Faculty
of Economics and Research School of Social Sciences.

Dervis, K., R. Martin and S. van Wijnbergen (1984): "Policy Analysis of
Shadow Pricing, Foreign Borrowing, and Resource Extraction in Egypt".
World Bank Staff Working Papers no. 622.

Dornbusch, R. (1980): "Open Economy Macroeconomics". Basic Books, Inc.
Publishers. New York.

Dornbusch, R. (1983): "Real Interest Rates, Home Goods, and Optimal External Borrowing". Journal of Political Economy. Vol. 91, no. 1. pp.
141-153.

Drud, A. and A. Meeraus (1980): "CONOPT. A System for Large Scale Dynamic Nonlinear Optimization. User's Manual". Development Research Center. World Bank.

Eide, E. (1973): "Virkninger av statens oljeinntekter på norsk økonomi". Sosialøkonomen, no. 10. (Impacts of Government Oil Revenues on the Norwegian Economy).

Johansen, L. (1960): "A Multi-Sectoral Study of Economic Growth". North Holland Publishing Company. Amsterdam.

NOU 1983:27: "Petroleumsvirksomhetens framtid". Universitetsforlaget, Oslo. (On the future extent of petroleum activitis on the Norwegian continental shelf.)

NOU 1983:37: "Perspektivberegninger for norsk økonomi til år 2000". Universitetsforlaget, Oslo. (Perspectives for the Norwegian Economy up to Year 2000.)

CERTAINTY EQUIVALENCE PROCEDURES IN THE MACROECONOMIC
PLANNING OF AN OIL ECONOMY

BY

IULIE ASLAKSEN AND OLAV BJERKHOLT

ABSTRACT

The theme of this paper is how to cope with the macroeconomic
exposure to risk in the Norwegian economy entailed by the increased
reliance upon the extraction of petroleum resources. A framework for
long-term macroeconomic planning based on optimal management of national
wealth under uncertainty of future oil price and rates of return on non-oil
assets is suggested, and a formal optimization model based on dynamic
programming is presented. The model is solved under simplified assumptions
and some properties of the solution are presented. The last part of the
paper is devoted to numerical explorations in applying certainty equvalence
procedures in optimizing the consumption path and capital accumulation.

1. THE ISSUES: OIL AND UNCERTAINTY

1.1 OIL IN THE NORWEGIAN ECONOMY

Norway has been a net exporter of crude oil since 1975 and of natural
gas since 1977. The current level of production of oil and gas amounts to
18 percent of GDP. The oil production at present corresponds to 3-4 times
the domestic consumption of petroleum, while the production of natural gas,
of which all is exported, is higher than the oil production (as measured in
toe). Proven reserves amount to 35-40 times the current annual level of
production, while more liberal assessments of oil and gas still in the
ground indicate that there may be considerable more: 100 times the current
annual production is a frequently quoted figure. With increasing
production and growing real price of extracted oil and gas it is thus well

within the range of possibilities that Norway may become dependent upon oil
and gas production for 20-30 percent of its GDP for an extended period of
time.

The theme of this paper is how to cope with the macroeconomic
exposure to risk in the Norwegian economy entailed by the increased
reliance upon the extraction of petroleum resources. It has been stated
that the Norwegian economy has never been so dependent upon one single
price as it today depends upon the international crude oil price. This may
well be so, but exposure to risk is nothing new in Norwegian economic
history. Over the last hundred and fifty years Norway has reaped benefits
and incurred losses from such diverse circumstances as the Navigation Act,
the elusive migrations of enormous shoals of herring and world wars as well
as the exposure of a small, open and not very diversified economy to the
ups and downs of world markets.

The current and future reliance upon extraction of petroleum
resources differ from these earlier circumstances in a number of important
ways:

- the long-term perspective of oil in the Norwegian economy,
- the macroeconomic importance of petroleum as measured e.g. by the
  share of GDP,
- the large scale of the resource base as compared e.g. with total
  national wealth,
- the high rent share of petroleum revenues, and
- the high government share of net revenues.

In the short-run context the rent of oil and gas production is a
source of national income. In the long-run perspective the stock of oil
and gas in the ground is a part of national wealth - an extraction of an
amount of oil and gas represents not income, but only a running down of a
large but limited stock. The real source of income connected with
petroleum resources is the increase in value of these resources, (although
the national accounts ignoring stocks of natural resources will tell a
different story). The rate of return on the stock of petroleum in the
ground is the increase in the net price.

Most of the attention given to uncertainty in connection with the
increased reliance upon petroleum extraction in the Norwegian economic and
political debate has been related to short- and medium-term consequences of
a volatile oil price. This has been natural in view of OPEC I and II and
the downward adjustment of the oil price from 1981. (It has also played a

prominent role that the government at an early stage grossly overestimated the rise of the overall production profile, but a lesson has been learnt and the importance of this incident now seems to fade). Countercyclical use of oil revenues, ratchet effects, "protection" of oil income booms from political misuse have been among the issues in this debate. Less attention has been given to uncertainty in the longer term perspectives. However, two recent reports from government appointed committees have i.a. dealt with these perspectives (NOU 1983:27, NOU 1983:37).

Our work is related to that of these two committees and may be regarded as suggestions of how the analyses could be brought further. We are well aware that answers given are very tentative to say the least, both theoretically and empirically. Our own attitude to them can be well expressed by a quote from the late Professor Leif Johansen (his share in our work is quite formidable) who wrote in the introduction to his book on the MSG model: ".... if I were required to make decisions and take actions in connection with relationships covered by this study I would (in the absence of more reliable results, and without doing more work) rely to a great extent on the data and the results presented in the following chapters." (Johansen, 1960).

In Norway macroeconomic medium- and long-term planning is based on quadrennial government White Papers presenting a four-year plan and a less detailed and less committing projection for the ensuing 20-30 years. It is in this context that the management of the long-term uncertainties of the Norwegian economy derived from the petroleum sector has its natural place. In section 1.2 we take a peek at earlier government projections of the Norwegian economy toward 2000. Section 1.3 discusses the notion of a strategic approach to long-term macroeconomic planning.

In section 2 we suggest a framework for overall long-term macroeconomic planning based on optimal management of national wealth under uncertainty of rates of return. A formal optimization framework based on dynamic programming in discrete time is presented and the model is solved under simplified assumptions. Some properties of the solution are discussed and some suggestions of how this framework can be applied in national economic planning are put forth.

In section 3 some ideas drawn from an article by Leif Johansen (1980) on certainty equivalence procedures in decision-making are applied in an attempt to analyze the implications of the projections drawn up by one of the committees referred to above when uncertainty is taken explicitly into account. The numerical explorations are based on very rough estimates of risks associated with the distribution of national wealth.

1.2 THE NORWEGIAN ECONOMY TOWARDS 2000: THE CURRENT STATE OF ANALYSIS

Official government projections for the Norwegian economy in 2000 have been presented on four occasions since their first appearance in 1973. These projections have all been elaborated by means of successive versions of the MSG model, originally constructed by Leif Johansen in 1960. The MSG model is a large general equilibrium model which combines an overall macroeconomic framework a with considerable amount of details. The MSG model is wholly deterministic, it does not deal explicitly with the many uncertainty aspects of the projections for the future. The most prominent uncertainty factor in our context is the future crude oil price.

Deterministic models are, however, often employed to illustrate uncertainty, either by presenting alternative broad scenarios or by using sensitivity calculations varying the assumptions about exogenous influences. Such methods can give interesting illustrations of the uncertainty. But in a planning context the uncertainty as it propagates from the exogenous influences must be evaluated in view of what can be governed or influenced by means of economic policy, and the important question is what conclusions can be drawn for current and future planning decisions.

An illustration of the uncertainty of future prospects of the economy can be found by comparing earlier projections. In table 1 the aggregate results for the development of gross domestic product and private consumption 1980-2000 in four official projections are put together. The presentation is merely for illustrative purposes, as an adequate comparison of these projections would require a more thorough treatment of the background and assumptions of the individual projections. The first projection had "high" and "low" alternatives while the ensuing projections had "high", "medium" and "low" alternatives. The figures given in the table are year 2000 figures as percentage increase over 1980 and average annual growth rates.

Table 1 conveys an impression of cyclical change in the assessment of the future from modest future growth rates in 1973 to a peak of optimism in the mid-1970's, and down to low prospects in 1981. The use of high-low intervals has been the method of exposing the uncertainty in these projections. Note, however, that the medium growth rate of GDP in the 1981 projection is outside the high-low interval in all the preceding projections. If one is interested in studying the confidence with which a government projects the future, one may ask whether the fluctuations in estimated long-term growth rates as revealed by table 1 reflects short-term changes in the economic climate and mood more than any real change in the evaluation of growth factors.

Looking back on earlier projections for a period that is still ahead of us, such as those included in table 1, one may search for better ways of assessing and presenting the uncertainty around the projected paths. A lot more is, of course, said about this in the respective publications. There is also a not too encouraging record of how well long-term projections have

Table 1. Official government projections for the Norwegian economy. Gross Domestic Product and Private Consumption in 2000 as percentage increase over 1980. (Average annual growth rates in parentheses).

Source	Year	Gross Domestic Product			Private Consumption		
		High	Medium	Low	High	Medium	Low
Long-Term Programme 1974-1977	1973	119.2 (4.0)		75.7 (2.9)	80.7 (3.0)		61.5 (2.4)
White Paper on Natural Resources and Economic Development	1975	132.1 (4.3)	106.8 (3.7)	67.1 (2.6)	136.6 (4.4)	119.1 (4.0)	60.7 (2.4)
Long-Term Programme 1978-1981	1977	99.8 (3.5)	92.5 (3.3)	85.6 (3.1)	100.2 (3.5)	85.9 (3.1)	85.9 (3.1)
Long-Term Programme 1982-1985	1981	83.1 (3.0)	59.3 (2.4)	38.3 (1.6)	92.4 (3.3)	71.7 (2.7)	49.7 (2.9)

Note: The figures are derived from published data in the following publications: St.meld.nr. 71 (1972-73), St.meld.nr. 50 (1974-75), St.meld. nr. 75 (1976-77) and St.meld. nr. 79 (1980-81). Some recalculations have been necessary to achieve comparability because of changes in the base year for volume figures and different periods of projection. The 1980 figures used are those implicit in the respective projections. For the first three projections the 1980 figures overestimated GDP in 1980 with 5,9 and 6 per cent and Private Consumption with 0,5 and 6.5 percent. A comparison of absolute year 2000 figures would thus make the 1975 and 1977 projections stand out as even more optimistic compared with the 1981 projection. In the latter projection the 1980 figures used were the preliminary national accounts figures available at the time.

performed compared to the actual development. A survey is given in an annex to the 1981 projection.

In this article we shall focus not so much on the treatment of uncertainty in macroeconomic projections in general, but more specifically on the implications of uncertainty for the selection of "optimal" or "good" paths. In the projections referred to above no explicit welfare function or preference indicator has been applied. The projections were presented in government papers as an annex to a medium-term programme. Usually the long-term projections are referred to as being elaborated by planning experts without the political commitments given to the medium-term programme.

Our analysis in section 3 is based on projections in a report called the "Perspective Analysis" (NOU 1983:37), published in 1983 by an appointed committee of experts relying to a great extent on the model tools and data

Table 2. Selected projections from the Perspective Analysis. Gross Domestic Product and Private Consumption in 2000. Percentage increase over 1980 and average annual growth rates.

	Gross Domestic Product		Private Consumption	
	Percent increase	Percent p.a.	Percent increase	Percent p.a.
1. Reference path	43.0	1.8	60.7	2.4
2. Higher petroleum income				
2.1 Increased domestic use	46.2	1.9	70.6	2.7
2.2 Increased capital exports	43.2	1.8	57.5	2.3
3. Sluggish world economy				
3.1 Tight policy	39.9	1.7	55.9	2.2
3.2 Lax policy	42.7	1.8	64.9	2.5

Note: The figures are derived from NOU 1983:37, table 7.1b. The reference path is based on full employment and an increase in the production of oil and gas reaching 80 mill. toe in year 2000. The crude oil price is in the reference path assumed to grow with 2 percent p.a. in real terms. Non-oil export grows with less than 2 percent p.a. In the two higher petroleum income scenarios the production of oil and gas is assumed to reach 90 mill. toe in year 2000, while the crude oil price grows with 3 percent p.a. In 2.1 the increased income is used to promote growth in domestic demand. Employment and the rate of technical progress increase, while in 2.2 the increased income is accumulated as foreign assets. The sluggish world economy scenarios depict developments where non-oil exports grow even less than in the reference path, only 1 percent p.a. In 3.1 the balance of payments is maintained by means of tight demand management. Employment falls off compared with the reference path. In 3.2 on the other hand priority is given to employment. Private and Government Consumption are increased with adverse consequences for the balance of payments. This table reveals, in fact, little about the differences between the alternatives. The Perspective Analysis also presented 3-4 other alternative scenarios.

289

sources used by the government for its projections. The committee stated views on the methodology of using macroeconomic models for long-term projections as well as presenting its own projections in the form of a reference path and alternative scenarios reflecting both uncertainty issues, policy alternatives and policy performance. The methodological part included remarks on how to cope better with uncertainty in macro-economic projections, but refrained from introducing new procedures in the preparation and presentation of projections compared to earlier government projections. Results corresponding to those in table 1 for the reference path and four alternative projections are summarized in table 2. As can be seen from the table the reference projection entails a considerable further revision downwards from the 1981 projection.

These alternative projections of the Norwegian economy towards year 2000 results in different states of the economy by the end of the planning period. In the highly simplified representation of these alternatives in

Figure 1. Selected projections from the Perspective Analysis. Percentage increase in consumption in 2000 over 1980 (C) and accumulated wealth in 2000 (W).

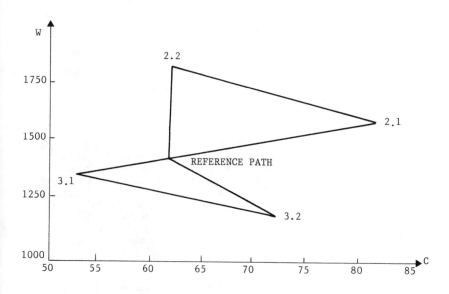

C = Total consumption (private and government) in 2000 as percentage increase over 1980.

W = Net foreign reserves in 2000 plus value of proven oil reserves in 2000

our further dicussion we ignore most structural and other aspects of the
differences between these alternatives and focus on only two variables:
consumption level (or rather increase over 1980) and wealth position.
Figure 1 plots all five projections with regard to these two
characteristics.

1.3 THE CONCEPT OF STRATEGY IN LONG-TERM MACROECONOMIC PLANNING UNDER UNCERTAINTY

Long-term economic planning is undertaken by enterprises, multinational corporations, municipalities, branches of govenment and households with
regard to their respective decision areas and responsibilities. Long-term
macroeconomic planning is the logical counterpart for the supervisory
branch of government responsible for the management of economic policy.
While short-term macroeconomic planning activities are day-to-day tasks of
governments exerted within well defined frameworks, long-term macroeconomic
planning is a somewhat more elusive concept. Much of what is presented as
long-term plans seem to be less operative and less committing than one
would normally expect of a plan worthy of its name. The term "projection"
is often used to convey a such more subdued intention. Sometimes
government will ask expert forecasters to draw up a projection on which the
government will base its long-term policy considerations. The forecasters
will then, at least implicitly, have to make assumptions about what the
government's decisions will be. This constitutes a puzzle which was posed
and answered by the late professor Ragnar Frisch in an article written many
years ago and wellknown to Norwegian economists (Frisch, 1961):

"How can it be possible to make a projection without knowing the
decisions that will basically influence the course of affairs?
It is as if the policy maker would say to the economic expert:
"Now you expert try to guess what I am going to do, and make
your estimate accordingly. On the basis of the factual
information thus received I will then decide what to do". The
shift from the on-looker view-point to the decision view-point
must be founded on a much coherent form of logic. It must be
based on a decision model, i.e. a model where the possible
decisions are built in explicitly as essential variables".

Frisch here rejects the idea that a government can adopt what he
calls an on-looker point of view. It should instead adopt a decision point
of view, that is, use techniques such that the analysis of the effects of
government decisions are integrated in the preparation of projections.
The preparation of long-term projections is a very demanding task. It
entails to bring together a large amount of data, much of which is not

normally easily available, about the future course of exogenous influences. It requires, furthermore, the application to a future period of model tools representing the functioning of the economy, but which often turn out to be insufficient, inadequate and inaccurate. The length of the horizon of the projection is often longer than the time series on which the estimated coefficients are based. These issues which are quite formidable are not dealt with in the sequel.

The <u>strategic</u> problem faced by the long-term macroeconomic planner is the implications of taking sequential decisions when there is uncertainty about a number of the exogenous influences. This has two important aspects. One is that the room for possible action at a future point of time may, and normally will, be narrowed down as a consequence of earlier actions and external influences. The irreversibility of extraction of oil and gas is a case in point. A diagram, borrowed from Johansen (1977, p.117) illustrates this. In figure 2 $A_{t(s)}$ is the set of possible acti- at time t, possible before decisions taken at time s (<t).

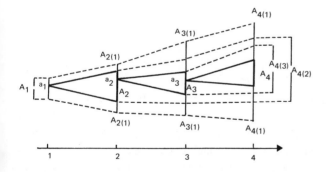

Figure 2. Sets of possible actions in a dynamic strategy.

until called for. This implies that future decisions can be based on more information than is available at the time of plan preparation, in particular the realization of uncertain events in the period between plan preparation and the decision point will be known. The problem is how to integrate this dynamic flexibility into an integrated plan.

Johansen (1978, p. 326) summarizes these points:

(1) In a dynamic context, in which there are interrelationships between what happens in the various periods, it is clearly not

advisable to determine the policy for some period without at the same time thinking of which policies one should pursue in the following periods.

(2) Since information continues to accrue in every future peri- od, it would be inadvisable to decide already in an early period what to do in later periods; decisions should rather be post- poned until they have to be taken, in order that this information, which is not available right from the beginning, can be utilized.

The answer is to search for strategies, i.e. policy functions which are decision rules stating how policy should be determined in each period on the basis of information available at the time. Perhaps the main purpose of long-term macroeconomic planning exercises should be the search for strategies. Unfortunately, the solution of this problem in the form of explicit policy functions are almost impossible to find except in very simplified cases.

Consider the following problem. An economy has at the outset an accumulated wealth given by W_0 and plans for two periods ahead. The wealth is invested abroad at a given certain interest, r. Income in each period, R_t is uncertain with known expectation and variance. The planning problem is to determine consumption, C_t. The optimization criterion is given as

$$\text{Max } EU(C_1, C_2, W_2)$$

where W_2 is the wealth remaining at the end of period 2. This problem can be solved as a static problem giving optimal solutions C_1^S and C_2^S. The dynamic optimization problem is to determine C_1 when the decision on C_2 is postponed one period. The solution to this problem entails finding the strategy for C_2, i.e. the policy function determining C_2 when R_1 is known.

Using the exponential preference functions we shall employ in section 2, the maximization problem above can be reformulated as a non-stochastic problem:

$$\text{Max } U(C_1, C_2, \tilde{W}_2)$$

where $\tilde{W}_2$ is an uncertainty adjusted expection of W_2, i.e. the real expectation adjusted downwards with an amount which depends both on the uncertainty of income in the two periods and the risk aversion implicit in the preference function. The problem is solved by first considering the second period decision based on a known value of W_1. This problem gives the strategy function for C_2. Then C_1 can be solved on the basis of the known strategy. How is the dynamic solution, C_1^D and C_2^D, compared with the static solution? The answer depends upon the choice of preference function. With a linear model and quadratic preference function the answer is given by the wellknown certainty equivalent result of Theil (1964): the first period decision on C_1 is the same in both cases. Using the additive exponential preference indicator of section 2, implying constant absolute risk aversion, it can be shown that the dynamic optimization implies higher consumption in period 1 and higher expected consumption in period 2.

Why is this so? Optimal consumption comes out higher in period 1 because less emphasis is put on the uncertainty of income in period 1. If this turns out to be different from expected income, it can to some extent be counteracted by the second period decision. The second period consumption comes out higher because this decision is based on more information: income in period 1 is not uncertain any longer. (The higher consumption in period 1 will have a slight negative influence on consumption in period 2 because of reduced interest income but not enough to counteract the effect of reduced uncertainty). Thus strategies are worth searching for.

The rationale of this approach is a major theme in Johansen (1977, 1978). After commenting on the many intractable aspects of solving planning problems in terms of strategies, he concludes (Johansen, 1978, p. 328-329):

> (1) Although analytical derivation of strategies for strict optimization is usually not feasible, the general understanding of the nature of the problem and its solution may help to formulate the policy in a better way than without this understanding.
> (2) Concrete questions of economic policy are often posed and debated as strategy problems, although they are not necessarily formulated in the terminology of this theory.
> (3) In spite of the point made under (1) above, under certain conditions optimal strategies are really simple.

2. A MODEL FOR OPTIMAL MANAGEMENT OF NATIONAL WEALTH

2.1 NATIONAL WEALTH AND RATES OF RETURN

We assume that the national wealth is distributed over a number of assets - physical and financial assets as well as natural resources. Assets are measured in terms of the purchasing power of consumption goods. The planning horizon is divided into periods of equal length. At the beginning

294

of each period the returns on the various assets are added up and distributed between consumption and accumulation in the same assets. For the decisions to be taken at the beginning of each period we have the following budget equation

$$(1) \qquad R_t \;=\; C_t \;+\; \sum_{i=0}^{n} I_{it}$$

where I_{it} is the investment in asset no. i and C_t is the rate of consumption in period t. Consumption is defined as the sum total of private and government consumption. All income is assumed to be capital income, accruing from investment undertaken one period earlier, hence

$$R_t \;=\; \sum_{i=0}^{n} r_{it} W_{it-1}$$

where W_{it-1} is the amount of asset no. i invested at the beginning of period t and r_{it} its rate of return. In asset terms the budget equation can be written:

$$(2) \qquad G_{t-1} \;=\; C_t \;+\; \sum_{i=0}^{n} W_{it}$$

where $G_{t-1} \;=\; \sum_{i=0}^{n} W_{it-1} + R_t \;=\; W_{t-1} + R_t$

Total wealth G_{t-1} at the beginning of period t hence consists of stocks of assets inherited from the past as well as capital income. The rates of return are stochastic variables. We assume that when decisions are to be made at the beginning of period t the outcome of the stochastic rates of return dated t is known with certainty whereas the uncertainty regarding future periods has to be taken into account.

Oil reserves still in the ground can be considered as one type of assets although they are not usually counted as part of national wealth. The value of the oil reserves can be measured as the product of the amount of reserves S_t and the price net of marginal extraction costs, $q_t = p_t - b_t$

where p_t is the current oil price and b_t is marginal extraction cost. We assume that marginal cost is constant with respect to the rate of extraction but is a hyperbolic function of the reserve level. The rate of return on the oil reserves is equal to the rate of growth of the net oil price. Introducing oil as an additional asset in (2) and redefining total wealth G_t and total stock of assets W_t to include oil reserves give:

$$(3) \qquad G_{t-1} = C_t + W_t$$

where
$$G_{t-1} = \sum_{i=0}^{n} W_{it-1} + R_t + q_t S_{t-1}$$

and
$$W_t = \sum_{1=0}^{n} W_{it} + q_t S_t$$

In the numerical explorations in section 3 we shall distinguish between four assets apart from oil:

W_S = real capital in the sheltered sector (i.e. non-tradable goods production, protected sectors, and government)

W_E = real capital in the export sector

W_H = real capital in the import-competing sector

W_U = foreign assets

Foreign assets are assumed to yield a risk-free rate of return of 3 percent. The variance-covariance matrix for the estimated rates of return in the respective estimation periods is given in table 4.

This choice of breakdown of non-oil national wealth is - as the other specifications in the model - rather tentative. A priori we would expect capital in the non-tradeable sector to be a more certain asset (i.e. lower rate of return, but also lower variance) than investment in the tradeable sectors, while foreign reserves are assumed to be a risk-free asset.

For a small oil exporting country like Norway the oil price is exogenous, independent of domestic reserves and rate of extraction. It may not be so obvious whether the rates of return are independent of the stocks of the respective assets, and whether the stochastic rates of return on assets other than oil also are time independent as assumed in the formal

Table 3. Average rates of return. Percent.

	Estimation period 1962-81
Sheltered sector (excluding government)	7.53
Import competing sector	10.00
Export sector	5.45

Table 4. Variance-covariance matrix 1962-81.

	Sheltered sector	Import competing sector	Export sector	Real oil price
Sheltered sector	1.65685	-0.088861	-1.84331	-1.28275
Import-competing sector		2.30443	1.93291	-0.897742
Export sector			13.8807	0.621457
Real oil price				16.789

model in section 2.3 below. In the following we assume that real capital
by sector has constant expected rates of return as set out above. This
exceedingly simplified picture of a national economy can only be defended
on the ground that it serves a higher purpose!

2.2 RISK AVERSION AND PREFERENCES

The planning problem is defined here as the maximization of the sum
of discounted expected utility from consumption over a planning horizon of
length T, taking into consideration the discounted utility of terminal
wealth. The utility of terminal wealth must be interpreted as derived from
the consumption possibilities it represents beyond the planning horizon.

The objective function at the beginning of period t can thus be
written as

(4)
$$\sum_{\tau=t}^{T} U(C_\tau)(1+\delta)^{t-\tau} + V(G_T)(1+\delta)^{t-T} \qquad t=0,1,\ldots,T$$

where U and V are the utility functions for instantaneous consumption and terminal wealth respectively, and δ is the rate of time preference.

The decision problem at the beginning of each period is deciding on the reinvestment of total wealth and the rate of consumption to be maintained in the period. The results of earlier decisions are represented in period t through the stock of assets inherited from the previous periods. We assume that total wealth can be reallocated between assets. The decisions to be taken in the following periods up to T have to be taken into account when deciding on consumption and investment at the beginning of period t. Decisions in all periods should reflect an appropriate trade-off between consumption and investment, as well as between consumption in the planning period and terminal wealth.

For the instantaneous utility function we use the exponential function

$$(5) \qquad U(C_t) = - Bexp(-\beta C_t) \qquad B,\beta > 0$$

which implies constant absolute risk aversion. The absolute risk aversion coefficient is given by $-U''/U' = \beta$. For terminal wealth we likewise assume constant absolute risk aversion, i.e

$$(6) \qquad V(G_T) = - Gexp(-\gamma G_T) \qquad G,\gamma > 0$$

There is no strong apriori arguments for choosing constant absolute risk aversion as an assumption (and empirical tests of planners' preferences are hard to come by). The big advantage of the exponential utility function is that it combined with normally distributed risk factors has very pleasant properties in terms of certainty equivalence.

A well-known certainty equivalence result (e.g. Johansen, 1980) states that when x is normally distributed and f(x) is an exponential function, then

$$E f(x) = f(\hat{x})$$

where $\hat{x}$, the certainty equivalent of x, is given by

$$\tilde{x} = EX - \frac{1}{2}\ \alpha\ var\ x$$

where α, the exponential coefficient of $f(x)$, also expresses the absolute risk aversion.

2.3 OPTIMIZATION BY MEANS OF DYNAMIC PROGRAMMING

The optimization problem given by maximization of (4) under the budget constraint (3) and given initial values of oil stock and non-oil wealth can be solved by the method of stochastic dynamic programming. For a planning horizon starting at t=0 from given values of G_0 and S_0 the optimization problem is solved by beginning at the end of the planning horizon and solving the decision problem for each period recursively. At the beginning of period T the optimal W_{iT}, S_T and C_T are determined, given the initial condition G_{T-1} and S_{T-1}. Having found the optimal solution for the last period contingent on any initial condition G_{T-1} and S_{T-1}, we solve the two-period problem for the last two periods by choosing the optimal W_{iT-1}, S_{T-1} and C_{T-1}, contingent on the initial condition G_{T-2} and S_{T-2}, and so on. In the last stage the optimal W_{i1}, S_1 and C_1 are determined, given the initial values G_0 and S_0 available at the beginning of period 1. A crucial assumption for the optimality of this procedure is stochastic independence between rates of return, including the oil price, in different periods. Our approach follows Samuelson (1969) and Chow (1975), see also Aslaksen and Bjerkholt (1984).

In the dynamic programming fashion we denote the maximum expected value of (4), contingent on G_{t-1}, by $J_t(G_{t-1})$. The decision problem at the beginning of period t can now be more precisely stated as

(7) $J_t(G_{t-1}) = Max\ E\{U(C_t) + J_{t+1}(G_t)/(1+\delta)\}$

where the maximization is with respect to W_{it} and S_t and subject to (3). Before proceeding to the solution procedure, the stochastic assumptions must be specified.

The stochastic assumptions concerning future oil prices and rates of

return are of considerable importance for the optimal solution. We shall
assume that the rates of return are multinormally distributed with expected
values ϱ_i and variances and covariances σ_{ij}, $i,j=0,\ldots,n$. The oil price is
assumed to be normally distributed with expected value π_t and variance τ^2.
Covariances between the oil price and the rates of return on non-oil assets
are given by τ_i, $i=0,\ldots,n$. By the method of dynamic programming we start
by solving the maximization problem given by (7) for t=T, i.e.

$$(8) \qquad J_T(G_{T-1}) \;=\; \text{Max } E\{U(C_T) + V(G_T)/(1+\delta)\}$$

$$= \; \text{Max } \{U(C_T) + EV(G_T)\}$$

where the maximization is with respect to W_{iT} and S_T and subject to (7).
The expectation is contingent on the initial conditions G_{T-1} and S_{T-1}
at the beginning of period T. The expected value operator is applied only
on the second term since current consumption C_T is known once we have made
our decision.

Applying the certainty equivalence result referred to in the section
2.2 above to (8) gives:

$$(9) \qquad J_T(G_{T-1}) \;=\; \text{Max } \{U(C_T) + V(\hat{G}_T)\}$$

where:

$$\hat{G}_T \;=\; EG_T - \frac{1}{2}\gamma \text{ var } G_T$$

$$EG_T \;=\; \sum_{i=0}^{n} W_{iT}(1+\varrho_i) + (\pi_{T+1} - b_{T+1})S_T$$

$$varG_T \;=\; \sum_{i=0}^{n}\sum_{j=0}^{n} \sigma_{ij}W_{iT}W_{jT} + \tau^2 S_T^2 + 2\sum_{j=0}^{n} \tau_j W_{jT}S_T$$

Evaluating the terminal value of the oil reserves should take into account
future oil price uncertainty beyond the planning horizon. The approach of
measuring the terminal value by certainty equivalent net price at the beginning of period T does not capture this future uncertainty. However, the

<u>marginal</u> value of the terminal oil reserves is equal to the certainty equivalent net oil price, provided that the terminal level of oil reserves is optimally weighed against consumption throughout the planning period and terminal stocks of non-oil assets.

The first order conditions for the solution of (9) are:

(10a) $\beta U(C_T) = \gamma V(\hat{G}_T)(1+\hat{r}_i)/(1+\delta)$ for non-oil assets

(10b) $\beta U(C_T) = \gamma V(\hat{G}_T)\,\hat{q}_{T+1}/q_T/(1+\delta)$ for the oil asset

where

$$\hat{r}_i = \frac{\delta \hat{G}_T}{\delta W_{iT}} - 1 = \varrho_i - \gamma \sum_{j=0}^{n} \sigma_{ij} W_{jT} - \gamma \tau_i S_T \qquad i=0,\ldots,n$$

and

$$\hat{q}_{T+1} = \frac{\delta \hat{G}_T}{\delta S_T} = \pi_{T+1} - b_{T+1} - \gamma \tau^2 S_T - \gamma \sum_{j=0}^{n} \tau_j W_{jT} - b'_{T+1}(S_T) S_T$$

$\hat{r}_i$ is the certainty equivalent rate of return on assets no. i, i.e. the marginal increase in certainty equivalent wealth by a marginal increase in asset no. i. $\hat{q}_{T+1}$ is the certainty equivalent net oil price in period T+1. The difference between the certainty equivalent net oil price and the expected net oil price consists of the correction terms due to the uncertainty as well as a term due to the dependence of marginal cost on the reserve level. With a hyperbolic marginal cost function, $b_t = m/S_{t-1}$, cost function terms in $\hat{q}_{T+1}$ cancel out, and $\hat{q}_{T+1}$ appears as

$$\hat{q}_{T+1} = \pi_{T+1} - \gamma \tau^2 S_T - \gamma \sum_{j=0}^{n} \tau_j W_{jT}$$

To obtain an explicit solution for the optimal portfolio and consumption we make the crucial assumption that asset no. 0 is risk-free, yielding a certain rate of return r_0. Hence, $\hat{r}_0 = r_0$ and from the first-order conditions we get:

(11a) $\hat{r}_i = r_0$ $i=1,\ldots,n$

(11b) $\tilde{q}_{T+1}/q_T - 1 = r_0$

Optimal accumulation in the uncertain assets is determined by the condition that certainty equivalent rate of return should be equalized for all assets. Oil extraction is determined by a modified Hotelling rule: certainty equivalent net oil price should grow at a rate of return equal to the certain rate of return.

Substituting the first order conditions into (9) using (11) gives the maximal expected utility at the beginning of period T

(12) $J_T(G_{T-1}) = U(C_T^*)(1+\beta/\gamma(1+r_0)) = U(C_T^*)\mathcal{E}_1$

where C_T^* is optimal consumption in period T and $\mathcal{E}_1 = 1 + \beta/\gamma(1+r_0)$

From (12) it is seen that optimal consumption C_T^* can be expressed as a function of total wealth G_{T-1} at the beginning of period T. The explicit solution for optimal consumption C_t^* will be derived in a similar way from the general solution for $J_t(G_{t-1})$. To realize the recursive nature of the solution, it is elucidating to consider the decision problem for t=T-1 and then derive the general solution for $J_t(G_{t-1})$ by induction. The decision problem at the beginning of period T-1 is

(13) $J_{T-1}(G_{T-2}) = \text{Max } E\{U(C_{T-1}) + J_T(G_{T-1})/(1+\delta)\}$

where the maximization is with respect to W_{iT-1} and S_{T-1} and subject to (3). Observing that J_T is an exponential, we apply the certainty equivalent result to (13):

(14) $J_{T-1}(G_{T-2}) = \text{Max}\{U(C_{T-1}) + J_T(\hat{G}_{T-1})/(1+\delta)\}$

However, the appropriate risk aversion coefficient in the certainty equivalent expression for G_{T-1} is not γ. J_t is an exponential function with time dependent absolute risk aversion coefficient. Differentiating (9) with respect to G_{T-1} and applying the first order condition (10) gives

(15) $\quad \dfrac{dJ_T(G_{T-1})}{dG_{T-1}} \;=\; U'(C_T^*)$

and by using (12) we get:

(16) $\quad \dfrac{J_T'(G_{T-1})}{J_T(G_{T-1})} \;=\; -\beta/(1+\beta/\gamma(1+r_0)) \;=\; -\beta/\mathcal{E}_1$

The appropriate risk aversion coefficient for $\tilde{G}_{T-1}$ is thus $-\beta/\mathcal{E}_1$ and

$$\tilde{G}_{T-1} \;=\; EG_{T-1} - \dfrac{1}{2}\,\beta/\mathcal{E}_1 \,\operatorname{var} G_{T-1}$$

The first order conditions for the solution of (14) can hence be stated as

(17a) $\quad \beta U(C_{T-1}) \;=\; \beta/\mathcal{E}_1(1+\delta)\;J_T(\tilde{G}_{T-1})(1+r_0)$

(17b) $\quad \beta U(C_{T-1}) \;=\; \beta/\mathcal{E}_1(1+\delta)\;J_T(\tilde{G}_{T-1})\ddot{q}_T/q_{T-1}$

The solution for J_{T-1} is found by substituting (17) into (14)

$$J_{T-1}(G_{T-2}) \;=\; U(C_{T-1}^*)(1+(1+\beta/\gamma(1+r_0))/(1+r_0)) \;=\; U(C_{T-1}^*)\mathcal{E}_2$$

Comparing the solutions for J_T and J_{T-1} the recursiveness of the solution for J_t appears through the coefficient $\mathcal{E}_{T-t}$, which is recursively determined by the difference equation.

$$\mathcal{E}_{T-t} \;=\; 1 + \dfrac{\mathcal{E}_{T-t-1}}{1+r_0}$$

The solution for $\mathcal{E}_{T-t}$ is given by

$$\mathcal{E}_{T-t} \;=\; \left(\dfrac{1}{1+r_0}\right)^{T-t}(\beta/\gamma - \dfrac{1+r_0}{r_0}) + \dfrac{1+r_0}{r_0}$$

with $\xi_0 = \beta/\gamma$

By induction it can be shown that the generalizations of (12), (15) and (16) are

(18) $\quad J_t(G_{t-1}) = U(C_t^*)\xi_{T-t+1}$

(19) $\quad J_t'(G_{t-1}) = U'(C_t^*)$

(20) $\quad \dfrac{J_t'(G_{t-1})}{J_t(G_{t-1})} = -\beta/\xi_{T-t+1}$

From (19) and (20) it follows that C_t^* is a linear function of G_{t-1}, i.e.:

(21) $\quad C_t = a_t G_{t-1} + b_t$

a_t is easily found to be $1/\xi_{T-t+1}$, while b_t can be solved from the difference equation

$$b_{t+1} = (\xi_{T-t+1}/(\xi_{T-t+1} - 1)) b_t + \alpha/\beta$$

to give

(22) $\quad b_t = -\{ \dfrac{1+r_0}{r_0} \dfrac{\alpha}{r_0} + \dfrac{1}{(1+r_0)^{T-t}} \left[-\beta/\gamma(1+r_0)(\ln(\beta/\gamma)-\alpha-\ln(1+\delta)) \right.$

$$+ \dfrac{T-t}{1+r_0} (\dfrac{\beta}{\gamma} - \dfrac{1+r_0}{r_0}) \alpha - \dfrac{1+r_0}{r_0} \dfrac{\alpha}{r_0} \left. \right] \}/\beta\xi_{T-t+1}$$

where $\alpha = \ln \dfrac{1+r_0}{1+\delta} - \chi$

and

$$\chi = \frac{1}{2} \sum_{i=1}^{n} \sum_{j=1}^{n} (\varrho_i - r_0)(\varrho_j - r_0)\hat{\sigma}_{ij} + (\frac{\bar{q}_{t+1}}{q_t} - 1 - r_0) \sum_{j=1}^{n} (\varrho_j - r_0)\hat{\tau}_j$$

$$+ \frac{1}{2}(\frac{\bar{q}_{t+1}}{q_t} - 1 - r_0)^2 \hat{\tau}^2$$

$\hat{\sigma}_{ij}$, $\hat{\tau}_j$ and $\hat{\tau}^2$ are the elements of the inverse of the variance-covariance matrix of σ_{ij}, τ_j and τ^2, and $\bar{q}_{t+1}$ is the expected net price (equal to $\pi_{t+1} - b_{t+1}$). One can use the approximation $\ln((1+r_0)/(1+\delta)) = r_0 - \delta$, which means $\alpha = r_0 - \delta^*$, where $\delta^* = \delta + \chi$. Thus as an implication of the certainty equivalence procedure, the stochastic parameters appear only in the risk-adjusted time preference rate δ^*.

In the solution of b_t the coefficients B and G in (5) and (6) are assumed equal to one. The marginal propensity to consume out of current wealth is the reciprocal of the recursion coefficient ξ_{T-1}. By rewriting the expression for ξ_{T-1} it is easily seen that:

$$(23) \qquad \xi_{T-t} = \beta \left[\frac{1/(1+r_0)^{T-t}}{\gamma} - \frac{1-1/(1+r_0)^{T-t}}{\beta \frac{r_0}{1+r_0}} \right]$$

β/ξ_{T-t} can be interpreted as a weighted harmonic average of the terminal wealth risk aversion coefficient γ and the risk aversion coefficient β adjusted by the term $r_0/1+r_0$. As the time interval from the present date until the planning horizon is increasing, the effect of γ on current consumption is diminishing. In the limiting case where $T-t \to \infty$, ξ is a constant given by

$$(24) \qquad \xi = \frac{1+r_0}{r_0}$$

In this case the marginal propensity to consume is independent of γ as well as β. However, γ and β appear in the constant term of the consumption function.

When the optimization problem has been solved step by step, optimal consumption is implemented by recording actual development and inserting, period by period, the outcome of the stochastic rates of return, i.e. G_{t-1}, in the consumption function (21). The optimal solution can thus be interpreted as a **strategy**; decision rules for optimal consumption are calculated initially, whereas actual consumption decisions are postponed until current wealth is known with certainty.

This consumption strategy is consistent with a long-term consumption path given by

$$(25) \qquad C_t = \frac{r_0 - \delta}{\beta} t + C_0$$

were C_0 is initial consumption.

From the first order conditions for the optimization problem follows a relation between marginal utility of consumption in two successive periods,

$$U'(C_t) = \frac{1+r_0}{1+\delta} U'(C_{t+1})$$

hence the optimal C_t is derived by taking logarithms on both sides and solving the resulting difference equation for C_t.

Given the optimal consumption, the accumulation in the uncertain assets is determined as a one-period portfolio problem.

$$(26) \qquad W_{it} = \frac{\xi_{T-t+1}}{\beta} \{ \sum_{j=1}^{n} (\varrho_j - r_0) \hat{\sigma}_{ij} + \hat{\tau}_i (\pi_{t+1} - (1+r_0) q_t) \}$$

$$(27) \qquad S_t = \frac{\xi_{T-t+1}}{\beta} \{ \sum_{j=1}^{n} (\varrho_j - r_0) \hat{\tau}_j + \hat{\tau}^2 (\pi_{t+1} - (1+r_0) q_t) \}$$

Hence, optimal oil extraction in period t is given by

$$(28) \qquad X_t = S_{t-1} - S_t$$

where S_t is determined by (27) and S_{t-1} is given from the previous period.

Due to the strong assumptions regarding the utility function and the stochastic parameters as well as the production structure and the cost function for oil extraction we have thus obtained explicit solutions with intuitive interpretations.

3. NUMERICAL EXPLORATIONS IN APPLYING CERTAINTY EQUIVALENCE PROCEDURES IN OPTIMIZING THE NORWEGIAN ECONOMY

3.1. PREFERENCE FUNCTIONS DERIVED FROM MACROECONOMIC PROJECTIONS

The intended application of the stochastic optimization framework outlined in this article is mainly as a means for evaluating and corroborating long-term projections from the MSG model. Although stochastic elements are not included in the MSG model, the model is a valuable means for illustrating the wide range of possible long-term projections under alternative oil price assumptions. Model calculations are performed with alternative oil price scenarios and exogenously stipulated oil and gas production profiles. The consequences of alternative oil revenue scenarios are traced out by model calculations. These long-term projections illustrate the considerable impact on sectoral development and accumulated foreign reserves under alternative oil price assumptions. A consistent evaluation of these long-term equilibrium growth paths under uncertainty requires a stochastic optimization framework.

In order to apply the stochastic optimization model outlined above, we have to make an assessment of the risk aversion coefficients β and γ. Before facing this cumbersome task, a quote from an early paper on certainty equivalent procedures by Freund (1956) may be appropriate: "The estimation of the risk aversion constant a is a purely subjective task, and any chosen value is exceedingly difficult to defend". However, in our approach to applying certainty equivalence procedures to long-term macroeconomic planning, the estimation of the risk aversion coefficients should not be based on subjective judgements, but rather reflect current political preferences.

The analysis of this chapter is based on the MSG projections in the report of the Perspective Analysis (NOU 1983:37). As stated in section 1.2 these long-term projections are elaborated by a group of experts without the political commitments that are given to the projections presented in e.g. the medium-term programme. However, for our purpose it may not be totally misleading to interpret them as reflecting current political preferences. The projections of the Perspective Analysis do not easily lend themselves to the assessment of preferences. Little is said about the evaluation of the alternative projections, and no precise guidelines are given for the trade-off between consumption and wealth accumulation.

The present analysis is based on the reference path and the four alternative projections which are summarized in table 2. These five projections illustrate a wide range of possibilities for the choice between consumption and accumulation of foreign assets. The two triangles in figure 3 indicate the feasible sets under the assumptions of either higher petroleum income (2.1 and 2.2) or sluggish world economy (3.1 and 3.2). Little is said about the choice between increased domestic use and increased capital exports in the case of higher petroleum income, and the choice between tight and lax policy in the case of a sluggish world economy.

Based on the information provided in the report of the Perspective Analysis we have however established the following crucial assumptions.

Consider the following stochastic experiment with two possible outcomes: Either the outcome of higher petroleum income is realized, where the feasible set is represented by the line segment between 2.1 and 2.2, or the outcome of a sluggish world economy is realized, where the feasible set is represented by the line segment between 3.1 and 3.2. These two outcomes are assumed to have an equal probability. The alternatives 2.1 or 2.2 and 3.1 or 3.2 thus represent extreme policies in view of the uncertainty, and to reveal the optimal policy we state the following assumptions:

a) Sluggish world economy: Given a feasible set of all points between 3.1 and 3.2 the best choice is to pursue a policy aiming at a result midway between the two extreme policies.

b) Higher petroleum income: Given a feasible set of all points between 2.1 and 2.2 the best choice is to pursue a policy aiming at a result slightly closer to 2.1 than the midpoint.

c) Reference path: The reference path is considered as the certainty equivalent of the stochastic experiment described above. Given the

308

two optimal policies described in a)-b) the expected utility of
these two outcomes is equal to the utility of the reference path.

These assumptions are formulated in view of a preference function
given by

(29) $U(C,W) = -B\exp(-bC) - G\exp(-gW)$

C = Total consumption (private and government) in 2000 as percentage
increase over 1980.

W = Net foreign reserves in 2000 plus value of proven oil reserves
in 2000.

To simplify the estimation of the risk aversion coefficients, the
preference function (29) has been formulated as a static analogy to the
multi-period preference function (4) of the dynamic optimization problem.
In (29) preferences are attached to the percentage increase in consumption
over the planning horizon, rather than the sum of discounted utility of
consumption in each period. However, this reformulation does not alter the
main conclusions for the trade-off between consumption and terminal wealth
under uncertainty. The numerical estimate for the risk aversion
coefficient b will differ from the risk aversion coefficient β of the multi
period preference function, and the appropriate estimate for β will finally
be derived.

The wealth concept W defined as net foreign reserves plus the value
of the oil reserves is highly tentative, to say the least. It does not
properly reflect the concept of national wealth as defined in the
optimization model. According to the preference function (4), consumption
should be weighed against total wealth at the end of the planning period,
i.e. production capital, financial assets and natural resources. The role
of terminal wealth in the preference function is to represent the
production potential for future consumption beyond the planning horizon.
The discussion of the Perspective Analysis is however more explicitly
related to the trade-off between consumption growth and net foreign
reserves at the end of the planning period. The point of foreign reserves
in this connection seems to be as a safeguard against the risk inherent in
the oil reserves. In order to accommodate the views expressed in the report
as a guideline for our estimation of the risk aversion coefficients, the
value of petroleum reserves and net foreign reserves are included in our

wealth concept here while other assets are disregarded. This is perhaps a dubious interpretation and inclusion of real capital would have given different estimation results.

The assumptions a)-c) give three relationships to determine the parameters b, g and G/B. The level of utility is arbitrarily chosen by setting B=1. Furthermore, the parameter values are adjusted to yield G=B=1. The following parameter values are thus obtained:

b = 0.1426

g = 0.00589

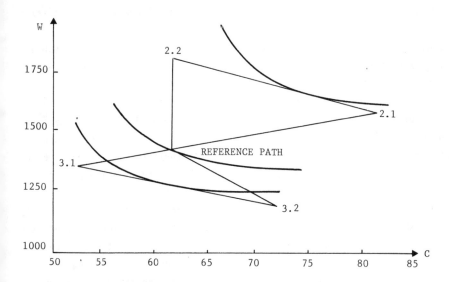

Figure 3.   Indifference curves with b=0.1426 and g=0.00589

Given these parameter values, the numerical application will be pursued in two directions. First, the indifference curve approach outlined in this section will be elaborated as an illustration of a more general certainty equivalence procedure developed by Leif Johansen (1980). The idea of this approach is to incorporate uncertainty in the decision-making by a modification of the parameters of the objective function. The effect of uncertainty on the trade-off between consumption growth and terminal wealth is thus clearly exposed. Based on our estimates of the risk aversion parameters and the standard deviations, the optimal trade-off between consumption growth and terminal wealth under uncertainty will be discussed.

Secondly, the relationship between the preference function given by (29) and the multi-period preference function of section 2.3 will be established, and some tentative numerical results will be given with regard to the optimal consumption path.

3.2. THE JOHANSEN APPROACH TO CERTAINTY EQUIVALENCE PROCEDURES IN DECISION-MAKING UNDER UNCERTAINTY

The simple certainty equivalence procedure introduced in section 2.2 as a means for solving the stochastic dynamic optimization problem and the assumption of constant absolute risk aversion and normally distributed stochastic elements permit a transformation of the stochastic optimization problem to an optimization in terms of certainty equivalents. The certainty equivalent of a stochastic variable is the expected value minus a correction term, which is proportional to the variance and the risk aversion coefficient.

In this section the preference function (29) will be examined in terms of certainty equivalence. It may be elucidating to analyze the consequences of uncertainty in the static analogy to our dynamic optimization problem, before proceeding to illustrate the consequences of uncertainty on the decisions taken year by year in the planning period.

This section is based on some ideas from an article by Leif Johansen (1980). In economic theory certainty equivalence procedures have mainly been elaborated in the case of a quadratic objective function combined with a linear structural model. One of the many contributions of Leif Johansen in this field is the generalization of the usual certainty equivalence procedure to the case of an objective function expressed in terms of combinations of exponential functions. The idea of this approach is to modify the original parameters of the objective function in order to incorporate the variances and covariances of the stochastic elements. This parametric certainty equivalence procedure, as developed in Johansen (1980), gives a procedure which is the same as under certainty, but the decisions actually taken will generally be different under uncertainty than under certainty because the modified parameter values will depend on the probability distribution.

Consider the preference function given by (29). If there were no uncertainty involved, we would choose from the feasible points so as to maximize (29). The indifference curves of (29) are characterized by the marginal rate of substitution between C and W given by

(30) $\dfrac{dW}{dG} = -\dfrac{bB}{gG} \exp (gW - bC)$

Given the assumption of normal probability distributions, the parametric certainty equivalence procedure entails the following transformation of (29)

(31) $U(EC,EW) = -\hat{B} \exp (-b\ EC) - \hat{G} \exp (-g\ EW)$

where $\hat{B} = B \exp (1/2\ b^2 \sigma_c^2)$

and $\hat{G} = G \exp (1/2\ g^2 \sigma_w^2)$

The standard deviation of C and W is denoted by σ_c and σ_w respectively. The certainty equivalence procedure consists in choosing EC and EW so as to maximize (31). The marginal rate of substitution is now expressed as

(32) $\dfrac{dEW}{dEC} = -\dfrac{bB}{gG} \exp (1/2(b^2\sigma_c^2 - g^2\sigma_w^2)\ \exp (gEW - bEC)$

First it can be noted that uncertainty has no effect on the actual decisions in the case where:

$b\sigma_c = g\sigma_w$

If this is not the case, the indifference curves of (31) will be twisted as a consequence of uncertainty. Furthermore, a partial increase in σ_w will make the indifference curve flatter while a partial increase in σ_c will make the indifference curve steeper. This will in general mean that a larger σ_c tends to induce a change in the decision in the direction of a larger value of EC, while a larger value of σ_w tends to induce a change in the decision in the direction of a larger value of EW.

To illustrate the parametric certainty equivalence procedure, a tentative calculation is performed based on the risk aversion coefficients derived above and the stochastic parameters estimated over the period 1962-81, cf. the data given in section 2.1. The following values are used:

b = 0.1426
g = 0.00589
σ_c = 12.5
σ_w = 364.2

which implies that $g\sigma_w$ > $b\sigma_c$.

Our parameter values indicate that the risk adjustment term of terminal wealth is the larger, which implies a flatter ´indifference curve compared to the indifference curve when uncertainty is disregarded. In figure 4 the consequences of uncertainty are illustrated in the case where the feasible set is given by a line corresponding to the 2.1-2.2 line of figure 3. This means that we consider a situation with higher petroleum revenue in 2000 than in the reference path, and the question is how the uncertainty should influence the trade-off between consumption growth and terminal wealth.   The extreme alternatives 2.1 and 2.2 represent respectively increased domestic use and increased capital exports.

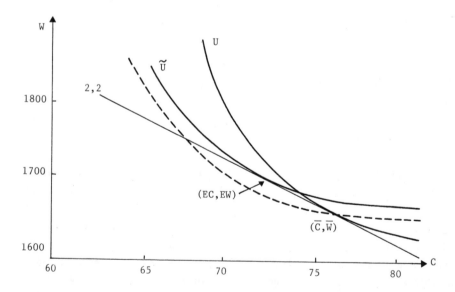

Figure 4. Consequences of uncertainty when $g\sigma_w$ > $b\sigma_c$.

The indifference curve U corresponds to the case where uncertainty is disregarded, and in this case ($\bar{C}$, $\bar{W}$) represents the optimal trade-off between consumption growth and terminal wealth. The dotted curve illustrates how the indifference curve is twisted due to the certainty equivalence transformation of the parameters. However, we assume that the feasible set of (C,W) combinations is not influenced by the uncertainty, and the relevant indifference curve is thus $\tilde{U}$. A flatter indifference curve thus entails a change in the decision in the direction of a larger expected value of terminal wealth and a smaller expected value of consumption growth. This is indicated by the point (EC,EW) in figure 4, which represents the optimal trade-off between consumption growth and terminal wealth in terms of certainty equivalence. The parametric certainty equivalence procedure implies that the decision maker will tend to safeguard against uncertainty by taking a decision which implies a higher expected value of the variable which has the higher uncertainty, i.e. uncertainty as measured by the product of the standard deviation and the risk aversion coefficient.

3.3 A STRATEGY FOR OPTIMAL CONSUMPTION UNDER UNCERTAINTY. NUMERICAL RESULTS AND TENTATIVE CONCLUSIONS

The empirical application of the dynamic programming model can be outlined. Based on the stochastic parameters given in section 2.1 and the risk aversion coefficients derived in section 3.1, the conclusions of the model will be tested against an actual long-term projection. The reference path of the Perspective Analysis is chosen as our point of departure. The questions we are addressing are the following:

- To what extent should current and future consumption be influenced when the value of the oil reserves is considered a part of national wealth?
- How should the uncertainty regarding the value of the oil reserves - as well as the non-oil assets - influence current and future consumption?
- To what extent should a shift in the variance and the expected oil price influence current consumption?
- How should the trade-off between terminal wealth and consumption be

affected by uncertainty?

In these tentative calculations, the consequences of uncertainty are
examined only with regard to the consumption path and the trade-off between
total consumption and terminal wealth. At present we have not made any
attempts of estimating an optimal oil extraction path under uncertainty. In
our model the principle of estimating an optimal oil extraction path under
uncertainty is straightforward: Certainty equivalent net oil price should
grow at a rate equal to the risk-free rate of return. However, we have not
yet resolved the difficulties in making appropriate cost assumptions.
Hence, we have applied the oil extraction path and the accumulation in
non-oil assets as given by the reference path.

First of all we need to establish the correspondence between the
preference function (4) of the dynamic model and the static analogy given
by (29). In the dynamic model which is to be applied now, preferences are
formulated in terms of the sum of dicounted utility from consumption over
the planning period, whereas in the static preference function (29), the
relevant concept is percentage increase in consumption over the planning
horizon. In order to find the appropriate risk aversion coefficient in a
dynamic context, we make the assumption that the sum of discounted utility
from consumption over the planning period is equal to the utility of the
percentage increase of consumption. The annual growth rate of consumption
in the reference path is 2.4 percent. We assume that the time preference
rate is 1 percent. Given the estimate of b=0.1426 an estimate of β=0.0352
is obtained for the risk aversion coefficient of the dynamic model. The
estimate of the risk aversion coefficient g=0.00589 is calibrated in order
to include the production capital. An estimate of γ= 0.0027 is thus
obtained.

The optimal consumption path of the dynamic model is given by the
consumption function (21), where optimal consumption in each period is
related to wealth. As an implication of the certainty equivalence
procedure, uncertainty regarding future income influences the current
consumption decision through a risk-adjustment of the time preference rate,
which enters the constant term of the consumption function. This consumption function can be expressed as a strategy in the sense discussed in
secction 1.3. According to the strategy, decision rules for consumption are
elaborated at the beginning of the planning period, whereas actual
consumption decisions are implemented by recording the outcome of the
stochastic rates of return and inserting, period by period, actual wealth
in the strategy function (21). Under uncertainty there is a gain in

elaborating a strategy where consumption decisions can be revised, when more information is available, instead of determining the consumption path at the beginning of the planning period.

An increase in uncertainty has the effect of reducing expected consumption in all periods to safeguard against future income loss. A partial increase in a standard deviation implies less risk-adjustment of the time preference rate and thus a partial decrease in the consumption path. The consequence of uncertainty for the optimal consumption path is illustrated by the following calculation. Consider an increase in the oil price uncertainty, which is measured by the standard deviation of the trend-adjusted real oil price. In the estimation over the period 1962-81, the standard deviation is 4 dollar/barrel. The question is now how current consumption is affected by a 100 percent increase in the standard deviation from 4 dollar/barrel to 8 dollar/barrel. The stochastic parameters are given in table 3 and 4, and the expected growth rate of the real oil price is set at 4 percent. This growth rate is exceedingly high, but still small compared to the risk-free rate of return which is set at 3 percent.

The marginal propensity to consume out of current wealth is time dependent and depends on the risk aversion coefficients and the risk-free rate of return, cf. (22). It is estimated to 0,04 by the beginning of the planning period and increases as the planning horizon is approached.

The main assumptions of the calculations are given in table 5.

Table 5. Assumptions for calculating optimal consumption.
Billion 1980-Nkr.

	1980	2000
Production capital..............	938.9	1726.6
Net foreign reserves	-97.3	58.3
Estimated value of oil reserves .	2782.5	2407.5
Gross domestic product	282.4	403.7
Balance of interest and transfers	-12.1	-0.3
Total wealth	3894.4	4595.8
Optimal consumption	196.9	328.1
Actual consumption/projected consumption in the reference path of the Perspective Analysis ...	186.8	303.0

The risk adjustment terms of the consumption path is illustrated in figure 5. A 100 percent increase in the standard deviation of the real oil price hence has the effect of reducing optimal consumption at the beginning of the planning period by approximately 10 billion Nkr.

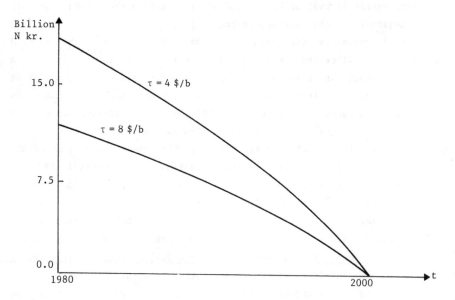

Figure 5. Risk adjustment of the optimal consumption path.

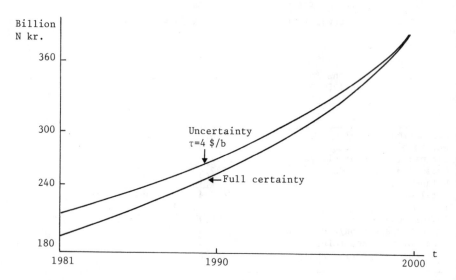

Figure 6. Optimal consumption path.

Figure 6 illustrates the optimal consumption path under the assumptions in table 5, compared to an optimal consumption path where uncertainty is disregarded.

The interpretation of the strategy implies that only the current consumption decision is to be influenced by the uncertainty. The indicated
value for consumption in 2000 has the interpretation as an estimate of a
future decision. The idea of formulating a consumption strategy under
uncertainty is that future decisions can be based on more information about
the realization of uncertain events than is available at the time of plan
preparation. However, the initial decisions should be adjusted to account
for future uncertainty.

REFERENCES

Aslaksen, I. and O. Bjerkholt (1983). A framework for evaluating planning
strategies for an oil exporting country under uncertainty of future
oil prices and rates of return. In Basar and Pau (Eds.), Dynamic
Modelling and Control of National Economies. Pergamon Press, Oxford
and New York, pp. 353-358.

Bjerkholt, O., L. Lorentsen and S. Strøm (1981). Using the oil and gas
revenues: The Norwegian case. In T. Barker and V. Brailovsky (Eds.),
Oil or Industry? Academic press, London. Chap 7, pp. 171-184.

Bjerkholt, O., S. Longva, Ø. Olsen and S. Strøm (Eds.) (1983). Analysis of
Supply and Demand of Electricity in the Norwegian Economy. Central
Bureau of Statistics, Oslo.

Chow, G.C. (1975). Analysis and Control of Dynamic Economic Systems. John
Wiley & Sons, New York. Chap. 8. pp. 197-201.

Chow, G.C. (1979): Optimum control of stochastic differential equation
systems. Journal of Economic Dynamics and Control, pp. 143-175.

Freund, R.J. (1956). The introduction of risk into a programming model.
Econometrica, pp. 253-263.

Frisch, R. (1961): A Survey of Types of Economic Forecasting and Programming and a Brief Description of the Oslo Channel Model. Memorandum,
13 May 1961.

Johansen, L. (1960). A Multi-Sectoral Study of Economic Growth. North-
Holland Publishing Company, Amsterdam.

Johansen, L. (1978). Lectures on Macroeconomic Planning, Part 2. North-Holland Publishing Company, Amsterdam. Chap. 8.

Johansen, L. (1980). Parametric certainty equivalence procedures in decision-making under uncertainty. Zeitschrift für Nationalökonomie, 40, pp. 257-279.

Merton, R.C. (1969). Lifetime portfolio selection under uncertainty: The continous-time case. Review of Economics and Statistics, LI, pp. 247-257.

Merton, R.C. (1971). Optimum consumption and portfolio rules in a continous-time model. Journal of Economic Theory, 3, pp. 373-413.

NOU 1983:27. The Future Extent of Petroleum Activities on the Norwegian Continental Shelf. Summary and conclusions of the Report from Commision appointed by the Royal Decree of 5 March 1982.

NOU 1983:37. Perspektivberegninger for norsk økonomi til år 2000.

Pindyck, R.S. (1981). The optimal production of an exhaustible resource when price is exogenous and stochastic. Scandinavian Journal of Economics, 277-288.

Planning Secretariat (1981). Norwegian Long-Term Programme 1982-1985. Report no. 79 to the Storting (1980-81).

Samuelson, P.A. (1969). Lifetime portfolio selection by dynamic stochastic programming. Review of Economics and Statistics, LI, pp. 239-246.

Theil, H. (1964). Optimal Decision Rules for Government and Industry. North-Holland Publishing Company, Amsterdam.